A Second Shot

The Pursuit of Justice in Maryland's Oldest Cold Case Murder

Michael F. Weisberg, M.D.

A Second Shot
The Pursuit of Justice in Maryland's Oldest Cold Case Murder

Copyright © 2025 Michael F. Weisberg

All rights reserved. No part of this publication may be reproduced, distributed, or transmitted in any form or by any electronic or mechanical means, including photocopying, recording, or information storage and retrieval systems, without prior written permission in writing of Intelligentsia Books, or its duly authorized agent, except in the case of brief quotations embodied in reviews and certain other non-commercial uses permitted by copyright law.
For information regarding permission, contact the publisher.

Disclaimer: This book is a work of nonfiction. All information presented is based on publicly available records, court documents, interviews, and journalistic accounts. While every effort has been made to ensure accuracy, some identifying details such as names or personal characteristics may have been altered or omitted to protect privacy.

The author and publisher do not intend to harm or defame any individual or entity. Any errors or omissions are unintentional. The views and interpretations expressed are those of the author and are not intended as legal conclusions or accusations.

Published in paperback by Intelligentsia Books
ISBN: 979-8-9927859-0-6

Intelligentsia Books
18208 Preston Road #D9335 Dallas, Texas USA
www.intelligentsiabooks.com

Dedication

This book is dedicated to Captain James T. Hall and to all the other law enforcement officers who have lost their lives protecting Americans.

BOOK ONE

CHAPTER ONE

The Butterfly Effect

I have always been fascinated by the notion of the butterfly effect and its place not only in our world but also in my life. The butterfly effect rests on the idea that the world is deeply interconnected—so that one small occurrence can influence a much larger system. It proposes the theory that a butterfly flapping its wings in Kansas could, theoretically, cause a typhoon in Japan.

What are examples of the butterfly effect in real life? Random encounters with strangers can lead to life-changing events. The events that lead to such encounters can be traced back, one by one, to their origin-and one is left realizing that even if one of the long line of events hadn't occurred, the ultimate encounter would never have taken place.

I met my wife, Sheryl, at a Jewish singles party in 1992 at the Columbian Club, the Jewish country club in Dallas, Texas. It was a Sunday afternoon event, and although I had known about the event for some time, I'd decided not to go. Friends of mine—who were as close to me as my parents—were visiting from Houston for a Bar Mitzvah. When I went out with them on Saturday night for dinner, I told them I was canceling my plans to go to the singles event to spend more time with them.

Arnold and Jan Greenspan were my friends, and they vehemently argued against my change of plans. I was thirty-three years old, still single, and not dating anyone—and I might meet my future wife at the event. It was rare for the Greenspans to come to Dallas; I usually visited them at their home in Houston. I might have found another excuse for not going if not for their insistence. I was tired from working all week and wanted to relax. I had never gone to a Jewish singles party before, so this would be a first. After much debate, I decided to go and they went to their Bar Mitzvah brunch.

Sheryl Steinberg, my future wife, knew about the singles party but also had decided not to go. She had gone to a lot of these parties, and it was always the same men whom she was tired of meeting and making small talk with. Two hours before the event, her friend Stephanie Silverberg called her and told her she wanted to go to the event but didn't want to go alone. After considerable discussion, Sheryl decided to go and drive with Stephanie to the club.

The Columbian Country Club was a beautiful venue with a large clubhouse and pristine golf course. We were all assigned tables to sit at for the luncheon and speaker afterward. At my table were eight women and one other man. The women were all attractive, but the one who caught my eye was a dazzling redhead with blue eyes who sat directly across from me. We joked and talked across the table and then moved our chairs together to hear the speaker. I got her phone number at the end of the event off her business card. Her name was Sheryl Steinberg. She was a beautiful, intelligent attorney with a great sense of humor. We went out on our first date two days later and were married within a year. That was thirty-two years ago, and if not for a random series of events (which included being persuaded to attend the event and being seated at the same table), we would never have met, gotten married, and had three children together. I'd like to think a small butterfly flapping its wings somewhere initiated a series of events that changed two lives and brought three children into this world.

Dr. H.C. Chancellor was one of the most respected and prominent physicians in Plano, Texas, a suburb north of Dallas. He'd served in the Air Force during World War Two as a gunner. He was a family practice physician, and all his patients loved him. He practiced medicine for fifty years, the last thirty-two in Plano, where I joined a practice after finishing my fellowship in gastroenterology in 1991. I met him and was impressed by his sense of humor and his confident demeanor. He liked the Texas Rangers Law Enforcement Department and would have coffee with them every Wednesday. He was a true Renaissance man, even doing things like sewing his daughters' dresses. I sent him my business cards and looked forward to getting referrals from him. He did have other gastroenterologists in Plano that he had worked with for years, including my two senior partners, and he typically sent all his patients to these other physicians.

Two years into my practice, in 1993, I received the only referral I ever got from him in the fourteen years that our careers overlapped. The patient's name was Anna Hall, and she was a seventy-five-year-old white female who had suffered a heart attack in the past. She had curly white hair, brown glasses, and was overweight. She also had an engaging personality and smiled frequently. When she did, her smile radiated across her entire face. She carried a black purse and took out two doctors' cards from it-mine and a young cardiologist friend of mine. She said that Dr. Chancellor had sung our praises and told her that we were the only doctors to see in Plano. She put the cards away and spent the next thirty minutes telling me about all her gastrointestinal problems and what had been done previously for testing and treatment.

Accompanying Mrs. Hall was her daughter, Carolyn Philo. Carolyn was an attractive forty-eight-year-old woman with red hair and sparkling blue eyes. She had worked in the medical field for years and worked for Dr. Chancellor from 1984 to 1995. She informed me that her mother had been married twice-first to her husband who died in 1971, and then to her second husband, who died in 1990. She filled in whatever her mother left out and was quick to reassure her mother that things weren't so bad and that I was the one to fix the maladies that had plagued her for years. At the end of our encounter, I ordered some tests, and on Mrs. Philo's advice, I prescribed a medicine that had helped Mrs. Hall in the past. I continued to see Mrs. Hall as a patient until her death in 2005 from heart disease.

The butterfly effect: I first saw Mrs. Hall's daughter, Carolyn Philo, as a patient three years later, in 1996. She only came to see me because her mother was my patient, and she liked the way I took care of her. This started a doctor-patient relationship that has continued to this very day and was the second step in my journey to becoming the author of the book detailing the most critical event in the Hall-Philo family history.

The butterfly effect had again nudged my life in a new direction.

Had I not gone to that Jewish singles event, I would not have met Sheryl. If I hadn't married Sheryl, we wouldn't have settled in Plano. If I hadn't joined that particular practice, I wouldn't have crossed paths with Dr. Chancellor. Without him, I likely never would have met Anna Hall or her daughter, Carolyn Philo. And without Carolyn, I wouldn't have had the opportunity to write this book.

It's easy to overlook the quiet chain of small decisions and moments that shape the future. But in hindsight, the connections are undeniable—and they serve as a reminder that we are all part of something far more complex and beautiful than we often realize. The butterfly flapped its wings, and years later, here I am—telling the story of a man whose life was ended too soon, and a family's relentless pursuit of justice.

CHAPTER TWO

The Ask and My Decision

I saved Carolyn Philo's life by accident. Due to her complaints of abdominal pain, I ordered a CT scan of the abdomen and pelvis in 2009. The abdomen and pelvis looked okay, but there was a nodule—a small mass-seen in the right middle lobe of her lungs. Two months later, on a repeat CT scan, the mass had increased in size, so I referred her to an oncologist and a thoracic surgeon. She underwent a right middle lobe lobectomy on October 26, 2009. The pathology revealed a well-differentiated neuroendocrine tumor, 1.2 centimeters in size. There were also scattered, smaller nodules of metastatic tumor identified throughout the remainder of the specimen. The tumor was found in lymphovascular spaces, but the pleural and bronchial margins were clear. She has been followed by oncology since then and, fortunately, has had no recurrence. Blood markers for the tumor have remained negligible.

Over the years, I treated Mrs. Philo for a range of gastrointestinal issues and performed her colonoscopies. I was very familiar with her mother's medical history, but I never asked about her father, James J.T. Hall. On her family history forms, she simply listed her father as diabetic and noted that he died at age fifty-three. Looking back, I wonder how many significant stories we doctors miss by not probing more deeply. I routinely asked about family history of gastrointestinal or related cancers, but I rarely looked beyond that.

Carolyn came in for an office visit prior to her endoscopy and colonoscopy on January 11, 2023. She was seventy-nine at the time, and I liked to speak with and examine elderly patients before performing procedures. She now had wavy white hair like her mother's and wore glasses. She walked with a slight limp due to years of back problems and spinal surgery. Her attitude was upbeat, and she answered all my questions without hesitation. There was something strikingly youthful about her-her face was unlined, she wore no makeup, and her complexion remained clear.

At the end of our visit, as I was about to walk her to my medical assistant's office to schedule her procedures, she asked if I had time to hear something. I said, "Sure," as I sat back down.

Her father had been a sheriff's deputy who was murdered in 1971 while patrolling a country club in Maryland. The case had gone cold and, by its fiftieth anniversary in 2021, was the oldest unsolved murder in the state.

That year, a team of cold case detectives reopened the file. They identified a person of interest who had never previously been considered a suspect living under a different name in New York state. When questioned, the suspect confessed to murdering Sheriff Hall. He waived extradition and was brought back to Montgomery County, Maryland, where he remained in jail awaiting trial for first-degree murder.

Carolyn said she and her husband Bob-himself a former Maryland police officer turned Texas lawyer-met with the detectives and were shown a timeline of the murder and investigation. Now, after more than half a century, her father's murderer would be tried and sentenced.

I was riveted by this story. When she finished, I sat quietly, processing what I'd heard.

"I want you to write the book," Carolyn said.

"What?! Why me?"

"Bob and I both enjoyed *The Hospitalist and In the End*," she said, referring to my two published novels. "You're the right person to tell this story."

"Those books are fiction," I said.

"I have confidence in your ability," she replied. "Think about it. The story is tied up with a bow. The murderer confessed. The detectives will walk you through how they solved it-without physical evidence or eyewitnesses. Even the State's Attorney, Donna Fenton, will speak to you about the charges and the trial. Please just think it over."

I led Carolyn out of my office and out to my medical assistant's desk. While I wouldn't have ordinarily considered writing a true crime book, this was an incredible story. I couldn't help but continue to think about it.

Over the next month—between that office visit and her scheduled procedures-—I went back and forth. At first, I was certain I didn't want to take it on. I wasn't a journalist. I wrote fiction because it allowed me the freedom to explore problems in society through imagination and storytelling.

Both of my previous novels began with a core issue. *The Hospitalist* addressed the shift in American healthcare in the late 1990s and early 2000s-when personal physicians stopped following patients into the hospital, passing them off instead to hospitalists. That book evolved into a broader commentary on how the art of medicine became a business (which was also the subject of my TED Talk in 2016).

In the End had a wider scope, beginning as a search for life's meaning. Along the way, the five main characters confronted heavy social issues-abortion, abuse, homosexuality, grief, and more.

At the time, I was also tinkering with other projects. "Tinkering" is the right word-I only worked on them during vacations or long weekends. One was a screenplay about Daniel Mendoza, the first Jewish heavyweight boxing champion of England. The other was a sequel to *The Hospitalist*, set fifteen years after the first book.

Carolyn's story felt like a departure from all of that. Was this a true crime murder mystery? Was this book supposed to be a police procedural? Should it be a courtroom thriller? It didn't seem like it fit my style or skillset. Still, I watched the press conference that followed the suspect's arrest. There on the screen was my patient, Carolyn, speaking about her gratitude to the detectives and the closure their investigation brought her family. She explained how hard she had worked to get the case reopened and how meaningful it was to see justice finally within reach.

I read everything I could find online about the case and its resolution. The more I read, the more I realized how rare it was for a fifty-year-old case to be solved-especially one with no physical evidence or DNA evidence or eyewitnesses.

Something in this family's story really touched me. I felt called to follow and explore where it would lead me. Also, I have to admit, it sounded, frankly, as if once I got started, this would be an easy book to write. The facts were there. The key people were willing to talk. It was a matter of gathering the material and shaping it into a narrative. I began to trust that, ultimately, the story would dictate the shape.

On the day of her procedure, Carolyn came in smiling, her usual polished self. When she spotted me in the procedure room, she called out, "Well, Doc, what did you decide about writing my book?"

"Well," I said, "it's usually me who asks the first question in this setting. Do you have any questions about the procedure? Anything you want to tell me?"

"Nope. Been here, done that. I'm ready to get a good nap after you tell me your decision."

I smiled. "I'm going to Maryland with you and Bob," I said. "I'm going to write the book."

CHAPTER THREE

On the Plane
May 1, 2023

One of my favorite things to do in life is to sleep on an airplane. There is something very soothing about the motion of the plane and the whirring of the engines that drops me off to sleep. I put in my AirPods, select a favorite mix that I've made on Spotify, and lean back and fall asleep.

On Monday morning, May first, I was on an American Airlines flight heading from Dallas to Washington, D.C. I was going to meet the Philo's and their family and be with them for the Candlelight vigil and Memorial Service honoring the fallen police officers and sheriff's deputies who had died in the line of duty. I was also looking forward to meeting and talking to the detectives, the state's attorneys, the confessed murderer, and the Philo/Hall extended family.

I knew that I would have very little problems with writing this book. I'd already spent hours interviewing Carolyn and Bob and their daughter Carrie to get background on J.T. Hall and his murder. I knew from talking to them that the following things would be given to me in Rockville, Maryland:

1. Details of what the State's Attorney planned to do in this already closed case
2. A written copy of the confession or a tape to listen to
3. Interviews with Lisa Killen, Katie Leggett, and Sarah White, the three cold-case detectives who solved the murder.
4. Possibly an interview with the confessed murderer

Besides combing the internet to learn about the case and the key figures involved, I'd also read about the city of Rockville in Montgomery County, Maryland where the murder took place. Rockville is located near Washington, D.C. and it takes thirty minutes on the Metro train to go between the two cities. Rockville was named the "Best Place to live in Maryland" by Money magazine in 2018 and came in thirty-ninth on Money magazine's "Best Places to live in America" in 2017. It was settled in 1717, founded in 1803, and incorporated in 1860. It is the county seat of Montgomery County. The 2020 census lists Rockville's population as 67,117 making it the fourth largest city in Maryland. Along with neighboring Gaithersburg and Bethesda, Rockville is at the core of the Interstate 270 Technology Corridor which is home to numerous software and biotech companies. It is a prosperous city with a median income in 2020 of $111,797. It is a Democratic city, with 73.9 and 79.5% of voters voting democratic in the presidential elections of 2016 and 2020, respectively. The city is served by the Rockville City Police Department as well as the Montgomery County Police Department.

The actual site where the murder occurred was the Manor Country Club, which I'd also read about. The pictures of the country club and club house looked beautiful, making it easy to see why it was advertised as a popular wedding destination. The golf course was kept immaculately and the houses surrounding the golf course looked magnificent.

Before going on the trip, I'd also read Mark Bowden's book, The Last Stone, to familiarize myself with the area and the law enforcement officers. *The Last Stone* is about the abduction of the Lyon sisters, aged ten and twelve, from a Montgomery County shopping mall in broad daylight in March of 1975. The girls or their remains were never found, but the case was reopened in 2013 by the Montgomery County Cold Case Detectives and the murderer was found and convicted. The very well-written book concentrates on the interrogation techniques used by the detectives over a period of years to figure out what had happened to these girls. One of those detectives, Chris Homrock, had overseen reopening the Sheriff Hall murder case and selecting the detectives to investigate it. Another of the detectives, Katie Leggett, was the senior detective on the Sheriff Hall murder case. I got a good feel for the area where these two crimes had occurred from Bowden's book and began to realize all the work and luck that goes into solving cases that are cold for forty to fifty years.

I woke up just as the airplane touched down at Reagan National Airport. I pulled my carry-on down from its overhead compartment and walked to the underground Metro station in Reagan Airport. I bought my ticket to the metro station in Gaithersburg which is five miles from Rockville and where Bob and Carolyn would pick me up. They had driven to Gaithersburg from their home in McKinney, Texas and we would all be staying in the Homewood Suites Hotel in Gaithersburg. As I rode the Metro I had the feeling of being an adventurer, a journalist who would tell an amazing story about a crime that took over fifty years to solve. I'd seen pictures of Deputy J.T. Hall and now I was about to find out more about the man himself and how he was murdered on that night of October twenty-third, 1971.

CHAPTER FOUR

The Night of the Murder
October 23, 1971

Carrie Philo could hardly contain her excitement as their car came around the last corner and her grandparents' house was in view. She saw her grandfather, J.T., mowing the lawn of the house next door to his house with his push-mower. He stopped for a second and waved at their car.

Carrie opened her door and ran over to her grandfather. She grabbed him around his waist and started squeezing.

"Grandpa, I love you. It's great to see you."

A moment later Carrie's brother Eddie, who was two years older than her at age ten, grabbed J.T. around the waist from the other side and began squeezing.

"Grandpa, grandpa! Can we play tetherball in your backyard? Can we play Rollie-Pollie down the hill?"

"Well, of course, but I've got to finish mowing the Ross's lawn first and I'm only halfway done."

"I'll take over for you, J.T.," said Bob Philo as he walked up to J.T. and shook his hand.

J.T. was an average-sized man at five foot ten inches and one hundred and eighty pounds. Bob towered over him at six foot two inches.

"You take the kids out back and I'll finish mowing and rake up the grass. How's Doug Ross doing?"

"Not so good, "J.T. answered. "Ever since his stroke a year ago he can't talk or feed himself or do anything but just sit in that chair by the window. Laverne spends twenty-four seven taking care of him. It's such a shame since he was a good plumber until that stroke. Now he just sits there, and Laverne feeds him and cleans him and tries to get him to watch television. You know, without ever having any children there's no one to help her. If you don't mind finishing the mowing, I'll take these rascals into the backyard and see what we can play with." J.T. handed the mower to Bob.

"Where's your mother?" J.T. asked the children as they walked to J.T.'s house.

"She's already inside, "replied Carrie. "She made a scrumptious salad for dinner."

"That's perfect," replied J.T., "because Grandma is whipping up a potful of delicious spaghetti."

Every Saturday night Carrie and Eddie would have dinner with their parents and grandparents at their grandparents' home in Wheaton, Maryland, and then the grandchildren would spend the night there. Their parents would stay for dinner and then leave to spend time together on a date.

Carrie loved her grandfather who everyone called J.T. He now wore glasses and a white T- shirt and tan work pants. When they got inside the house J.T. picked up Carrie and swung her around high in the air.

"I can see your donut, "Carrie shouted joyfully. The donut was what Carrie called the perfectly round bald spot on J.T.'s head.

"What flavor is it today?" asked J.T. as he put her down and picked Eddie up and swung him around.

"I think it's chocolate," she replied.

"Maybe we'll have some chocolate donuts for breakfast. We should go outside. I saw some dark clouds moving this way and they're predicting rain."

The children ran out the back door with J.T. in pursuit. He winked at his wife, Anna, and daughter, Carolyn, as he passed them in the kitchen.

"Can we play tetherball? Can we please, please, please," asked Carrie.

"Sure," replied J.T.

"I'm going to beat Carrie at tetherball today," said Eddie.

The backyard was small and hilly, and the grass was still green. J.T. had put up a tetherball pole on the left side of the yard and the three ran over to it. At eight years old the backyard seemed enormous to Carrie with the separate tetherball court and one enormous hill. When she went back as an adult to see the house, she couldn't believe how small it really was and how the "mountain" was just a tiny incline.

The tetherball pole had been sunk into the ground with cement by J.T. The ball hung from a long rope attached to the top of the pole. J.T. Had put it in two years before after hearing someone at work talk about how much his grandkids loved playing the game.

"Okay, "said J.T. "Who wants to play first?"

"I want to play you, Grandpa James," said Carrie. "I'm going to beat you."

"I want to play first, too," said Eddie.

"You'll both get a turn, "said J.T. "We'll do eenie, meenie, miney mo to see who plays first."

J.T. did this and Carrie won. Eddie shrugged his shoulders and sat down on the grass to watch. He looked up at the dark clouds which now covered the whole sky.

"Those clouds look like a dragon breathing fire," Eddie said pointing up at the sky. "I wonder if it's going to try and get me."

Carrie and J.T. had already started playing their game and didn't hear Eddie. J.T. would hit the ball gently with the palm of his hand to return the ball to Carrie, while Carrie cocked her right arm back and hit the ball as hard as she could with her fist. Eventually, J.T. let the ball go over his head enough times that Carrie won.

"I won, I won!" Carrie shouted.

J.T. picked her up in his arms.

"You're just too good. I'm proud of you." He kissed her on the top of her head.

"Can we roll down the hill, can we roll down the hill now?" asked Carrie.

"Wait a minute," answered J.T. "We gotta give Eddie a turn also. Let's see if he can beat Grandpa."

Eddie wasn't as coordinated as Carrie and missed several times when attempting to punch the ball. However, after five minutes J.T. had let enough of Eddie's strikes go by him that the ball tethered, and Eddie won.

Eddie was beside himself with joy. "Grandpa, I can't believe I beat you. Maybe I can beat Carrie, too."

"Let's play for the championship, Eddie," said Carrie. "You and I will play, and the winner will be the world champion."

They picked their sides and began hitting the ball back and forth. Within a few minutes, even though Eddie tried furiously to hit the ball, Carrie won. Eddie was upset and frowned.

"She always wins," he complained.

J.T. put his arm around Eddie's shoulders. "You're getting better and better. Your sister is just a wiz at this. You're gonna keep getting better and better and you'll be able to win sometimes."

"Let's roll down the hill. Let's roll down the hill!" Carrie shouted as she made her way up the hill which overlooked the alley behind the house.

It suddenly got darker outside, and J.T. looked up at the sky. "It looks like we've got some rain coming our way. We'll play a few minutes and then go inside for supper"

"You call out the different things you want us to roll down as," said Carrie as Eddie trudged to the top of the hill.

Carrie and Eddie both wore jeans, red short-sleeve shirts, and white Keds sneakers. Carrie's shirt was neatly tucked into her jeans, while Eddie preferred his shirt untucked and blowing in the breeze.

"Okay," said JT, "Eddie you roll down first."

"I want to go first," said Carrie.

"We're going to let Eddie go first now, and next time you'll go first."

"Okay," said Carrie half-heartedly. Usually, Grandpa and Grandma spoiled her and let her do what she wanted, but Grandpa always stood up for Eddie. Carrie had overheard grandpa say to her mother that Eddie was his "special grandchild."

"Eddie, you roll down the hill like you are a..." Just then Bob walked out the back door.

"All finished and I bagged the grass and put it in the trash," he said.

"Eddie, you roll down the hill as a lawn mower," said Grandpa. Eddie lay down on the ground. He was chubby and with his shirt out his belly flopped out a little bit, too. He loved grandpa so much. Grandpa always looked out for him and tried to make him feel better. He loved spending time with him. It was so different from the kids at school who bullied him and made fun of him. He loved the stories J.T. told about growing up poor in the Depression and being a star baseball player.

Eddie started rolling down the hill like a lawn mower. He was one of the gasoline lawn mowers that made a noise like "run run" as it cut the grass. He pulled at the grass as he rolled over and over and finally reached the bottom of the hill.

"What am I, Grandpa?" shouted Carrie from the top of the hill.

"All right. I want you to roll down the hill like you're a sausage like we're going to have for breakfast in the morning."

Carrie grabbed her knees with her hands, turning her body into the shape of a sausage. She rolled down the hill in this position and said, "oink, oink" to show she knew sausage came from pigs.

Both children ran back to the top of the hill.

"Okay, Eddie. I want you to roll down the hill like you're a meatball."

"A meatball," repeated Eddie, "how does a meatball roll?"

"You hafta get into a round shape when you roll, "explained Carrie. "And you're delicious to eat."

Eddie tried to turn his body into a round shape, but it was hard. He could grab his legs but couldn't hold onto them for long. He did his best to come down like a meatball.

"Sure looks delicious," J.T. shouted.

Eddie started laughing and let go of his legs as he rolled down the hill.

"Okay, Carrie," said Grandpa, "I want you to roll down the hill like a bird."

"A bird," said Carrie, "that's a hard one. How would a bird roll down the hill?"

"Well, I guess the bird would be chirping and talking and flapping its wings," answered J.T.

"Oh, I can do that." Carrie rolled down the hill chirping as loudly as she could and flapping her arms like wings in between rolling.

Just then Grandma Anna came to the back door. "Hey, everybody, spaghetti is ready. C'mon inside and eat."

"Can't we play some more?" asked Carrie.

"How about we play some cards and board games after dinner," said Grandpa, "so Grandma can play, too."

They walked into the house, took turns in the bathroom washing up, and then walked into the dining room. The house was a small house painted white on inside and out with black shutters. You walked through the front door into the dining room where there was a wooden table with six high-backed wooden chairs around it. On the right side of the dining room was the living room where a card table was set up with four bridge chairs around it. This was where they played cards and board games. There was also a small white sofa in the living room right behind a front window. Straight back from the dining room was the kitchen which overlooked the backyard. If you took a left from the dining room, you entered a small hallway which led to two bedrooms each with its own bathroom. The house was bright and cheerful. The dining room table always had a red or blue tablecloth and the white paint used on the inside of the house seemed to sparkle with the lights on. The living room had shelves on one side going from the floor to the ceiling which were filled with books, carved pieces of wood, dolls from Anna's childhood, and framed certificates of awards that J.T. had won working as a sheriff's deputy. J.T. had removed the original kitchen floor himself, and with Bob's help had replaced it with a shiny black and white patterned tile. On their street there were identical houses painted different colors to differentiate them.

They sat down for dinner and ate salad and spaghetti. This was always Carrie's favorite meal of the week. Tonight, as a special treat, Grandma had added meatballs to the spaghetti which tasted delicious. Carrie ate slowly, enjoying the flavor of the large meatball on her plate.

They talked and talked about their jobs, their relatives, and about the children's school.

"Grandpa, Grandma, you're not going to believe this," interrupted Eddie.

"What?" asked J.T.

"I got my report card, and I got three B's and three C's."

"That's wonderful," said J.T. "I'm so proud of you, Eddie."

"That's the best I've done. All my teachers say I'm doing a really good job."

"How about you, Carrie?" asked Grandpa, "How did you do?"

"I made all A's."

"Very good. We're so proud of you both," said Grandma.

"I don't understand," said Carrie. "Mom and Dad always praise Eddie and say how great his report card is and I bring home all A's and it's like they expect it."

Carolyn looked at Anna. "You know, honey, how proud your father and I are of you and your great grades. We think the world of you and are so happy about how you do in school."

Grandma Anna chimed in, "You're so smart, Carrie. And Eddie, you're doing better and better with each report card. We have the smartest grandchildren around."

Carrie felt better. She loved the weekend ritual of spending Saturday nights with Grandma and Grandpa and then sleeping over at their house. After dinner they cleared the dishes and Carolyn and Anna went into the kitchen to wash and dry the dishes. Bob and J.T. and the children walked to the living room and took their seats around the card table.

"Let's play cards," said Eddie. "I want to play War. I like War the best."

"Okay," said J.T.

J.T. took a deck of cards from one of the shelves behind the table. Next to the decks of cards were the board games Monopoly and Checkers. J.T. shuffled the deck of cards and dealt them four ways. They had been playing for ten minutes when Anna and Carolyn walked into the living room.

"Daddy and I are going to be here for a few more minutes and then we need to go," said Carolyn.

"That's okay," said Eddie, "you can go. We love being at Grandma and Grandpa's house." Carrie looked over at her brother lovingly. She always took care of him and watched out for him even though he was two years older. It always felt like he was the younger brother.

"Grandpa," she said as she lay down the king of clubs to win that hand of War, "How were the garbage trucks today?"

One of Carrie's favorite things to do whenever she and Eddie slept over on a Friday instead of Saturday was to sit in J. T's lap on the sofa that faced the front window and watch the garbage truck pick up their trash. The truck had a huge mechanical arm that picked up the cans, emptied them into the body of the truck, and then the two sides of the truck came together and crushed the garbage.

"It was awesome," said J.T. "It could only have been better if you were here watching with me."

Then J.T. lowered his voice to a whisper and put his hand next to his mouth, shielding his voice from Grandma Anna. "But we can still drink coffee together tomorrow morning. How would you like that?"

For breakfast, sometimes, J.T. would give Carrie a little bit of coffee in her milk. Carrie didn't like the taste, but it made her feel grown-up. Grandma Anna didn't think an eight-year-old should be drinking coffee even if it was barely more than a sip. It was their little secret, and it bonded her even more to her grandfather.

"Okay, okay," she whispered back.

Just then they heard raindrops pinging against the roof tiles. It was a slow ping, just a light rain. It was much darker in the house now, so Grandpa turned on the wooden floor lamp next to the bridge table.

As Grandpa turned the floor lamp on, the telephone rang. Grandpa walked to the other side of the dining room to answer it, Grandma Anna said, "It's going to be a rainy night. Bob, be careful driving. I'm glad we don't have to go out in this weather."

Grandpa picked up the phone. "Hello," he said. "Oh hey, Jim."

Carrie watched Grandpa listen for a moment on the phone.

"Hold on a second, Jim. I've got to ask Anna if it's okay. Anna, Jim Young is supposed to work security at the Manor Country Club tonight and he's got a family issue come up and he can't make it. He needs me to work for him. That okay with you?"

"If that's what you need to do, I'm fine with you going," said Grandma Anna. "Just stay in your car as much as you can and be careful driving back and forth. I'll stay with the grandkids, and we'll play games."

"Okay, Jim," said J.T. speaking into the phone, "I'll get over there and work for you tonight. Need a little extra money for Christmas so that Santa can bring all the grandkids the presents they want." He smiled at Carrie and Eddie and hung up the phone.

"I gotta change," J.T. said looking at his watch. It's six-thirty now and I gotta be there by seven. Seven to one am shift. Six hours."

Grandpa walked down the hallway to his bedroom and closed the door. Carolyn took his seat and his cards, and the four of them continued to play War. Within a few minutes, J.T. came out wearing his Deputy Sheriff's uniform. He had wrapped plastic over his Sheriff's hat and carried his long yellow Sheriff's raincoat.

"You got everything you need, honey?" asked Anna.

"Oh, sure. I'm sure it will be another boring night at the country club. Rain will probably keep away those delinquents who have been breaking into the Coke machines on a regular basis. May be a little more difficult watching the clubhouse and parking lot if it starts raining harder. I've got my pipe to smoke and plenty of tobacco in the glove compartment."

"Take good care of yourself," said Anna.

"You know I will," J.T. replied. He walked over and kissed Anna on the lips and then kissed Carolyn and Eddie and Carrie. As he kissed the children on the forehead, he cradled their faces in his big powerful hands. He patted Bob on the back.

"Bob, I forgot to tell you how proud Anna and I are of you. Not only are you an outstanding police officer, but now you've graduated from law school while working full-time. You're going to practice law after you pass the bar."

Bob looked over his shoulder at J.T. "Thank you, J.T. It's a great accomplishment that I never could have done without the entire family's support and understanding. You and Anna have been wonderful helping with the kids."

"You know how much we love them, "said J.T. "You and Carolyn and the kids and Melvin and Judy and their kids are our lives."

Carolyn got up from the table and walked over to kiss her father goodbye again.

"Dad, you take care of yourself in this weather. It sounds like the rain is picking up. Stay in your car as much as you can so you don't get soaking wet."

"I will." J.T. patted the inside of his jacket where he kept his gun. "That new flashlight the department bought me will come in handy tonight. It's so dark outside. Goodbye." He walked out the front door and got into his 1967 two-door Ford Galaxie that was painted Army green. He picked up the flashlight under the passenger seat and put it on the seat. He turned on the car and drove off.

* * * * * * * *

They continued to play War until Carrie won the game. Carolyn and Bob announced that they were going to leave for their date night. They kissed the children goodbye and started walking out of the house. Carrie always loved seeing the two of them together. Dad was so tall and handsome, and mom was just beautiful with her red hair and blue eyes and creamy complexion.

Carolyn stopped and said," Now you kids be good and listen to grandma. Do what she tells you to do and go to sleep when she tells you."

"Oh, mom," said Carrie, "we always do what they tell us to do."

Carolyn's face broke into a smile and Bob said, "All right Carolyn, let's go." They left the house and Bob immediately opened their huge umbrella and held it over Carolyn and himself. They walked to their station wagon carefully dodging the puddles that were already forming.

The rain soon began pelting the house even harder. Carrie and Eddie played a game of Go Fish with Grandma and then grew tired of playing cards.

"Is it okay if we go down to the basement and play?" Carrie asked.

"Sure," replied Grandma. "You just be careful and don't mess up Grandpa's office or break his new desk chair."

Carrie and Eddie loved to play with Grandpa's new swivel chair on wheels in the basement. They opened the door in the hallway and ran downstairs to the basement.

"I'm going to go first," said Carrie, "I want you to push me, Eddie. Tonight, I'm going to be driving a garbage truck all over the city and squishing garbage in the back."

"Okay," said Eddie, "but you always go first."

"I know," replied Carrie, "but I'm a girl and girls get to go first."

She sat in the chair and Eddie pushed her around the basement as she picked up trash cans with the long arm of the garbage truck and then squished the trash bags together in the back of the truck.

Eddie spun the chair around in circles as they went around each corner in the neighborhood and Carrie laughed with delight. Eddie loved to hear his sister laugh and that made him spin the chair even harder.

After ten minutes of pushing, Eddie said, "It's my turn now, Carrie."

Carrie got out of the chair and Eddie sat down.

"What are you going to be tonight?" she asked Eddie.

"I'm going to be like Grandpa, a sheriff chasing bad guys and criminals around the streets of Rockville," answered Eddie.

Carrie wasn't as big and strong as Eddie, but she worked hard pushing him around the basement as he caught criminals and took them to jail. He had to use his gun a few times to get the criminals to behave and to get into the car so he could take them to jail.

The door to the basement opened and Grandma shouted down the stairs, "Now you kids be careful with that chair. Grandpa loves it. Don't break it."

"Okay," they chimed in together.

They were tired, so they went back upstairs to be with Grandma to play another card game. They played Go Fish until it was bedtime. Carrie and Eddie laughed and yelled with excitement as the games were played.

"All right children, it's eight-thirty and time to go to sleep. Change into your pajamas and I'll come and kiss you good night."

The children walked into the bedroom, got undressed, put on their pajamas and got into bed. There were two single beds in the second bedroom, perfect for sleeping over. Grandma came in and gave them both a good night kiss. By now it was pouring rain outside. They could hear the rain as it pounded the roof.

"I hope Grandpa doesn't get wet," said Carrie, "I hope he stays nice and warm in his car."

"Me, too," said Eddie.

"Don't you worry about Grandpa. He'll be fine. We'll have a great breakfast in the morning with Grandpa." Grandma Anna closed the door, and the room was dark.

CHAPTER FIVE
The Final Shift
October 23, 1971

J.T. drove through the neighborhoods separating his house from the Manor Country Club. The closer he got to the club, the bigger the houses were and the further apart the houses were from each other. Finally, driving into the country club grounds, he passed several gorgeous mansions which were built right on the golf course. It was a dark, rainy night and even with his windshield wipers going full blast, he drove slowly due to difficulty seeing the road. He pulled into the parking lot for the clubhouse and backed into a parking spot from which he had a great view of the clubhouse and of the rest of the parking lot.

The clubhouse was a beautiful two-level brick structure which was well-lit on this dark, rainy night. On the lower level was the large party room, which was considered one of the most desirable locations for weddings and was frequently rented out for this purpose. Also on the lower level was the large golf pro shop which sold golf and club merchandise and was where tee times and lessons with the golf pro could be arranged. There were also separate rooms on the lower level that could be used for card games, birthday parties, and other smaller gatherings. The upper level of the country club had a beautiful entrance with stone columns holding up a black triangular overhang. The doors were enormous and made of solid oak with beveled glass and with the country club's logo carved into the middle of each door. There was a restaurant on the top level as well as a bar and offices for the people who ran the club. Several smaller rooms were also available to rent for parties on this level. Parked behind a huge mahogany desk in the main foyer was a receptionist who was there to answer questions, book restaurant reservations, and keep non-club members out.

From where J.T. was parked, he could see both levels of the clubhouse straight ahead and to his right and left he could see the entire parking lot. The lot was full tonight; on the phone Sheriff Young had said there were high stakes poker games going on in the clubhouse which attracted a lot of the male members. The parking lot was full of expensive cars including a Rolls Royce and a couple of Lamborghinis. There was even a brand new 1971 Stutz Blackhawk parked 2 spaces down from J.T.

J.T. put on his raincoat, zipped it up, put on his hat and grabbed his flashlight. He got out of his car and walked around the parking lot to get to the clubhouse. The parking lot was already filled with puddles, so he walked carefully to avoid stepping in them. The lavish front doors opened with the push of a button on the wall next to them, and J.T. walked into the clubhouse and right over to the receptionist's desk. She was a small, blonde woman whose name was Joan.

"Hello Sheriff Hall," Joan greeted him. "You working tonight? On our schedule it said Sheriff Young would be here."

"He's got some family issues so he couldn't make it and asked me to take his place."

"Well, we're glad to have you on this miserable, rainy October night. For my kids' sake, I hope the weather gets better for Halloween and trick or treat."

"Me, too," J.T. replied. "Any problems I should know about or anything going on at the club that I should be aware of?"

"Big poker night," replied Joan. "We've got at least five games going on in the restaurant and in private rooms. Also, the bar is busy as usual on a Saturday night. But nothing bad. No reports of any attempts to break into the Coke machines tonight."

"Sounds good, sounds good. I'll keep my eyes out for anyone trying to break into those machines. Bad weather may keep troublemakers inside, so we won't have a problem. I'll walk by the bar and check out the poker games. I'm parked directly across from the clubhouse in a green Chevy. If there's any problems and I'm not in the clubhouse, just walk out the front doors and wave to me."

"Will do," Joan replied. "Have a pleasant night."

J.T. walked across the lobby to the restaurant where poker games were already going on and a few stragglers were still enjoying their dinner. He checked out the restaurant and everyone seemed to be having a good time. He walked by the bar and nodded his head at the few people who greeted him. There were two open doors in the rooms down the hall from the bar where other poker games were going on, which J.T. slowly walked past.

Then he left the clubhouse and started patrolling the parking lot. He knew he couldn't have patrolled effectively tonight if he didn't have his long raincoat, Sheriff's hat, and powerful flashlight. The rain had increased in intensity, so he couldn't wait to get back to his car. He still walked back and forth across the parking lot twice, using his flashlight to illuminate the cars to make sure no one was trying to break into them.

He got back into his car and sat down in the driver's seat. He picked up his pipe from the central console and reached into the glove compartment for his tobacco. He put three pinches of tobacco into the pipe and then lit it with a match. He enjoyed smoking the pipe when away from the house and grandchildren. He loved the smell of tobacco and the slow rise of smoke from the pipe as he puffed. He pulled out his pen and notepad from the console, ready to write down the license plate number of any unknown or suspicious cars or cars driven by suspicious looking people. Everything was quiet now except for the sound of the rain hitting the car. He would turn the car on every five to ten minutes so he could use the windshield wipers to clean off the front window.

The golf course was to his right as he sat there smoking in the car. With the rain, darkness, and dim parking lot lighting he had poor visibility. However, he knew that beyond where he could see was the green for the ninth hole and the tiny outdoor covered bar called the "Clubhouse Turn" where thirsty golfers could stop and get a soda or alcoholic beverage as they finished the first half of the course. Beyond that were trees and sand traps and other holes and at the farthest point away from him were the mansions that were built framing the golf course.

At the top of J.T.'s bucket list was having the opportunity to play one round of golf at the country club. J.T. had never played golf before, but he had been a great baseball player when younger. He felt that hitting a stationary ball with a club had to be a lot easier than trying to hit a ninety mile per hour fastball with a baseball bat. He knew that as a non- member he'd have to be invited by a member to play, but he had picked out a couple of regular poker players who he'd joked around with as possible members to invite him.

After a couple of hours, J.T. decided to get out of the car and patrol again. Everything looked good from the car. He opened the door of the car and patted the pipe against the side of the car to empty the tobacco. He put the pipe in his jacket pocket and got out of the car. He walked around to the Coke machines, and there was no one there. He looked out onto the golf course and through the darkness he could see lights coming from the houses on the other side. He couldn't make out anything more than the lights; even the trees seemed to be swallowed up by the darkness.

He walked to the lower level of the clubhouse and checked the doors to make sure they were all locked. He then went up to the main entrance and walked in. He dried off his shoes on the massive gold and green embroidered rug in the lobby and shook the rain off his raincoat. Joan was on the phone making a reservation for Sunday brunch as he walked by her and into the restaurant.

Everyone was gone now except for the men playing poker. The tables were covered with alcoholic drinks, poker chips, money, and playing cards. As J.T. walked around the tables he was greeted with "Hello Deputy" from just about everyone.

"Well, if it isn't Deputy Dawg," said Chris Clark who was seated in his usual place at his usual table. Clark was one of the wealthier country club members who owned a business in Washington, D.C. that supplied weapons to the Department of Defense.

"How are you doing tonight, Deputy Dawg?"

Deputy Dawg was the nickname that some members called J.T. when he worked at the club. Deputy Dawg was a Terrytoons cartoon character featured on the animated series of the same name from 1960 to 1964. The cartoons were between four to six minutes and were packaged three at a time and shown as a half-hour program. Deputy Dawg was a dog who was a deputy sheriff in the South and had to battle with local varmints to please the Sheriff. He also had to fight off animals who tried to steal his garden's produce. His favorite pastime was fishing for catfish. His catchphrase was "it's possible, it's possible". Deputy Dawg was always a step behind the varmints and his so- called friends, so although the nickname was endearing it also carried a sense of a stumbling, bumbling human being.

J.T. looked at the nickname positively. He felt that it showed that the ultra-rich country club members were trying to connect with him and give him a nickname they could laugh at together.

"Deputy Dawg is kind of wet tonight," he answered with a smile. "But I'm doing my job, and everything looks peaceful."

"I'm glad to hear that," said Clark. "Any way you can arrest that varmint across the table who keeps taking my money?"

J.T. laughed just as someone at another table shouted out, "Deputy Dawg".

J.T. looked over at them and waved and tipped his wet hat towards their table. He walked around the room and then went out to the now empty bar. He took a glass from behind the bar counter and poured himself water from the faucet and drank it. He was satisfied that the clubhouse was safe, so he made sure his hat was down over his head and walked out of the clubhouse into the heavy rain. His flashlight guided him across the parking lot to his car and he sat down in the front seat.

He decided to smoke his pipe again, so he took it out of his jacket pocket and reached over to get tobacco from the console. He looked at his watch. It was about ten twenty-five now, two and a half hours from when his shift would end at one a.m. While he was putting tobacco in his pipe something moved in the periphery of his vision on the right near the golf course. It was dark out, so at first he wasn't certain, but then he saw something move again as he looked right at it. There was something stacked up in the grass separating the golf course from the parking lot that hadn't been there before.

J.T. put his pipe back into his jacket pocket, picked up his notepad and pen and got out of the car. Instinctively he patted the pocket in his jacket that held his revolver to make sure it was there. He grabbed his flashlight and quietly closed the car door. He silently crept through the ongoing deluge of rain toward where the pile was located. When he got twenty feet away, he turned on his flashlight and saw that the pile consisted of household items and included what looked like a jack-o-lantern.

Suddenly his light outlined a man dressed in dark clothes. The man had been taking things off the Formica table that was in the center of the pile. The man froze.

J.T. shouted, "What are you doing? Come closer where I can see you and put your hands over your head."

J.T. reached into his pocket for his gun and just as he got his hand on the grip, he heard a gunshot and felt his flashlight being forcibly knocked backwards out of his hand. They've got a gun, he thought. He turned quickly away from the assailant to try and seek cover until he could get out his gun from under the raincoat in his jacket pocket. As he took a step in the rain, he heard a second gunshot and felt a new wetness on the back of his scalp and then an explosion in his head. He tried to take a step, but his body suddenly went limp as he fell face-first onto the soaked parking lot. The area around him was soon a sea of red. Instead of getting his gun out, he'd managed to pull his pipe out from the same pocket. The pipe skittered away from his hand as he fell and rolled to a stop next to a storm drain. He could feel the gun loose under his raincoat, but he knew he would never be able to use it. He was having problems breathing and maintaining consciousness. The last thought that passed through his brain was that Carrie and Eddie would be disappointed that he wouldn't be home in the morning to have breakfast with them.

CHAPTER SIX
Deputy Sheriff J.T. Hall

I never got to meet Deputy Sheriff J.T. Hall. I never spoke to him or heard him laugh. I never saw him hug his wife or kiss her goodbye when he left for work. I never got to see him teach his son, Melvin, to play baseball or see him cheat at croquet by kicking his ball to improve his position. I never saw him get down on the floor of the house to play Hot Wheels with his grandson, Eddie. never saw him interact with other family members, co-workers, or friends. All I have left to accurately record his life are the interviews I did with family, co-workers, and friends, and records I've read and pictures I have looked at hundreds of times.

Yet, I feel I know him. I feel that I understand him from the background he grew up in and from the relationships he formed. I feel that I know him from his work ethic displayed throughout his life and the various ways he always tried to provide for his family. Finally, I feel that I know him because after fifty years his daughter, Carolyn, still loved him and missed him so much that she continued to ask, cajole, and beg the Montgomery County Police Department to try and find his killer.

J.T.'s father, Frank P. Hall, was a conductor and a guard for the railroad. He would chase bums off the trains. Melvin described his grandfather as an "old, mean man who scared me." He was born in Prince George, Maryland and died at the age of ninety-two on October twenty-third, 1964. Due to his personality/meanness, all his sons rotated taking care of him in his later years. He would spend a year at each son's house, wear out his welcome, and then move on to the next lucky son.

J.T.'s mother, Lillie L. Hutcherson Hall, was of Irish descent and was a first generation American. She had flaming red hair as her most outstanding feature. She was born in Washington, D.C. and died young at the age of fifty-six on May fourth, 1944.

J.T. or James Tappen was the seventh of eleven children. He had seven brothers and three sisters. J.T. was born in Cherrydale, Arlington, Virginia in 1918. Settlement in this area was initiated in 1906 by the establishment of the Great Falls and Old Dominion Railway line which ended up being abandoned in 1935. J.T.'s father worked for the railroad, but the family moved around a lot. J.T. mainly grew up on a farm in Arlington around animals including cows, horses, and pigs.

Tappen was his middle name, and no family member knew where it came from. Looking up Tappen, it can mean to tap, draw liquid from a vessel. Tappen is also the name given to a fecal plug observed in bears during their winter hibernation. Translating Tappen from German to English yields the meaning "apologizing and attracting someone's attention".

James dropped out of school after fifth grade and began working to earn money for his family. They were very poor and didn't have enough money to buy James the eyeglasses he needed. None of his siblings went much further in school. James always worked hard and did all kinds of odd jobs.

James excelled at sports. There are pictures of him boxing with other boys. According to his son, Melvin, "J.T. was an incredible baseball player". He played pitcher and played minor league baseball. Melvin said the New York Yankees sent a scout to watch J.T. pitch before J.T. was drafted into the Army. He grew to be five foot eleven inches tall and weighed one hundred and eighty pounds. He had a chubby, kind face and curly brown hair. He was powerfully built with a broad chest and muscular arms.

J.T. was fixed up on a blind date with Anna Louise Garletts who was six months his junior and had graduated from a two-room country school. She had been born in Selbysport, Maryland and worked as a biological technologist. They got married when J.T. was twenty years old. Anna ended up working at the National Institutes of Health for a long time. Carrie, her granddaughter, described her as "amazing, the coolest woman around". She loved baseball and in later life was in love with Pudge Rodriguez, the catcher for the Texas Rangers baseball team. She had a life-size poster of Pudge on her closet door.

J.T. was drafted into the Army at age twenty-three. He went to boot camp in Florida and served stateside. He was found to be flat-footed, so his time in the military was short.

After J.T. was released from the military, he moved with his family to Silver Spring, Maryland and took a job working at D.C. Transit Company as a mechanic. He was a self-taught mechanic, and his specialty was fixing the transmission on buses. He was a hard worker and was well-respected by his co-workers. He became the shop steward at D.C. Transit and always maintained a good relationship with the union bosses.

J.T., like many people who grow up poor, was driven to keep his family from going through the same struggles he had endured growing up. He always worked two to three jobs at a time to pay the bills. It wasn't enough, and he couldn't pay for their home in Silver Spring which was taken away from them by the bank. They moved to a more affordable house in Kensington, Maryland and this is where they lived until J.T.'s death.

One of J.T's jobs was having two paper routes with Melvin. They passed the Washington Post in the morning and the Washington Star in the evening. They made fifteen to twenty dollars a month depending on how collections went. J.T. also had a job at the Glen Echo Amusement Park loading customers onto the roller coaster and making sure they were buckled in. The amusement park needed more security, so they eventually asked J.T. to be a Special Deputy Sheriff. This started his career in law enforcement.

The entrepreneurial bug bit J.T. and he bought an ice cream parlor named Shirley's and owned it for five years. J.T. would work hard to make the ice cream in huge vats in the back of the store. Carolyn and Melvin sold the ice cream in the front of the store. Carolyn remembered riding her bicycle to the store at a young age to sell ice cream. Customers would ask, "How much for a double dip chocolate cone?" Carolyn would answer, "How much do you want to pay?" Often the answer was twenty-five to fifty cents which Carolyn happily accepted as she scooped out the ice cream.

Working as a bus mechanic, deputy sheriff, volunteer fireman, owner of an ice cream store would seem to leave little time for J.T. to spend with his family. But he was an incredibly devoted father and husband who adored his family and loved spending time with them. I listened intently as Melvin and Carolyn told me about their father:

Melvin- "He was very, very kind. He never raised a hand at me."

Melvin- "When he got older, he was a great baseball coach."

Melvin- "He would spend every second with us when he wasn't working."

Melvin- "He was disappointed the day I decided not to stay with the police department. He understood why I wanted to go to the CIA, and he was very proud of me. I ended up in the White House. I was the duty officer at the CIA Headquarters the night he was shot."

Melvin- "He insisted I go to college. I was the first person in my family to ever get a college degree. I got my degree while I was working in the White House. I went to school part-time. All of that comes from the quality of life my father instilled in me. I worked with five different Presidents. I was hoping my dad would know that, but he didn't."

Melvin- "In my opinion dad was great and I've tried to be as good as he was."

Carolyn- "When I was six years-old Mom and Dad took us to the Amusement Park. They had a big dance floor that was very intimidating. Dad said, "Let's dance." I said, "I don't know how to dance." Dad replied. "Just put your feet on top of mine." He took me all around the dance floor and I felt so proud of myself and my dad."

Carolyn- "There was a terrible snowstorm and Bob was out on patrol and I had no milk for my two children. Dad drove ten miles through the snow to bring me milk and bread."

Carolyn- "My car was old and falling apart. Dad put a new engine in it, fixed up everything, and painted it a hot pink."

Both Melvin and Carolyn talked about the family tradition of making fudge over the stove. The tradition was started by Anna, their mother, but it was J.T. who kept it alive. The tradition lives on today as Melvin and his wife, Judy, and Bob and Carolyn make fudge whenever they are together at Melvin's house.

J.T.'s closest friends as an adult were his siblings. They loved to spend time together. His brother, Frank, was the fire chief. When they got together, they loved to play records and dance and have parties. This was the only time that J.T. would drink alcohol. J.T. loved to dance. On Saturdays a group of family and friends would go to a dance hall in Cottage City. They would drink, talk, and spend most of the time out on the dance floor dancing to the latest songs.

J.T. always had a keen interest in police work. He had his full-time job as a mechanic when Echo Park Amusement Park needed more security and asked him to be a Special Deputy Sheriff. The deputies worked at the amusement park, Manor Country Club, and at parades providing security. There was absolutely no training involved. J.T. had experience shooting a gun from his time growing up in the country and his time in the military, but he had no formal training for his new role. He was more of a security guard with a gun. The full-time sheriffs spent their time serving civil processes, running the jail, and providing security for the courtroom. They did not do any investigation. J.T. eventually was promoted to captain, the highest possible rank.

Melvin- "He loved the sheriff's job. He wanted to be a police officer, but he didn't have the education. When he had the chance to become a deputy sheriff he took it."

J.T. was never concerned about his health. He smoked cigarettes until he had to have an operation to remove vocal cord polyps. He quit cigarettes and moved on to smoking a pipe. He was diabetic as an adult and took a pill to control diabetes. He never drank much alcohol but loved drinking coffee and the stronger the better.

J.T.'s greatest love, according to everyone, was his family. He loved his wife, children, and grandchildren, siblings and their families, and his wife's family. Carrie vividly remembers her relationship with her grandfather, even though it ended when she was only eight years-old:

Carrie- "J.T. couldn't read well, but he loved to read us bedtime stories. When he read a book, it was his own story. We didn't dare interrupt or correct him since his story was more exciting than what was written in the book."

Carrie- "Eddie and I spent a lot of weekends at J.T. and Anna's house. Sometimes Friday night, sometimes Saturday night, and sometimes both. Grandpa loved to have us outside playing games like croquet, badminton, and tetherball. J.T. would always participate in the games."

Carrie-"J.T. loved to play Hot Wheels with us. He had the orange Hot Wheels tracks which he would put together so we could race the cars. He'd also play any card game we wanted: Fish, Old Maid, Canasta, War, or Crazy Eights."

J.T. was a man in love with life. He was a family man and yet devoted to his community. He was uneducated and yet raised a son to be a top CIA agent and a daughter who had successful careers in a variety of jobs. He was competitive at everything, yet he knew when to back off and let his children and grandchildren feel the pride of winning. He was raised dirt-poor and went through some tough financial times as an adult, but neither of his children said they ever felt poor. He was universally loved and respected and positively impacted many people during his lifetime.

CHAPTER SEVEN

Weekend in Rockville, Maryland
Day One
May 1, 2023

I grabbed my blue carry-on bag from the overhead compartment of the plane and quickly exited. I followed the signs at Reagan National Airport to the Metro Rail System which took me to Gaithersburg, Maryland, where Bob and Carolyn Philo met me in their SUV. I was excited and a little nervous. However, I was looking forward to getting the inside scoop from the detectives and prosecutors and the timeline of the investigation for the last fifty-two years.

Bob parked the SUV across the street from the courthouse in a parking lot and we walked into the courthouse. The courthouse is a large, imposing building seven stories high and made of large white stones. It houses the courts of the county as well as the people who work there including sheriff's deputies, clerks, prosecutors, and their back-up staff. We passed through security including metal detectors and were met by a sheriff's deputy who took us up to a conference room. After a few moments, the Sheriff of Montgomery County, Maxwell Uy, walked in and introduced himself.

Sheriff Uy (pronounced you) is the first Asian-American to hold the office of Montgomery County Sheriff. His father was Chinese, and his mother was Irish. He was about six feet two inches tall and solidly built. His black hair was cut short on top and shaved on the sides. He talked with authority but was very pleasant and easy to talk to. From his bearing and strong voice, I could picture him as a hostage negotiator, a post he held from 1997 to 2012. He had also been an instructor at the police academy for seven years.

Sheriff Uy sat in the conference room across the table from us flanked by two high-ranking deputy sheriffs who smiled as they were introduced to us but didn't smile again. The deputies looked straight ahead as Sheriff Uy went through the history and duties of the sheriff's department. The sheriff's office had been around since 1777 and until 1922 they were the sole law enforcement agency in Montgomery County. In 1922 the Montgomery County Police Department was formed. Sheriff Uy had won election to his post in December of 2022, becoming the sixty-second sheriff in the two-hundred- and forty-six-year history of the sheriff's department. He broke down for us the sheriff department's duties in Montgomery County. They are not the primary law enforcement agency in Montgomery County; that role is filled by the Montgomery County Police Department. For emergencies if you call 911 in Montgomery County you will almost always get a police officer who responds. There are twelve hundred police officers in the county and one hundred and fifty-five deputy sheriffs. Everything that the sheriff's department does has a connection to the court system. They are the law enforcement arm of the courts. Sheriff Uy stressed how significantly the department had grown since Deputy Sheriff Hall had served. Its jurisdiction was the largest county in Maryland by population with 1.1 million residents.

After he had told us about the history and workings of the sheriff's department, I decided it was time to focus on the reason I was there. I asked him about his knowledge of J.T. Hall's murder case.

"I had always known of Captain Hall's murder. Only unresolved law enforcement murder in Montgomery County. Oldest. My predecessor as the chief deputy was Mark Burbano. He told me that when Captain Hall was assigned to support the country club in an approved employment detail that maybe he came upon some type of criminal activity and ultimately was murdered. There wasn't a whole lot of additional information that I had been privy to. Everything seemed to come out thanks to these hard-working detectives, these young ladies with the county police. On a side note, I had the chance to teach several of them at the Academy. They have had wonderful careers. If not for their tenacity going back through the files, looking at the interviews that had been done at that time, looking through the notes, they could never have reached their findings."

Just then the state's attorney, John McCarthy, walked into the room accompanied by the assistant state's attorney, Donna Fenton who would be prosecuting this case. John had been the state's attorney, an elected position, for seventeen years, and was a deputy state's attorney for ten years before that. He looked and sounded like a politician. He had long white hair and wore a well-tailored suit. He moved with energy and was charming and self-assured. He acted like someone who had known success in life but hadn't let it keep him from still being able to fit in with the common man. He talked about staying up until midnight the night before and binge-watching a PBS Country Music program about Willie Nelson. It registered in my brain that Willie Nelson was from Texas as were the Philo's and me. He talked about Willie Nelson's album, Stardust, which he felt was one of the greatest albums of all time. "They didn't want to release it," he said, "and when they released it the album was a top ten album for five hundred and twenty-four weeks." He talked about Howard Stern's radio interview with Bruce Springsteen which was made into an HBO special. It was two and a half hours long, but John had already seen it four times. "He sang Tougher Than the Rest," he told us. "He usually sings it in concert with his wife because it's a song to her." Then, just as quickly as he'd entered and seized the conversation, John McCarthy was saying his goodbyes and leaving the room, leaving Donna Fenton in charge.

The cold-case detective who had solved the case, Lisa Killen, walked in as John McCarthy left. John stopped to say, "I was friends with Lisa's mother and father before she was born."

Carolyn beamed at Lisa and Carolyn announced to the room, "Besides the love of my life, Bob, Lisa is the other love of my life."

John McCarthy, now halfway out the door, leaned his head back in and said, "There was limited information on Captain Hall's murder. If not for the tenacity of you guys (pointing to Lisa), we wouldn't have located him."

Lisa was six feet tall and thin and athletic. She appeared to be about forty. She was dressed very casually for a police officer wearing a plain shirt and blue pants. I later learned that her job on the police force was as a plain-clothes detective, which explained her appearance. I could tell that she and the Philo's had formed a special bond, and I could also tell immediately that she was somewhat wary of me and my mission of writing a book about the case. I could understand her perspective; this was the biggest case of her career and certainly one of the most important in Montgomery County and Maryland history. She didn't want to say anything that would jeopardize the year of painstaking work that she'd put into solving it.

I looked up Donna Fenton, the assistant state's attorney on the internet before I left Dallas. She graduated from The Catholic University of America, Columbus School of Law. She'd been a senior assistant state's attorney since July of 2000. She was married with four children and her oldest child was a freshman in college. She dressed conservatively in a dark blue floor length skirt with matching jacket and white blouse. She was tall and slender and wore glasses and had brown hair pulled back behind her face. She started talking and I leaned in, thinking that this was the start of the information to complete my book.

"I was working in my home office and Lisa (Killen) called. "Do you have five minutes?" she asked me. I think three hours later I'm on the floor of my home office surrounded by legal pads because this was not a short story. This is an active investigation."

She turned to Carolyn and said, "You were so sweet. You are hard to forget. It's our honor to do this on behalf of the family."

I interrupted Donna to tell her that I was recording this meeting to use in my book. Next came the point that my hopes were shattered.

Donna turned and looked at me and sighed for effect. "I cannot talk about anything involving the case if the recorder is running. I can talk procedurally and typically that's what I would do in a first meeting with a victim's family, but there's not going to be a lot of questions that I can answer on the record factually. Turn it off now."

I turned the tape recorder off. Donna explained that the accused killer had withdrawn his confession and was now represented by a prestigious law firm in Washington, D.C., Covington and Burling instead of a public defender. The lawyers of this firm were taking the case pro-bono to give their younger attorneys courtroom experience. The public defender, Michael Beach, was out, and the twenty-seventh largest law firm in the United States with twelve hundred attorneys was now defending the accused. Covington and Burling was considered one of the world's leading law firms with offices throughout the world.

I was stunned. The case would be going to trial and the whole idea of a book focused on the solving of a cold case murder by ingenious detectives would now have to be expanded to include motions, jury selection, a trial, and jury deliberation. I half-listened to Donna as she gave us the preliminary calendar for the case:

October third through October fourth-litigating the confession

January fourth to January fifth, 2024-jury selection

January eighth, 2024-trial starts and will last approximately five days

We left the conference room after Donna finished her remarks and were given a tour of the courthouse. We were shown two prominently displayed plaques dedicated to Deputy Sheriff Hall and his ultimate sacrifice. I took pictures of Carolyn and Bob standing on either side of the plaques.

We went out to dinner at a Tex-Mex restaurant that night. We were going to go for Italian food, but we missed the turn-off to that restaurant and turned into the next street which had the Tex-Mex restaurant. I ordered a Margarita to drown my sorrows and don't remember much about dinner except all three of us remarking that Texas still had the best Tex-Mex food in the world. We drove back to our hotel, the Homewood Suites in Gaithersburg, and checked in. As I sat in my hotel room getting ready to go to sleep, I resigned myself to the fact that I was not going to be handed a packaged book tied with a bow on this trip. Today was just the start of a long, bumpy road.

Tomorrow night was the Candlelight Vigil to honor all the officers who had been killed in the line of duty. Before that, Bob, Carolyn and I planned to visit the important locations for the Hall and Philo families in the area. Then we would meet Lisa Killen at the site of the murder where she would show me what had occurred and where. Finally, before the Candlelight Vigil, we would have dinner at the Manor Country Club with members of the Hall family who had come to town to honor Captain Hall during Montgomery County Law Enforcement Memorial Week. Before falling asleep, I thought to myself that it wasn't going to be easy to tell, but there was more of a story here than I had ever dreamed of.

CHAPTER EIGHT
Weekend in Rockville
Day Two
May 2, 2023

I am the child of a mixed marriage. My father, Fred Weisberg, was born in Brooklyn, New York and was Jewish. His father died when he was six months-old of Streptococcal sepsis, so he never got to know him. My father had a rough childhood with his mother, Gussie, becoming severely depressed after her husband's death. At one point my father was placed in an orphanage due to Gussie's inability to take care of him. He developed medical maladies due to neglect including Rickets. However, his mother fought through her depression, and she eventually took her son back and raised him. They were very poor, and my father started working at age six. Despite this tough upbringing, my father was the most optimistic, happy person I have ever met. No matter how bad the situation was, he would never be down or pessimistic. He always preached about the beauty of life, how lucky we were to be alive, and the importance of enjoying each day to its fullest. Even if today was a bad day, tomorrow will be better. He lived his life adhering to this philosophy. Life was an orange, and he sucked all the sweetness from it and then dealt with the pulp by devouring it. I never saw him sad or discouraged. I only saw him happy and upbeat and willing to try anything to make his life and the life of his family better. Even as he was dying and suffering from dementia at the age of ninety-seven, when he woke up and I asked him if he needed or wanted anything he would reply "Just take care of yourself and enjoy your life."

My mother was also Jewish and born in Brooklyn, New York. Her mother suffered from severe depression and spent quite a bit of her life in mental institutions. My mother's father sold women's shoes and spent a lot of his time at his company's factory in Maine and travelling around the country selling shoes. My mother was brilliant and seemed in a hurry to get out on her own. She graduated from high school at age sixteen, then was Phi Beta Kappa and graduated from New York University at age twenty. She then went on to Yale Law School and was one of the earlier women to graduate from Yale Law School. However, like her mother, she spent much of her life sad and depressed. She was able to function and raise three children, but I remember the times she was very down. Accompanying her depression was a vicious anger, and I distinctly remember the screaming and yelling fights she had with my father daily. Nothing was good enough for her, and nothing could make her happy. When I was six years old, she asked me what I wanted for my birthday. "Mommy, I just want you to be happy." She was never happy for long and was always ready to fight. Her public displays of anger were embarrassing. Once we took my parents out to a Mexican restaurant in Dallas that my wife and I enjoyed going to. My mom started screaming and yelling at my father first and then at the waiter about not getting a big enough portion of food. My wife and I crept out of the restaurant after paying the bill with our heads down, never to return.

I think I'm a combination of my parents. I like to think of myself as being eighty to twenty in favor of my father's disposition, but it may be closer to sixty to forty. My outlook, shaped as it was by such polar opposite parents, led me to having mixed feelings about my second day in Montgomery County. I was looking forward to seeing the various sites important in the life of J.T. Hall that I'd been told about by Carolyn and Bob. I was also excited about our scheduled afternoon meeting with Detective Lisa Killen. Lisa was going to meet us at the Manor Country Club and show us how and where everything happened that fateful night. On the other hand, I was discouraged and sad.

I was no longer going to have a book handed to me. Instead, I would have to become a journalist, an investigative reporter, to try and find out what had happened, when it had happened, and who was involved. There was a great deal of trepidation on my part; I was a physician who enjoyed writing fiction from my imagination, and now my first non-fiction book would have to be carefully researched and organized.

I met Bob and Carolyn in the lobby of our hotel and after having breakfast in their small, all you can eat buffet, we walked to their SUV. Carolyn was wearing a white sweatshirt with a circular purple line around the neck. There was a moose drawing on the left breast of the sweatshirt and the name 'Silverhorn' below the moose. Her white hair was perfectly coiffed, and she wore blue jeans. Bob was dressed in black with black sweatpants and a black jacket. The temperature was in the fifties, so I wore a long brown winter coat.

The first place we drove to was Damascus, Maryland where Bob and Carolyn had lived and raised their two children. Damascus was a twenty-minute drive from Gaithersburg. Along the way Bob and Carolyn pointed out various sites of interest. Some were buildings that still stood where they were in the seventies while other buildings had been torn down long ago and replaced by more modern structures. As you reach Damascus you find yourself out in the country and the number of houses becomes less and the distances between them becomes greater. We drove onto a street with a few small houses, and Bob parked in front of their old house. There was no answer to our knocking on the door or ringing the doorbell, so we walked through bushes and grass to the next-door neighbor's house. It was the same neighbor who had been there in the 1970's when the Philo's lived next door.

The neighbor answered the door and was a very fit, short, gray-haired man in his eighties. He was very happy to see Bob and Carolyn after over forty years. He was wiping sweat off his face and said he had just finished mowing his front lawn. He took us around to the back of his house and we again walked through bushes and grass to Philo's old house. The backyard of Philo's house was large, at least a couple of acres. There was a patio made up of concrete blocks that had a grill on it next to a white stone patio which abutted the house. Carolyn showed me the section of the backyard where Bob plowed yearly so she could plant her vegetable garden. There were huge trees covered in leaves sheltering the entire lot.

The lady who occupied the house now opened the patio door and came out to see who we were. Once she saw we were with her neighbor she relaxed. After Carolyn and Bob explained that they had been previous occupants of the house, and the current resident became extremely friendly and hospitable. She invited us in and showed us around the entire house. It was a small pretty home which looked very comfortable and lived in. There were three bedrooms and three bathrooms and a large basement that was filled with old furniture, bags overflowing with artificial flowers, and an assortment of other household items.

After thanking the owner for her hospitality, we drove to the Montgomery County General Hospital, which was built in 2004, thirty-three years after J.T.'s murder. I wanted to see if the hospital had any records of his time there, although I knew the chances were slim. There was some uncertainty over which hospital J.T. had been brought to, since in 1971 the previous Montgomery County Hospital had opened and replaced its predecessor, the original Montgomery County General Hospital which was built in 1920. The current hospital had pictures of both of its predecessors prominently displayed. The original hospital was built to look like a large house with eight white pillars holding up a front porch and residential windows on all sides. The pictures of the hospital from the 1920's were in black and white and the hospital looked large enough to hold twenty patients. The picture of the newly built Montgomery County Hospital from 1971 revealed a modern, large hospital which is where J.T. was brought. It was a five-story structure with a large parking lot surrounding it. The rectangular institutional windows were grouped into pairs on the upper four floors and unlike the original hospital, there was signage saying "Montgomery General Hospital' over the entrance which lit up at night. On the roof of the 1971 hospital was a large generator painted white. A three-story doctors' office building was next to the hospital.

The hospital we were in now had a huge generator on top with Montgomery General Hospital written across it which could be seen for miles when lit up at night. We went inside and looked around. No one working there was the least bit interested in interacting with me, even when I told them J.T's story and that we were there to learn more about what happened after J.T. was taken to the hospital. I was able to find the medical records department, but the door was locked, and no one answered when I rang the bell or knocked. I was able to get the phone number for medical records from a woman working at a desk in the lobby and I called it. The phone was answered by a man who let me speak for fifteen seconds before cutting me off by saying in a gruff voice, "There's nothing we can do to help you and don't you ever call this number again." There was nothing to be gained by staying at the hospital, so we left.

We drove to the police station where Bob worked when he was a member of the Montgomery County Police, the Wheaton-Glenmont Station. It was a brick building surrounded by a black fence with a push-button automatic front door. It was situated in the middle of a business district right on a highway. Bob took me inside the building to the front desk, but the policeman refused to allow us behind the desk to see the rest of the station.

We next drove to Connecticut Avenue Park in Wheaton and saw the house where J.T. and Anna lived at the time of his murder. It was a small white house looking from the outside to be fifteen-hundred square feet in size. The woman who lived there now came to the front door. She was a small, middle-aged woman who spoke only Spanish. I used my three years of high school Spanish and three semesters of college Spanish to communicate with her and asked to be let inside, but she refused. I took pictures of the outside. There were windows with black shutters on either side of the front door which contrasted sharply with the white house. The grass was cut neatly, but there was a large empty bag of fertilizer on the front lawn next to the stairs leading into the house. There were two sets of stairs; five steps led from the sidewalk to a landing and then another five steps which led from the landing to the house. There was a chimney and Carolyn pointed it out to me on the right side of the house when facing it, where the living room was where cards and board games were played. She told me the rest of the layout of the house. There had been no significant changes to the outside of the house since J.T. and Anna had lived there. I could see a tall tree to the left of the house and the upper half of another tall tree in the backyard whose branches touched the house's roof.

We left J.T.'s house and drove to Kensington where Shirley's ice cream store had been located. All of these cities were located within five to twenty minutes of each other. The shop was a three-story old house that was now a fitness club called 'The Sweat Shop of Kensington'. One of the windows on the second floor had YOGA painted in large white letters, and the other window had Namaste Yoga printed in purple letters. The third floor also had two windows, with 'Physical' painted on the one on the left and 'Therapy' painted on the one on the right. Behind the "Therapy" window the upper half of a human skeleton could be seen. The siding which covered the outside of the house was painted green and the front door and the rails for the steps leading up to the house were painted dark red.

We walked inside the house, and it was packed with work-out equipment. There were treadmills, stationary bikes, and weights. There were changing areas and lockers. We met the owner, and when he heard of our connection to the building, he took us on a tour. Carolyn pointed out the back of the building which housed the vats where J.T. made the ice cream. I pictured J.T. holding a long, wooden ladle and stirring the liquid inside the vat until its components gelled into ice cream. Hard work was all J.T. had known his whole life, and this was just another job that demanded it. I took pictures of Bob and Carolyn on the porch in front of Shirleys, and then the owner took pictures of the three of us, bundled up in our jackets.

It was around four o'clock, and our next stop was the Manor Country Club in Rockville. We would first meet Detective Lisa Killen who would show us where everything happened that night when J.T. was murdered. Then we would have an early dinner at the country club with many of Carolyn's cousins and their spouses who had come in from surrounding areas to see Bob and Carolyn and to attend the Candlelight Vigil for law enforcement colleagues who had died in the line of duty.

As we pulled up to the country club my gaze was directed to the perfectly manicured golf course with its immense trees. Everything was so green and full of life. There was a large parking lot and after we parked, I could see the stately clubhouse which was still two levels. Lisa Killen was waiting for us in the parking lot and got out of her car to greet us. She was in a difficult position because there was only so much she could tell me about what had happened due to the impending trial. But she did her best to lay out the scene that night, with help from Bob and Carolyn.

Lisa- "So this is it. This is the Manor Club. I know Carolyn can tell you a little more. I just know that your dad was working here as a security guard. What that entailed back then I do not know. This is the parking lot where he was murdered."

Bob- "Do you know where his car was parked?"

Lisa- "I do know." She showed us where the car was parked. I looked around. This was a great vantage point to see the entire parking lot, golf course, and the clubhouse. There was a down slope of the parking lot from where J.T. was parked to a storm drain where his pipe was found by police investigating the crime scene.

Carolyn- "Would you like to join us for dinner with the rest of our family in the clubhouse?"

Lisa- "I'd love to, but I've got other plans and have to go."

We left Lisa and walked across the parking lot for dinner.

CHAPTER NINE

Family Dinner at the Country Club

We walked into the clubhouse, and I was immediately taken by the grandeur of the décor. There was a giant lobby with beautiful furniture and impressive chandeliers. The pretty young lady sitting at a table on the right side of the lobby directed us to the dining room which was equally magnificent., The entire dining room looked out on the golf course and the tables were spread far enough apart to allow easy conversation with tablemates. The other eight members of the family, all cousins and their spouses, were already seated. Carolyn pointed to an empty seat between two men where she wanted me to sit. These were two cousins, Frank Jr. and John Michael, who Carolyn felt would give me the best idea of what the family was like and what J.T. was like.

Frank and John Michael looked like they were straight out of central casting. Both had been policemen, and Frank looked the part. Now seventy-five years old, he looked at least ten years younger. His full head of white hair topped a rugged, handsome face. He was about five feet nine inches and probably close to his weight as a policeman. He looked like he could get up from that chair in the dining room and resume active police duty now.

John Michael, on the other hand, reminded me of actors from old Western movies. He had white hair and a white mustache and goatee. His eyes were green, and he had just enough lines on his face to label him distinguished looking. He was about six foot one and had a slender but powerful build. Across from me was sitting John Michael's sister, Becky, who was a striking blonde woman in her sixties and who was being congratulated on her upcoming marriage.

Carolyn started the conversation:

Carolyn- "I don't know of any of the Halls who graduated from high school."

Me- "Eight boys and three girls."

Carolyn- laughing- "That we know of."

Frank-"Linda, my sister, is probably the most knowledgeable of the family. She took care of my father (J.T.'s brother, Frank Senior), and spent a lot of time with him. He did the genealogy thing. I was always working for the police, part-time jobs and trying to raise the family. Mike (John Michael) was the same way. Police officers work and do a lot of overtime. This county had a huge epidemic with heroin in the 1970's. Then in the late eighties it was crack cocaine. Now all of this stuff that's coming around. It's amazing how it goes in cycles. New stuff that even Narcan doesn't work on."

Bob- "Carolyn, did your dad have another wife?"

Carolyn-laughing-"Not that I know of."

Frank-"Our father was the fire chief of Montgomery County. That was Frank Hall Senior."

Bob- "Out of towners, these lawyers (referring to the accused's new lawyers). They think Rockville is so cute or so quaint. They can come up from D.C. on the Metro, get off, walk over to the courthouse. Quite frankly, if I was on trial, I wouldn't want those guys."

John Michael- "It's like a college football coach going to the National Football League. He'd do all kinds of tricks, hidden ball trick..."

Bob- "You get what you pay for. He did qualify for a public defender."

Frank- "I don't know if the public defender talked him into these guys or not. Unless he didn't like who they offered him. Because if you're indigent they give you a free attorney. These guys (the public defenders) know everybody in the courthouse. You get somebody from out of town, everybody is cliquey. Public defenders are paid by the taxpayers, while these guys work for a law firm. They're not paid by the taxpayers."

John Michael-"A lot of handouts discouraging people not to work. I was raised you work, and you get paid. Never ask anybody for anything. Family and friends would help each other out. Nowadays it is different. I mean, I worked extra hours for free. Now these guys punch a clock and can't wait to get out. It's scary."

Me- "What was it like when you worked?"

John Michael- "I've got so many stories. They put me up in Wheatsville, Maryland, a little country area (other people listening to John Michael laughed). It was the country. You gotta drive ten miles to get to a shopping center. Anyway, I didn't always know what was going on there, but I was used to getting along with everybody. So, they gave me a call for a family fight that was at Lewis' orchard, Jay Lewis was involved in it. Jay was an ole, burly boy. It was on Peach Orchard road. I pulled into his house, and he slammed the screen door wide open, and he came walking out. I had never met him before. He walked down towards me. I stuck out my hand, "How ya doing?" He shook my hand. He had this bewildered look on his face. He said, "You know, I could break your hand right now." He started that squeezing game, so I started squeezing back. I said, "Yeah, but I might break your hand. If you break mine, my wife's gonna come down here and kick your ass. And it looks like you can't control your own wife." We're still doing the squeezing. I said, "I bet there's a lot of deer around here. Do you hunt?" He says, "Damn right I do. Come on in the house." He let go of my hand and I followed him into the house. He's got this big deer head on the wall. I noticed that the antlers were broken off. I asked, "What happened to that deer head?" He said, "Oh, I got drunk one night and shot it again." I had turned my police radio volume down so it wouldn't get him all fired up. He asked, "Do you like cantaloupes?" I said, "Yes." So, I got an armful of cantaloupes. We're walking out towards my car, and I hear all these sirens. I said, "I better turn my police radio back on." He says, "They're coming to help you." I said, "To help me?" He says, "Yeah. Last week I had a problem here and the SWAT team was here." The police cars started pulling into the property and the first one who pulled in was Frank. They saw me with a whole armful of cantaloupes and peaches. Jay and I together. Jay would go down to that bar in Lewisville and get drunk and they'd call me to bring him home. I met his daughter a few years back. He'd passed away. He always said, "Don't wound a grizzly bear, you gotta kill it." That was his saying."

Our dinner came out and I started eating my chicken and potatoes. After a few minutes I asked Frank, "Can you tell me about your father?"

Frank-"My impression was he was very much like his brother, J.T. Pretty straight, direct, forward- going, well-behaved. As a boss I've heard many stories about how people liked working for my father as fire chief. They knew where they stood. He was hard but fair."

Carolyn-"That does sound like daddy."

Frank- "No nonsense and firm. Didn't tolerate any crap. No disrespect, not heard of. He was able to gather a large group of people in the rural areas of the county and it turned out they were all very loyal employees that had a good work ethic. When you see photos of my dad, Frank Senior, he was always a stoic-looking fellow. Very concentrated on his job. I found that to be his approach to everything. When he had grandchildren he would get down on his knees and play with them for hours and hours. Our oldest daughter had disabilities. He would build these block structures for her, and she would knock them down. He would build it again, and she would knock it down again. As long as she wanted to do it, he would do it. Just one heckuva loving person. Like I said, he was no-nonsense."

Me- "Do you think that was from his upbringing, being very poor and having to work at a young age?"

Frank- "During the Depression he was the youngest child. He was born just before the Depression and went out on his own after the Depression. He just barely qualified age-wise to be drafted in World War Two. The day he got married he came home and got his draft notice. He went to basic training and then he went to Austria. When he applied for the fire department he told them he was eighteen, but he wasn't quite there yet. He got hired. When he got back from the war he went to the fire chief and apologized and begged for forgiveness because he lied about his age. The fire chief said, "We couldn't have found anybody to work anyway, so we appreciate the fact that you did. Let's go upstairs and change the file so there's no discrepancy when it's time for your retirement. We'll get the accurate days and ages."

Frank- "My mom had been working and they didn't know how old she was. She retired, and she was an inspector. She was bored and did daycare at home, but that didn't keep her happy and Dad didn't like it. So, she got a job at KinderCare, and everything was great. She got her CPR and all of her classes. She was eighty-six when she retired. She told them that she was ten years younger, and she goes, "I've got to fill out some papers for my resume and you've got to come over and help me right now." I was like, "What do they think?" and she said, "They think I'm sixty-five." She never told anybody how old she was. She was ninety-eight when she passed and I'd say, "You're ninety-eight," and she'd say, "Oh, no I'm not. Who told you that?" One time I said, "You're ninety-eight mom," and she goes, "I don't know what age you think I am, but I am not that age."

Carolyn- "I remember Uncle Frank and Daddy sitting out on the porch in front of the house and talking all the time."

Frank- "The last time I remember Uncle Jim (J.T.) was over at the house and Melvin and his wife were there. I was working a lot of crazy hours, so I really wasn't home a whole lot, and if I wasn't working was probably off doing something I wasn't supposed to be doing. Dad did have a fantastic work ethic. He worked for the fire department. He drove a bus during the day. The only time we'd get to see him was when Mom would drive us over to the parking lot and he'd come out and visit unless he got a phone call. We wouldn't see him for a week."

Carolyn- "Dad had a work ethic like that and Uncle Bill, too."

Frank- "Dad also volunteered at the hospital. We were there the day... So, Mom raised us when she wasn't in the hospital because she had kidney problems. How did our dads learn their work ethic? Dad said he rode the horse up to Walter's Store as a boy to get something and he came outside, and the horse had come untied and gone home. Dad had to walk all the way home. You learned to tie up the horse properly. This was in Bethesda right across from Bethesda Naval Hospital on Georgetown Road. A few blocks up the road my father opened up the fire station there. Cedar Lane and Old Georgetown Road. Always would see him at that window. I worked with several of the guys who worked with my father, and they said he was one of the best bosses they ever had. He was a straight shooter and didn't take any stuff."

Frank- "My father's family including J.T. rented a farm on Bradley Boulevard just west of Bethesda. A lumber company, Gallagher Lumber Company, owned the farm. The family lived on their own during the Depression. They grew vegetables, had chickens and pigs. They were dirt poor. They moved several times, and it was hard to find out exactly where they lived. But up until my father was born, they lived in that house. They moved a lot. There were several houses I was able to trace them to through the census in Fairfax County, Virginia."

Frank- "My father lived with a couple of his older brothers until there was no place to go. He was dating my mother when she was only fifteen years old. Her mother, my grandmother, said, "Okay, you need a place to stay, you can live in our house. You're going to treat my daughter, Betty Jean, like she's your sister. I don't want any shenanigans. I've got to work." There was no father there because he'd passed away. They got married when she was fifteen and dad was eighteen. She was seventeen when she had me. They were together fifty-four years, and he gave her a rose for every year they were married, so he got her fifty-four roses."

Frank- "I've locked up our relatives. They had the audacity to ask me for bail money. I said, "I worked too hard to get you in there, I'm sure enough not going to bail you out." The standard line in our family was "you are either police department, fire department, or in jail."

Frank-"My memories of J.T. are very limited. He was a lot like my father. Very quiet and very low-key. Family-oriented man. Melvin was one of the first police officers in Montgomery County who had a degree."

John Michael- "I worked with some guys who could hardly read. When we went to the police department, I thought the chief of police had a college degree. I had an associate degree. Nowadays, you need a bachelor's or master's degree before you can be considered."

Frank- "It's a beautiful place where the ceremony for the fallen officers is tonight. I realized that I was at most of their funerals."

John Michael- "My father was married to a Hall, Frank's aunt Alice. She and my dad met at Glen Echo Amusement Park."

Frank- "Glen Echo was a neat place. Riots there burned it down. They had a huge amusement park with two roller coasters. A great pool called "The Crystal Pool".

Frank- "The police and sheriff's departments worked well together. The Sheriff's department mainly worked at the courthouse and serving papers. Montgomery County was your main police force and even state police just did traffic enforcement. I worked for the sheriff's office in Frederick County and they're the big agency there. Then you've got your city police, Gaithersburg, Rockville, Takoma Park. I also worked for the Secret Service at the end of my career."

Me- "Did you know O.W. Sweat?"

Frank- "I knew O.W. Sweat. I forgot he was the first detective in J.T.'s case. He was my supervisor for a while. He was a lieutenant investigating murders and robberies. I was there from 1972 till 1979. I was informed that I was not allowed to get involved in that (J.T. Hall's) case. Mike was told that also. All the files were there. We were told to keep our hands off of it."

Me- "How many people besides O.W. Sweat could have gotten that initial call?"

Frank- "I was still on patrol. I know that he was primary, but I didn't know who his assistant was. So long ago now., You could get transferred a month after you got a case, so someone else would have to take over. Before they did this specialized unit you worked on all murders, robberies, serious assaults. When a murder happened, everyone went in and worked together. Once we got all of the information and statements, then it was turned over to one person. They coordinated everything and you would have to feed them all of the information."

Me- "It was just by chance that he got that case?"

Frank- "He was probably working that day when it happened. At nighttime you usually only had one person working in the 70's."

Me- "Bob said they didn't start the investigation until the next day."

Frank- "That's probably true."

Me- "It was raining that night, so evidence like fingerprints could have washed away. Would that have been common that they would have let it go that night and waited until the next day? It seems now anytime you watch a police show on television it's nighttime and they're all out there investigating."

Frank- "Way back then they didn't even have a homicide unit. You had detectives who worked everything. That's why they had to have officers specialize in crimes, it's way too involved. I was training other officers and had a fifteen-year-old kid who hung himself. Mother felt terrible. The officer had been around for a hundred years. I got there with my trainee, and we walked in. The family had broken up and the kid committed suicide. Upset mom. I look at the scene. I look around. I said, "This isn't suicide, this is an accidental death." Old officer asked, "How do you accidentally hang yourself?" I said, "That is what he did. Have you ever heard of auto-erotic death? Well, that is what he did. You see all those other marks up on that door jamb up there? He's done this nine times. You had the mirror, the magazine. What happened is that whoever explained to him how to do this didn't tell him you need a break. In other words, if you black out the rope will break, and you don't hang yourself." The other officer said, "Whoah, whoah, whoah. Wait a minute. That's incredible!" The mother was devastated thinking it was suicide from the divorce. I asked her, "Did you ever notice any bruising around your son's neck?" She said, "A few weeks ago he went up to New Jersey to see some family. He came back and had bruises around his neck. I asked, "What's up with these bruises? Were you horsing around up there and got in a headlock?" He said, "Yeah, we were just horsing around, and I got in a headlock." Now I have a problem. There's a family up in New Jersey and I don't know them who are hanging themselves. The mother was shocked because she had never heard such a thing, but she was relieved that she wasn't responsible. I had to inform all of the family in New Jersey so they wouldn't kill themselves. The little female police officer that was training with me was shocked and said, "I gotta go home and tell my parents."

Me- "That case you solved right then. Are you surprised that a case like J.T.'s wouldn't be solved, that things would go on and on and on? Especially since he was part of the sheriff's department. Your whole family is prominent in law enforcement. You'd think that extra care would be taken to figure out what's going on."

Frank- "Well, I'm not saying they didn't because I never had access to the file, never had a chance to read it. Never allowed to, so I cannot express my opinion. Back then Montgomery County was so old-fashioned. They weren't up to the big city standards. All the money involved and training in the big cities wasn't here. Some of the officers involved had probably never worked a homicide and had no idea what to do. The other thing, the biggest problem police have is called 'tunnel vision'. You focus on a suspect, and you think that's it. That's the biggest problem with law enforcement officers that aren't well-versed and well-trained. You get that tunnel vision, and you focus on one thing. That's why a lot of the time cold case people come in and they've got a whole new picture based on what they are seeing, not what the original investigators were exposed to that night. These women on this cold case team were unbelievable. Lisa, oh my goodness."

Me- "It sounds like the kids who broke into the Coke machines that night were the suspects."

John Michael- "It's a good thing I didn't act on my impulses, because I was sure I knew who did it. There were burglars at the Coke machines.

One was the son of a police officer, and he was constantly in trouble doing burglaries and other crimes. So, he was a big-time suspect. Bob and Frank and I weren't privy to a lot of information at that time because they knew we were related. We heard lots of pieces and we heard the names that were involved in the Coke machines thing. Two plus two is four. I mean, they're there, they're the burglars. This is who did it. I was very shocked when I found out it was not them. Up until last year's news conference I thought I knew who was responsible for it."

Me- "So, do you know what happened to the son of the police officer who you suspected?"

John Michael- "He's still alive. He's done time for burglaries. He's been in and out of jail since then."

Frank- "He'd burglarize and then go up to Atlantic City and burn the money and come back down and do some more burglaries. Then he'd head back up there and party."

John Michael- "His father, the police officer, always felt we were picking on his son. His other son is a policeman in Fairfax County."

Frank- "What bothered me a lot is that the father would always come to the aid of the kid. Almost like enabling him. 'Don't talk to the police,' he'd tell his son.' Well, maybe if you talked to the police and cooperated you would have him eliminated as a suspect. See that's a problem a lot of people don't understand. If you're not involved it's good, I think, to talk to the police so you clear yourself. But when you look down and say I'm not going to talk to you, I want the right to an attorney, then you make me more suspicious. You've got something to hide. He just kept continuing his criminal behavior. I locked him up myself. And the first thing he said was, 'You gotta call my dad right away.'"

Me- "Is he still a criminal now?"

Frank- "No, no, no. He's too old."

Carolyn-"Lisa has talked to him. He's changed his ways. He's working. He told them when they interviewed him, "I know I was bad.""

Me- "Did he ever use a gun in his burglaries?"

Frank-"My understanding was he broke into a bank. Teller Bank. Drive through booth. They brought him in."

Me- "Amazing what this cold case team did. Reminds me of the Lyon sisters' case."

(Two sisters ages ten and twelve were abducted from a mall in broad daylight and raped, murdered, and their bodies burned. It occurred in 1975 and was solved by a Montgomery County cold case team in 2015.)

Frank- "I worked that case. I was at their house. Their son became a police officer."

Me- "Same person, Chris, who reopened this case reopened that case. Man came in not long after the girls went missing and gave details of what happened. But he contradicted himself, so they initially dismissed him."

Frank- "That was the biggest mistake. No training back in 1975. They didn't have the expertise. I was on the case. Once the case was resolved and charges were made they invited us back. We listened to four hours of testimony. We got a firsthand explanation of everything that happened. That was a very depressing thing. Horrible. The Lyon's case murderers lived near my house. They had a basement in the house with a pool table. After they had abducted the girls, on the way to their house a man was behind them in a station wagon, and he saw a girl with tape on her face. The car with the girls took off and the man in the station wagon didn't get the tag number. We would get weird calls from people saying, "Mommy, mommy, mommy." The FBI had taps on the phones. I got to know the parents. Matter of fact, several years later they helped me close a case. There was an incident at a swimming club, and they saw me and they told me what really happened. They were very nice people."

John Michael-"Whenever you have something like that the parents are interviewed first. I remember the parents were at a party and so was the detective who had to interview them and there was a little tension there."

Frank- "The night of J.T's shooting I went to the hospital and J.T. was alive and on a respirator. They kept him alive on the respirator for some time with no brain function."

John Michael- "We were all there when they took him off the ventilator. I came on in June of 1971 as a cadet. We were all standing there when they turned the ventilator off."

Frank- "His head was bandaged. It was tragic. Things will start moving quickly in this case if the suspect loses out on suppression of his confession. After the trial, the detectives can talk to you. But right now, they're between a rock and a hard place. If they talked to you, that could jeopardize their whole case. The defense could subpoena you to court and ask if the detectives really said this or that to you. I think the world of Lisa Killen. For a young woman to make a case like this, as many people as have handled that case. She deserves an awful lot of credit."

Carolyn- "Sheriff Uy said he taught Lisa in the academy."

Frank- "Lisa got creamed in a car accident. She got hit really badly. She was stopped at a light and someone plowed into her car. She was in the hospital."

Frank- "You remember George Wallace? He was shot here. He was put in the hospital in Silver Spring. Ended up in Holy Cross Hospital. I was assigned to protect his wife. I got a certificate that I'm a lieutenant colonel in the Alabama State Militia. I'll never forget his wife was drop-dead gorgeous. But he was stuck in the corner of the intensive care unit and the Secret Service had him. I was in charge of his wife's room. Nobody could come into her room. The Secret Service would escort her back and forth if she had to leave. Wallace had been here and gave a speech and was shot at a rally in Prince George County which is twenty to twenty-five minutes from here. This area of Maryland has had some high-profile cases over the years."

Carolyn- "It's time to go to the candlelight vigil. Just got a text that the vigil location has been moved to the rear of the building due to the weather. Let's go."

CHAPTER TEN

Candlelight Vigil

We drove over to the Public Safety Headquarters in Gaithersburg which housed the Montgomery County Police Department. It was dark and rainy, but I could see the massive four-story white building which was surrounded by trees and had a beautiful small lake in front of it. I was told the building was originally the National Geographic Headquarters and was built in 1968. General Electric bought the building and the site became known as the GE Tech Park.

After years of use, this landmark building needed renovation and at the same time the Public Safety Headquarters was in poor condition and overcrowded. The Public Safety Headquarters was moved to the GE Building and the building was renovated to fit its new occupants. The Public Safety Headquarters is the home of the Montgomery County Police and Fire and Rescue Departments, as well as the Office of Emergency Management and Homeland Security.

The candlelight vigil was held on the covered deck in the rear of the building, and at least two- hundred people attended. We were all given electric candles which we turned on and held. We listened to a speech from the police chief which not only brought tears to one's eyes but was also inspirational and uplifting. A couple of officers also spoke about the tragedy of their comrades' deaths and how the deceased loved what they did and had died to make our lives safer and better. An African American police officer with an amazing voice sang a song of tribute to the deceased, and then a large screen was brought into view.

On the screen there flashed pictures of each of the deceased, listing their date of death, their age at death, the department they were in, and what they were doing when they died. Almost all of the fallen officers had died in their twenties and thirties and had left behind wives and children. I felt a cold shiver run through my body as I thought of all the families standing around me whose lives had been shattered by this terrible loss. I was amazed to see how many of the deceased had died in motor vehicle accidents, either on their way to a crime scene or chasing after criminals in their cars.

Finally, J.T's picture was on the screen with the facts about him. He was the only sheriff who had been killed in the line of duty, and he wore his sheriff's uniform on the screen. He died October twenty-sixth, 1971, at the age of fifty-three. He died while investigating a robbery. Carolyn was weeping softly next to me and Bob used his hands to wipe his eyes. Then it was on to the next officer, and the next until all had been honored.

After the ceremony concluded, Bob, Carolyn, and I carefully made our way down to the Memorial Park which was built on the bank of the lake. It was cold and the ground was muddy, but we all felt it was important to visit tonight. We used our cell phone lights to illuminate the ground. The Memorial Garden had a large stone circle in the middle with marble walls extending out from the circle like spokes on a wheel. There was a white easel set up in the circle in front of one of the marble walls with a circular arrangement of sunflowers on the top of the easel. There were two statements written in bold white letters on the walls. One said, 'And If In Duty I My life Must Give' and the other said "Grant That By The Giving Others Live'.

We found the stone that honored J.T. and I made out its inscription:

Captain James Hall
James T. Hall
October 26, 1971, age 53
While attempting to make an arrest

There was a bouquet of red roses next to this engraving.

We drove back to the hotel in silence, with Bob or Carolyn occasionally breaking the silence to point out some landmark as we passed it. I quickly changed and washed up and almost immediately went to bed. I dreamt about the candlelight vigil and kept seeing pictures on a giant screen of young men and women whose time on earth had been brief, but who had been willing to give their lives so that we might live.

CHAPTER ELEVEN

Weekend in Rockville
Day Three
May 3, 2023

I wore a dark blue suit with a red tie to the Montgomery County Police Department Fallen Heroes Memorial Service. As we walked from our car to the Public Safety Headquarters front door we were greeted by four officers sitting on beautiful large horses. There were two horses on each side of the entrance to the building, facing the two horses on the other side. The horses moved their heads occasionally to look at us, but otherwise stood as still as statues. Their colors ranged from bay brown to brown to black and white. The saddles on the horses had the insignia of the Montgomery County Police Department proudly displayed. The officers were decked out in full dress uniform including tan Stetson hats. They looked straight ahead as they held the reins but did acknowledge us with a nod.

We met Brian Hall outside the doors. Brian was Melvin's son and the nephew of Carolyn and Bob. He, too, was a retired police officer and had driven from Virginia to attend the ceremony. He was about six feet tall with brown hair and brown eyes. He was in his fifties but looked forty. He wore a dark blue suit and patterned blue tie. This was my first time meeting him, so we exchanged greetings and then I took pictures of him with his aunt and uncle. I later noticed that without any intention, I included an American flag on top of a tall flagpole behind them in the picture.

We were taken by sheriff deputies to the large conference room where the service was to take place. Just inside the door was a large sign mounted on an easel. The sign had a black background and at its top it listed all of the officers who had died in the line of duty and the dates of their deaths. Below this was a large Montgomery County Police Department badge. On either side of the badge, black and white wings unfurled as if the badge was a bird in flight. Below the badge, on the bottom of the sign in big, white, capital letters it said, 'In Valor There Is Hope'.

We were greeted by Sheriff Uy and one of his deputy sheriffs who were wearing their full-dress uniforms and Stetson hats. At the front of the auditorium there were seats with signs on the back designating the family of the fallen officer. The sheriffs escorted the Philos and Brian to the seats designated for them, and I sat a few rows behind them in the seats for police officers and visitors. I looked to my right and saw the beautiful lake with tiny ripples running across it. It was a gorgeous day, and the sunlight brought the lake to life with its shifting reflections.

The ceremony started with a bagpiper in police uniform coming in and playing a poignant Scottish tune that I'd heard before at funerals. There were speeches given, including some by local politicians attending the ceremony. The focus of all of the speeches was that these brave, fallen officers had paid the ultimate price for their career choice, and although their lives were cut short, they would always be remembered and honored by a grateful community.

When the speeches were finished the last part of the ceremony began. Each of the fallen officers' faces and details surrounding their deaths were displayed on the screen in the front of the auditorium. Each family, accompanied by a police officer or a sheriff's deputy was escorted to the front of the room to light a candle. Each candle was in a beautiful glass vase affixed to a marble rectangular base. A gold police badge was on top of the marble base and the deceased's name and date of death engraved below it. Carolyn, Bob, and Brian went up and lit their candle, accompanied by a sheriff's deputy. The speaker at the podium called out "Deputy Sheriff James Hall killed while making an arrest in 1971." The entire ceremony was sad and tragic, but again, uplifting. The families of the deceased had been torn apart by their loved one's death but had managed to continue on in life and now were present to honor their loved one and hero. Knowing that this ceremony took place yearly to honor and remember the deceased reminded me of the Jewish tradition of lighting a Yahrzeit candle on the anniversary of the death of a family member. Lighting the Yahrzeit candle, like lighting these candles today, made one stop and think about the one who had died and kept their memories alive.

When the ceremony ended, the Philos and I again walked down to the Memorial Park. It was even more impressive in daylight as I could now make out much more of what was engraved in the granite. I could also see how beautiful the setting was for Memorial Park, flanked by trees on either side and the lake with noisy ducks in front of it. Across the lake was a line of tall oak trees and green grass. On the side of one of the granite spokes was written:

Diligently And Faithfully Without Partiality Or Prejudice

On the side of another spoke was engraved:

To Conduct Myself So That The Honor Of The Department Is Upheld

I thought of J.T. as I read these words. His whole life had been lived in a manner which upheld these codes of conduct. We were not here today to recall his tragic death, but instead we were here to honor the life he had lived and the ideals he upheld.

* * * * * * *

They had lunch for all of us in another large auditorium and I talked to Brian while we ate. He was married with children and grandchildren. He spoke about his father, Melvin, with reverence. I could tell how much he loved and looked up to his father. After retiring from the police force, Brian had taken a job heading up security for the elementary schools in a county in Virginia. The work was much slower paced than being a police officer, but he said he enjoyed his work and that it had its own unique set of problems.

After lunch, the Philo's, Brian, and I went upstairs to see the detectives' quarters where Lisa Killen, Katie Leggett, and Sarah White had worked solving the case. It was a huge room divided into cubicles with a large conference room on one end. We met Lisa at her cubicle which was close to the center of the room. I could only imagine how active and noisy it would have been on a working day. Sarah White soon joined us; she was a pretty, petite woman with brunette hair and a big smile. We praised her for the great work she had done helping solve the cold case, but she deflected all praise to Lisa. She told us Lisa was the detective who had spent hours poring over the files and interviewing anyone who could give information on the case. It was Lisa and Katie, we learned, who had travelled all over the country trying to chase down leads. Finally, it was Lisa who had obtained the confession from the alleged murderer. Lisa wasn't one to toot her own horn. She was very modest and said that it had been a collaborative effort between the three detectives that led to the solving of the murder. Before we left, the detectives showed us the conference room which the three had commandeered to work together without distraction. In the conference room they had laid out all of the evidence and figured out how it tied together leading to the one suspect. After this we said our goodbyes and got ready to go back to our hotel. Carolyn gave Lisa a big hug and said she was like a daughter to her. Lisa smiled and said she would see us again in October for the hearings on whether to admit the taped confession into evidence at the trial.

CHAPTER TWELVE

Weekend in Rockville
The Last Meal
Day Four
May 4, 2023

Bob, Carolyn, and I met in the hotel restaurant at seven a.m. to have our buffet breakfast before I left for the airport. I picked out cereal and low-fat milk, yogurt, and a cup of black coffee. I would be taking the Metro train to Reagan National Airport and flying back to Dallas from there. After we sat down, Bob and Carolyn started talking about themselves, their children, and their lives.

Bob- "Carolyn always worked, like her father. As for working in the school, Carolyn first worked In the cafeteria making biscuits."

Carolyn- "One time the baker was out so Margaret Reynolds said, "Carolyn, you've got to do biscuits." I had to make five hundred biscuits. I told Margaret okay. I'd made biscuits before, but never five hundred. Well, you're not supposed to melt the lard and I did it. The five hundred biscuits were like rocks. So, we made a lot of gravy and put it over the biscuits. But when I brought home what was left Bob left them out for the birds, and they broke their beaks trying to eat them.

Carolyn-"Growing up I was taught that you could either be a wife, a schoolteacher, or a nurse. That's what you're supposed to do, so that's what I did. My first job was at age twelve when I worked in Kensington at the Five and Dime. Then I worked at Shirley's Ice Cream. After that I would babysit for a family of eight children with two sets of twins. I even went on their vacations with them to help with the kids. We went to Florida, Canada."

Bob- "She sold Dutch Maid for a while."

Carolyn- "It was a line of lady's clothes, well-made clothes. I would pick my time to drive to different homes. Unpack the car, hang up the clothes and be a sales lady. They would have a party at their house. Just like a Tupperware party. I made pretty good money."

Bob- "We had a Volkswagen bus back then. It made it easier to hang the clothes in that because the doors opened on the side."

Carolyn- "Growing up, because Mom and Dad both worked, I would go to the farm with my grandparents (mother's parents) every summer. That's where I learned to drive a car; actually, I drove a truck because they would have to put the hay in the back of the truck and they didn't have enough people, so I would drive the truck. I learned how to milk cows. We had automatic milkers, but you had to clean the udders and then put the caps on. We also had to clean the milk machine. I worked hard all day, and since grandmother did not like weeds in her yard, I would pull out the weeds when I finished my other work. Every Thursday was 'Bake Day'. We made our own bread for the weekend and grandmother had a copper pot that we stored the bread in. We made pies and cobbler. We'd go out and pick the berries. I got to pick out my own dresses because we would go with Grandad to the Feed Store and the sacks had different designs. I would pick out the feed sacks that had designs I liked and that would be my new dress. Grandmother would make a dress out of the sack. We would dump the seed out of the sack and then we'd wash it. We didn't have indoor plumbing at the farm until I was twelve years old."

Bob- "Completely different background from mine growing up in the city."

Carolyn- "After Bob and I were married and living in Damascus, Maryland, I wanted a big garden because that is what I grew up with. So, Bob got that tractor and he'd plow it for me. The kids enjoyed it and would help with the plants."

Me- "Did you think you were poor growing up?"

Carolyn- "I never felt like I was poor. The fact that my dresses were made from sacks didn't bother me. Didn't think anything of it because there were pretty designs and I had buttons and bows. I wore them to school,"

Bob-"Her grandmother's farm was a beautiful place."

Carolyn- "Thousand acres on the Mason-Dixon line. They ended up selling all of the farm except for seventy acres. Grandma and Grandpa were wonderful, but of course, they're long gone. I remember their funerals."

Bob- "I think a funeral is for the living, not the dead."

Carolyn- "I felt total relief yesterday. I felt Daddy was okay. We did it! Even though I know the trial is not over and everything, I just felt this big relief in my heart. That was it. That's my closure."

Bob- "I guess in some ways when a parent loses a child to a disease and then they do something about that disease then that brings some closure."

Carolyn- "But you know when Eddie (their son) passed away, even though you are not supposed to lose your children... he suffered so much. It was a relief to him and to us. He was fun, but he kept getting worse and worse. He was smart and had a good memory. When he was sixteen he drove a car, went to the prom, and went to Spain. He took a class and learned Spanish. He could do geometry but he couldn't do algebra. For some reason...spatial versus numeric. There were periods when he would be really good, but then he kept progressing down. Instead of being forty he was more like sixteen in terms of his maturity. He was diagnosed with paranoid schizophrenia at age seventeen. At the time of his death at age forty-five he was on sixteen different medications. He came in one night and said he was the devil. I said, "What?" He said, "I'm the devil." Out of the blue."

Bob- "Which we learned is typical at that age. Something hormonal through adolescence into the late teens and early twenties. A lot of people are first diagnosed then."

Carolyn- "When he was four or five we took him to Children's Hospital in Washington, D.C. because he was 'slow'. I really don't know how to explain that. He was diagnosed from testing with Non-Specific Learning Disabilities. They didn't have special classes in school back then. He did well."

Bob- "He was a little slow to talk."

Carolyn- "He was a big boy. He was shy sometimes and sometimes he would just say what he thought. It could be inappropriate. He couldn't interact with other kids very well. He was more of a loner. I think he could have had autism. They didn't know as much back then. I think he had Asperger's."

Bob- "Eddie and I had a game naming streets. As a police officer, I had to know the streets. We didn't have GPS and so Eddie tried to memorize the streets. Wherever we'd go I'd ask, "Okay, Eddie, what's the name of the next street?" He would know it. His mind worked spatially if that makes sense. That's why he could do well with geometry but not well with numbers.

Carolyn- "Once he had his psychiatric break he'd hear voices. He would watch television and the basketball players were talking to him. Football players and baseball players didn't, but always basketball players. He did start sleepwalking and I caught him one time going out the front door. I said, "Eddie, go back to bed." He turned around and walked back to bed. I'm sure there were several things going on with him. But back in those days...fortunately it's come a long way in diagnosing and treating mental illness."

Carolyn- "After his diagnosis at age seventeen, he went to a special school at the Psychiatric Hospital. He actually graduated from that school and with his original class which was very nice. I remember one time I was in court with Bob and Eddie was at home so I decided to call and check on him. I asked him, "Eddie, are you okay?" He answered, "No, I was thinking of committing suicide." I asked, "What are you going to do?" He answered, "Well, I thought I'd jump off that step." I said, "Okay. That's one step. You'll be okay." He was seventeen or eighteen."

Bob- "It was a complete break. He regressed back to baby talk. Or not talking. He went catatonic at one time."

Carolyn- "So we've had quite a life. But we got through that. We had to stick together or we wouldn't have made it. I often wondered if it bothered Carrie (their daughter). It all started when Eddie went outside our house in Damascus and exposed himself. The policeman who lived down the street came and knocked on our door. The officer said to Bob, "Can we talk someplace, Bob?" He told Bob about what Eddie had done. We took Eddie to a psychiatrist who explained to us that he's trying to prove to people that he's a man. We've had some heartbreak."

Me- "Did it put a lot of strain on your marriage?"

Bob- "Yes. Only to the point where we disagreed on his abilities. It took me a long time to realize that Carolyn was right. Moms protect the kids. Dads want the kids to meet their ability. So, there was that conflict."

Carolyn- "I said to Carrie, "Are you okay going to school? If you want to stay home today that's okay." She said, "Why?" I said, "Has Eddie embarrassed you? Would you rather not go to school?" She said, "Oh no, mom. It doesn't bother me." And that's the way she is. She went into counseling to help others and she has throughout her life."

Me- "Was Carrie easy to bring up?"

Carolyn- "Yes. She did write us letters sometimes if she had a complaint. When she was little her spelling wasn't good."

Bob- (laughs) "That's right."

Carolyn- "When I was in school I was told I was in the 'Dumb Class'. My mom said, "No you're not." She went up to school and said, "I want her out of that class. She will go to whatever class she wants and she will not be in that class." I was told I was dumb. Mom said, "No you're not. You can do anything you want to do." So, they changed me to a regular class."

Me- "What's your philosophy?"

Carolyn- "There is always something good in everything. Eddie's situation did tear you up. The hard thing for us was back then mental illness was kept a secret. It was like walking on eggshells all of the time, hoping Eddie wouldn't act out if we were out doing something. We couldn't talk to anybody about it. It was really hard. Eddie took Spanish. I wasn't going to put him away in an institution. We did find the Psychiatric Institute in Washington, D.C. That was good."

Bob- "We were almost broke paying for Eddie's care in the 70's. It cost ten thousand dollars a month. Not all of it was coming out of pocket, but a significant portion did. We had to go down once or twice a week for family counseling. It's a long way from Damascus to Washington, D.C. It was about an hour drive back then. We went down to D.C. and the only place we could park cost four dollars."

Carolyn- "That was a lot to us."

Bob- "And I just blew it."

Carolyn- "We were in the counseling meeting. "Mr. Philo, what is your problem tonight?"

Bob- "I said, "I can't believe the ten thousand dollars a month you're getting paid does not pay for the parking!" But I didn't say it that nicely. I was so frustrated."

Carolyn- "She said, "I hear anger in your voice.""

Bob-" I said, "You're damn right I'm angry.""

Carolyn- "He got up and paced the floor.""

Bob- "It was total frustration and that was the last straw."

Carolyn- "They took Eddie roller-skating. The whole psychiatric unit of twelve. I thought they're taking Eddie roller-skating. He's not very well coordinated to begin with. Later they call, "Mrs. Philo, we just got back from the skating rink and Eddie broke his ankle." "Why did you take him there?" "We wanted him to be part of the group. He's out of the hospital and back with us." So, we've had quite a life."

Bob- "But we remember the good times."

....

As my flight back to Dallas was moving through the air, I thought back about my four-day trip to Montgomery County. There certainly had been some disappointments such as not getting the timeline the detectives used to pursue the case and not really learning anything new from the detectives or state's attorney about what happened that night. But on that flight and afterwards I decided to be like my father and focus on the good. I'd gotten to meet the Philo and Hall families and learn more about their histories and what made them tick. I'd gotten a good feel for what it was like to be a police officer or sheriff's deputy in the early seventies when J.T. was murdered. I could now put a face to the names of Lisa Killen and Sarah White and assistant state's attorney, Donna Fenton. I knew the lay of the land and saw where J.T. and Anna lived and where he spent his last night, as well as seeing where the Philos lived. I appreciated even more the ultimate sacrifice that those who are killed in the line of duty make whether they were police officers or soldiers. Finally, I decided that I would write the book about J.T's murder and I would follow the story to its end.

CHAPTER THIRTEEN
J.T. Found and Taken to the Hospital
October 23, 1971

At ten thirty-five p.m. on October twenty third a couple out on a date walked through the Manor Country Club parking lot to their car and saw what appeared to be a person lying face down in the parking lot. It was dark and the rain was pummeling the ground, so they moved closer for a better look. They saw the back of J.T.'s head, which was bleeding, and the yellow raincoat soaked with blood and rain. They ran into the country club and asked the receptionist to immediately call for an ambulance and the police for a man found down.

Within five minutes the ambulance arrived. Volunteer fire men manned the ambulance, and they moved J.T's head to the side to see if he was still breathing. He was, but barely. They picked him up and put him in the ambulance and took him to the new Montgomery County General Hospital.

Once he arrived at the hospital, the doctor working the emergency room saw how shallow J.T. was breathing so he intubated him and put him on a ventilator. A call went out to Bob and Carolyn's home from the emergency room, telling them that Carolyn's father had been shot and they needed to come to the hospital immediately. They got dressed and called Anna and told her briefly what had happened and that they would pick her up on their way to the hospital. Eddie and Carrie, who were sound asleep, were picked up by Bob's parents and taken to their home.

By the time Carolyn, Bob, and Anna had gotten to the hospital, x-rays had been done of J.T.'s head and the back of his head had been bandaged. The three of them stood at his bedside as a neurosurgeon in a tuxedo walked in to examine J.T. He did a brief neurological examination, and then motioned for Bob to follow him out of the room. Once they were out of earshot of Anna and Carolyn the neurosurgeon began speaking.

"I've reviewed the x-rays and the bullet ricocheted inside the Deputy's head. This doesn't look good. The bullet shattered his brain. The brain is gone from my exam. No operation can help him."

Bob tearfully asked, "Can anything be done to save him?"

The neurosurgeon replied, "There's no brain left to save. He'd be dead now, but the ventilator is keeping him alive."

Family members began showing up in the emergency room. Sheriff Jim Young got there around midnight. He was the man whose shift J.T. had agreed to take six hours before. Jim talked briefly to Bob and then spent the next few hours pacing the floor.

Eventually, J.T. was moved from the emergency room to a private room in the hospital. He spent three days there and didn't show any signs of returning brain function. After talking to all of the doctors who had been involved in J.T.'s care, Melvin and Bob made the decision to take J.T. off the ventilator. They told the family of their decision and they gathered around J.T's bedside to say goodbye.

The ventilator was turned off. Anna looked at her husband as she held his hand and thought back about their thirty-three years of marriage and how much she would miss him. She thought about the good times they'd had, and how tragic it was that such a good husband, father, grandfather, and friend could die so young.

Carolyn was twenty-eight years old and she sobbed as she held J.T's other hand. She thought about the force he'd been in her life and in the lives of her children. She kept repeating, "It's all right, Daddy, it's all right," even though she thought it never would be. But she felt it was important to give J.T. that reassurance while the monitor still showed his heart was beating and his chest slowly moved up and down with each agonal respiration.

After thirty minutes, J.T. stopped breathing and his heart stopped beating and he was pronounced dead. The family comforted each other as each one gave J.T. a final kiss or rubbed his shoulder on their way out of the room.

The autopsy on James T. Hall was done by Dr. Ronald N. Kornblum, the assistant medical examiner. Kornblum later moved to Los Angeles and did autopsies there on such celebrities as John Belushi, Natalie Wood, Truman Capote, William Holden, and Karen Carpenter. He also testified in the 'Preppie Murder Trial' as an expert in chokehold deaths. His final diagnosis for James T. Hall which was entered onto J.T.'s death certificate:

Gunshot wound of head

And under the section 'How Injury Occurred':

Shot while apprehending thieves.

CHAPTER FOURTEEN
J.T.'s Funeral and Aftermath
October 29, 1971

October twenty-ninth, 1971, was a beautiful day in Maryland. The sun was shining and the temperature was in the seventies. The weather contrasted sharply with the feelings of grief shared by the Hall and Philo families as they buried J.T.

The family held services for J.T. at the Collins Funeral Home in Silver Spring, Maryland. Over a thousand people attended including law enforcement officers, family, co-workers, and friends. He was buried in George Washington Cemetery in Prince George County. A second service took place with overflowing crowds at the cemetery. He was buried with full law enforcement honors. J.T. hadn't been religious, but both ceremonies were conducted by ministers. They talked about J.T.'s service to the community as a deputy sheriff for fifteen years, and how he had risen to the rank of Captain. They also talked of how he had been a hard-working and dependable mechanic for the D.C. Transit System. The ministers extolled J.T.'s virtues including his faith in God and his goodness to his fellow man.

Almost immediately the family and the Manor Country Club teamed up to offer a two-thousand- dollar reward for information that could track down and convict the killer of Special Deputy Sheriff James T. Hall. The Manor Country Club Board of Governors announced that it had voted to offer an initial reward of one thousand dollars. J.T.'s family requested that contributions of sympathy be made in the form of donations to the James T. Hall Memorial Fund with the money to be used as a reward. They eventually raised another thousand dollars bringing the total reward to two thousand dollars.

On Tuesday, November twenty-first, 1978, a story ran on the bottom of the front page of the Montgomery Journal newspaper. It was titled 'Reward Offered in 1971 Murder' and was written by Sandy Golden. On the right side of the story was a picture of J.T. wearing his deputy sheriff's uniform. The story said that a new police department 'crime solvers' program, in which rewards are offered for information leading to the capture of criminals, had inspired a Rockville lawyer to resurrect the unsolved 1971 murder of a deputy sheriff. Police had refused to cooperate in announcing a reward in the murder case.

The story went on to detail how J.T.'s son-in-law, Robert Philo Jr., who was now a Rockville attorney was offering a two-thousand-dollar reward for the arrest and conviction of J.T.'s killer. Philo said "The reward money had been raised seven years before, but area newspapers refused to publicize the reward offer without an official announcement from the police department and then police chief, Kenneth Watkins, would not make one. Hall's widow, Anna Louise Hall, is insecure, lonely, and very bitter that the murder has never been solved," Philo said.

'At the time of the murder, Philo was a detective with the Montgomery County Police Department stationed at the Wheaton-Glenmont police station that was responsible for investigating his father-in-law's death."

'Philo said he believes that police did not do a thorough job investigating his father-in-law's murder, and that belief was a "consideration" that led to his resigning from the police force to practice law. In addition, Philo said, two weeks after Watkins refused to call a press conference announcing the two-thousand-dollar reward, the police department held a press conference announcing a fifty-dollar reward for the capture of the murderers of two dogs who had been poisoned in Potomac.

"That hurt, that really hurt," Philo said. "It was like the police department was saying we don't care about people but we care about dogs."

Watkins could not be reached for comment.

CHAPTER FIFTEEN

The Philos

After J.T. was murdered and the case went cold, Carolyn Philo never gave up hope of finding the killer. She was twenty-eight years old when J.T. was killed, and the first couple of years after his death she let the police department do its job. She would call the department periodically and be told nothing was happening.

Bob Philo started out as a K-9 officer with the Montgomery County Police Department. His German shepherd was black and was named Midnight. Midnight became part of the Philo family, living in their house and being taken care of by the family. As a K-9 officer, Bob worked upper Montgomery county. If J.T. was working at the Manor Country Club on a weekend night and Bob was working, Bob would visit J.T. After he left J.T., Bob would go to a nice restaurant near the country club and get Midnight a bone.

After J.T.'s murder, Bob was promoted to sergeant and moved to another station. He was moved away from the Wheaton-Glenmont Police Station where the investigation into J.T.'s murder was taking place. Bob was extremely intelligent and hard-working. He decided to become a lawyer in the 1960's and graduated law school and was admitted to the Maryland Bar in 1971, the year of J.T.'s murder.

As an attorney, Bob was pigeon-holed doing DWI defenses. He was so good at DWI defenses because as a police officer he trained with the Breathalyzer so he knew the strengths and weaknesses of the machine better than anyone. He was a great attorney, but not a great manager. He felt he needed a career change, and decided they should move to

Texas in 1980. It wasn't Carolyn's first choice. She asked Bob, "Why do you want to move to Texas? It's nothing but rocks." It was also Carrie's senior year of high school.

Bob found a position working in Austin, Texas, and was admitted to the Texas State Bar. Bob tried civil cases all over the state. J.T.'s widow, Anna, remarried. Her second husband died and she moved to Texas in 1990 to join Bob and Carolyn. She lived in Texas until her death in 2005. Eddie also moved to Texas where he lived in his own home, group homes, nursing homes, and institutions until he died at the age of forty-five.

There is a biography of Bob Philo on the Internet. It tracks his work life succinctly:

"Bob is a former police officer (Detective Sergeant of Major Frauds Division) who went to law school and passed the bar while serving the public. He later opened his own law office and was licensed as a title agent in Maryland. He moved to Texas and regulated the Texas title insurance industry at the Texas Department of Insurance. He then joined Title Resource Guaranty Company when it was in formation and shortly thereafter was elected its President. He was also hired as a consultant to the New Mexico Insurance Department and wrote the title insurance regulations there. Later in his career he served as Texas Agency Manager for several different title insurance underwriters, as President of a title agency in Fort Worth, and as Regional Counsel for another underwriter. Bob has been a frequent speaker for the Texas Land Title Associates and other state and national organizations. He semi-retired and now acts as an expert witness in civil and criminal litigation involving title insurance, escrow, and real estate closings. He was one of the first people to receive the certification of Certified Title Insurance Associate (CTIA)."

Carolyn worked as a medical assistant in doctors' offices in Texas, doing everything from drawing blood to operating the x-ray machine. She loved her work, and the patients and staff loved her cheerful, outgoing personality. She was an attractive woman with short, wavy red hair and big, sparkling blue eyes. She never gave up on finding her father's murderer. She continued to call the Montgomery County Police Department every few months to see if there were any new leads but was always disappointed. After a period of years, it seemed as though the police department had decided to quit working the case, which Carolyn found unfathomable. She continued to call and plead with anyone she could speak with at the department to reopen the case and find the answer. Much of her motivation came from her love for her father. There was also the encouragement she got from watching Bob win one legal case after another by using his brilliance. If Bob could find the key, the trick, the method to win these cases, why couldn't the police department find a way to solve her father's murder? Nothing changed, though, and there was nothing to show for the work of all the investigators, starting with the original detective on the case, O.W. Sweat.

CHAPTER SIXTEEN

Interview with O. W. Sweat— Original Detective on the Deputy Sheriff Hall Murder Case

While we were in Rockville attending the events for the Fallen Officers Week, Bob made a phone call to O.W. Sweat who agreed to speak with me on the phone. He was now in his eighties and taking care of his ailing wife. He had a gravelly, rough voice that I'd always associated with smoking. He also sounded extremely confident in his abilities and proud of the work he had done as a police detective. I reminded myself that it had been fifty-two years since the murder, so it would be hard for anyone to remember all of the details accurately. Bob started off the phone call with O.W.:

Bob- "Dr. Weisberg has known Carolyn a long time."

O.W.-"That's his problem."

Bob- "Thanks for taking the time to talk to him."

O.W.- "No problem. Glad to do it."

Me- "Thanks O.W. Great to talk to you on the phone. Why don't you just tell me what happened that night as best as you can remember."

O.W.-"Got the call about J.T. while I was on another call. I was at the hospital when I got the call."

"They told me a deputy had been shot. I went to the crime scene of course and found a deputy had been shot in the back of the head. He was obviously shot in the back of the head which was really a brave thing to do."

Me-"Really?"

O.W.- "I'm being facetious. It was raining that night and dark. I saw the body. We found out that there had been some kids in the area. Some of them were caught burglarizing. Fifteen-to sixteen-year-olds; three of them. They were suspects until I talked to them., I don't want to say I'm cocky, but I was satisfied after talking to them that they had not shot or killed anybody. I spoke to each one of them separately and their stories were too much alike. It was obvious that they hadn't colluded. Their stories were alike but different. They hadn't shot anybody. We checked them out and their stories matched up. It was apparent to me that we had an unknown case on our hands. Whoever killed the Deputy Sheriff was unknown. Bob can tell you."

O.W.- "I don't know how many people I interviewed. I personally interviewed or interrogated...I don't know...a minimum of fifty to seventy-five personally. Me. Not counting the other detectives in the office. And, of course, it led nowhere. It just went into the cold case file."

O.W.- "Two reasons why I really felt bad about it. Number one was because of Bob being right in the same office and it being his father-in-law. I didn't know that right away. But having him in the same office. And number two, it's the only murder case that I ever worked that I didn't close. I must have worked thirty to forty. I worked a bunch of them. The lieutenant that was in charge of our section at that time called me whenever there was a homicide. For whatever reason, he put me on all of the murder cases. It's the only one that I never closed. The only one. Like I said, I investigated a ton of murder cases. The one that I probably wanted to close more than any of them I didn't close and I'm still unhappy about that."

O.W.-"I wouldn't even venture a guess regarding the caliber of bullet. Not a lot of blood on the ground, raining pretty hard that night. Wouldn't have been a lot. If there was, it would have been washed away. Wasn't a lot of blood on him or around the ground. And anybody who says there was is fabricating. It was a rainy, rainy night. It was a nasty night. The lighting was terrible in the parking lot. I used a flashlight to see things."

O.W.- "I can't remember how I found the three boys. I don't know how. They could have been breaking into the Coke machines. Yeah, I think they were. Now that you say that I believe they were breaking into the Coke machines. I wouldn't swear to it. It might be so. If someone else told you that, then they've got a better recall on that particular part of it than I do. These three boys were out in the middle of the night in that area. On a rainy night. That alone brought suspicion. They were found that night. How they were found I really don't remember. The officers found them that night. They might have been at the Coke machines, I don't recall. I cleared them."

O.W.- "There was one guy, a policeman's son, that I thought probably was the responsible party. But the policeman wouldn't let me talk to him. He was never interviewed; couldn't talk to him, couldn't talk to him. He was a juvenile and his father wouldn't let me talk to him. His background made me suspicious of him. I don't know if he was in the vicinity that night, he probably was, but I can't recall. I can't recall if he was one of the three boys from the Coke machines that I was able to clear. I have to look at my report."

O.W.-"I actively worked that case, day to day, for at least a couple of months. If you're talking about working the case, it would have been six months at least. And if you're asking about any time that anything came up on the case it would have been referred to me and that's indefinitely. It was my case because I was on that night."

O.W.-"It's hard to say how the people who were interviewed by me were chosen. Their name might have come up because they knew somebody in the area. A lot of them were people who lived in the area. The people who lived in the area, we interviewed all of them. Just to see if they knew anybody that was hanging around or anything. Or if they were hanging around."

O.W.-"When you go into a murder case you don't know who killed him. It could have been a neighbor that just got pissed off at him for walking around. You don't know. You just don't know. All murderers are not real bad guys that you see on TV. In fact, most murderers are not bad at all. That's what you do, you interview everybody. Everybody. I can't tell you specifically. You just start at the bottom and work your way up. I don't recall if any of the neighbors talked about having their houses burglarized that night. I think there were a couple of houses broken into. That might be why we went after those three kids. I didn't see a pile of things from houses that had been stolen. He was lying on the ground when found. Don't recall if head down. I didn't recall if face down or face up. He might have been face down. He did not have his gun pulled. I don't recall anything in his hands at all."

O.W.-"It was not reported to me who had seen him in the parking lot. I got a call from police communications. Said that there was a dead body, looked like a sheriff, and where it was and that was about it.

O.W.- "I didn't see where his car was in relation to where he was. No car door open. I think I did know that he was brought to the hospital and lived for three days on a ventilator, but I can't swear to that. I believe, now that you mention it, that he lived for three days and that a neurosurgeon was called."

O.W.-"I always got an autopsy report. He was killed by a single bullet to the brain. I don't know if a bullet was recovered at the autopsy, but I'm sure it was. It seems to me that it might be that one of the neighbors said they had a gun stolen from their house, but I can't say positively. I think that there was, but I'm not sure."

O.W.- "The murderer just walked up behind him and shot him in the back of the head. Just an out and out murder. Two bullets fired. One longer range hit the flashlight and then the person came up behind him and shot him. I don't know if more than one person was involved."

O.W.-"They always have churches for juveniles to stay in that are homeless. They're all over the place. That wouldn't have been unusual. Not one specific church. Churches provided a place to sleep. I could not get a judge's order to talk to the suspect I thought did it because he was a juvenile. Juveniles are sacrosanct. You can't talk to them and a judge is not going to do it. They're protected. If the parent says yes, the juvenile can still lie to you, but you can talk to them. But if the parent says no, it's game over. You can't even talk to them. That's it. That's Maryland law. Maryland law is the only one I dealt with. I would say that's pretty much nationwide. Juveniles are protected."

O.W. "The name Becker never came across my desk. I wasn't involved in Becker's interview in 1973. I'd been promoted by then. He was never a suspect. By then I was a lieutenant. Over the years, nothing additional was given to me about the crime. Believe me, I would have remembered it."

O.W.- "I was senior to Bob (Philo). We didn't patrol together. Usually, I had a partner. I may have worked with Bob a couple of times. But I was a senior investigator. Sometimes they had to have somebody with me."

O.W. "I enjoyed my career. I enjoyed police work and the Marine Corps. I had a good time. Certain times in the Marine Corps I didn't enjoy at all, but for the most part I enjoyed it. I was in the Marines a little over four years. While I worked on this murder I was probably not working on other murders. Most murders back then were not mysteries. Most murders back then were husband and wife type things. Most murders back then weren't mysteries. You opened the door and you got 'em."

O.W.-"I started police work in 1959. I was six feet one. One hundred and ninety pounds. Blonde, regular hair and blue eyes. Still got some. Not much chance of recovery for my wife. None at all. That's just the way it is."

CHAPTER SEVENTEEN

The Initial Suspect

The initial suspect in the murder was named Norman Shoemaker, Jr. He was born June second, 1955, making him sixteen years-old when Deputy Sheriff J.T. Hall was killed. His father was a police officer for the Montgomery County Police. O.W. Sweat locked in on him as the main suspect from the start, and word spread throughout the police department that he was guilty. He had been involved in other crimes and many in the police department felt that his father was an enabler who kept his son from getting the justice he deserved.

Norman grew up in Rockville and lived there most of his life. He attended Robert E. Peary High School and was the oldest of three brothers. The Shoemakers lived four miles from the Manor Country club and Norman had worked there as a caddy starting at age fifteen.

On October twenty-third, 1971, Norman and three of his friends were riding around smoking pot. The four of them decided to break into the soda machines at the Manor Country Club. In the car they had a screwdriver and a tire iron which they were going to use to break in and steal the quarters. They parked in the parking lot and made their way to the soda machines. They didn't see any law enforcement officers. They used the tire iron and screwdriver but were unsuccessful in breaking in. They heard sirens and ran back to their car and drove east to the service road. They saw fire trucks passing them with their sirens blaring. There were no police cars. They would have continued to flee the scene, but they saw that the screwdriver was not in the car but had been left by the soda machines.

Norman and his three accomplices turned the car around and went back to the country club to retrieve the screwdriver. They had been gone a total of ten minutes. As they drove into the country club parking lot their front lights illuminated what "looked like someone dropped a big trash bag in the parking lot". They got out of their car and walked up to it and realized it was the deputy sheriff in a yellow raincoat. His face was at a forty-five-degree angle pointing towards the soda machines. There was a puddle of blood around him. They ran to the clubhouse and had the attendant call the police and an ambulance. They all stayed with the deputy sheriff until the police and ambulance came.

Norman says he did speak to the police briefly and his father was aware he was speaking to the police. He never had a firearm, and he first shot a gun five years later at age twenty.

Because of his past history of run-ins with the law and his father's unwillingness to let Norman testify more extensively, O.W. Sweat and many others felt he was the murderer. The police would say to him, "Why don't you admit you did it?" Throughout his life Norman felt he was harassed by the Montgomery County Police Department and wrongfully blamed for the crime. He never denied being in the country club parking lot that night, but always maintained he had nothing to do with the murder of Captain Hall.

My only time to see Mr. Shoemaker was on the first day of the trial when he was the first of the 'Coke Machine Gang' to testify. He was stocky, approximately five foot nine and dressed completely in black. He was bald with a grey moustache and goatee. He was now living in South Carolina. After he testified and was standing outside the courtroom, Carolyn Philo went up to him and told him how sorry she was that the false accusation tying him to her father's murder had in many ways ruined his life. He seemed very grateful to hear her apology and looked like a man who had a great weight lifted off his shoulders.

CHAPTER EIGHTEEN

The 1970s as the Case Went Cold

O.W. Sweat worked the J.T. Hall murder case in the early 70's until he was promoted and moved to a different position. The case was assigned to different detectives who were never assigned to the case for too long. It slowly became what's known as a 'cold case.'

What is a cold case? The dictionary defines a cold case as "an unsolved criminal investigation which remains open pending the discovery of new evidence'. A case becomes 'cold' when all investigative leads available to the primary investigators are exhausted and the case remains open and unsolved after a period of three years. Among America's most notorious cold cases are the Zodiac Killer, the murderer of Jon Benet Ramsey, and the Black Dahlia. By far the most common type of cold cases investigated are homicides followed by sexual assaults and burglaries. Reported clearance rates for all types of cold case investigations are about one in five.

If the cold case is solved, the most common reasons are the advances in DNA technology. Advances in DNA technologies have substantially increased the successful DNA analysis of aged, degraded, limited, or otherwise compromised biological evidence. You do not have to be a police officer to become a Cold Case Investigator. Some individuals in this role may come from related fields such as forensic science, criminal psychology, or private investigator. Cold cases may be difficult to solve due to lack of hard evidence, recall accuracy, and witness credibility.

In 2023 there was an article published in 'The Hill' with the headline, 'Nearly Half of US Murders Going Unsolved, Data Show.

Thomas Hargrove, founder of the Murder Accountability Project, suggested that the reason for the low clearance rate is simple: there aren't enough people to solve them.

Carolyn Philo never gave up on finding her father's murderer. She would call the Montgomery County Police Department at least every six months and be told that there was nothing happening on the case. The detectives on the case kept changing, but Carolyn's insistence that the case be solved was the one steady factor.

CHAPTER NINETEEN
The 1980s
The Cold Case Grows Even Colder

J.T.'s wife, Anna, was single from the night of his death in 1971 until 1980. She was bitter and confused about why no arrests had ever been made in J.T.'s death. Her cousin living in Pennsylvania passed away and Anna and her cousin's widowed husband, Roy. began corresponding by mail. They became friends and talked on the phone and then visited each other. Roy would come to Maryland and play games and card games with Anna and her family while they were dating. They got married in 1980, just before Bob and Carolyn moved their family to Texas. Anna marrying Roy made Carolyn more comfortable moving to Texas. Anna moved to Roy's hometown of Somerset, Pennsylvania where he was a school teacher. It was great companionship for both of them. Anna became very involved with the church they belonged to in Somerset. With her new husband and involvement in the church, Anna was not as active in finding out who killed J.T. They stayed together until Roy's death in 1990.

Carolyn refused to give up. Her calls from Texas were frequent and she went up the ranks of the police department to as high as she could reach. No, nothing was new and there were no leads. It didn't deter Carolyn. She watched as Bob's law practice blossomed and saw how his use of intelligence and planning won all of his cases for him. Certainly, there were methods the police department could use like Bob did to unravel the mysteries of J.T.'s case. There had to be a year when one new detective would go back through the evidence and find the key. It didn't happen.

CHAPTER TWENTY
The 1990s and 2000s
The Cold Case Stays Frozen

Anna moved to Texas in 1990 after Roy died, close to Bob and Carolyn's house. She never dated again and was content to spend her time with family and friends. Bob's law practice and work with Title Insurance Companies continued to grow, and Carolyn worked as a medical assistant in a doctor's office. Anna Hall died in 2005, never knowing what had transpired on that miserable, rainy night in 1971.

Eddie lived independently sometimes, but flare-ups of his schizophrenia required hospitalization. His sister, Carrie, married and started a family of her own. She remarked that each time Eddie was hospitalized it took something out of him that he never regained. Carrie's husband, Ken, took Eddie under his wing and began jogging with him to improve his fitness. Ken became Eddie's idol and took Carrie's place as Eddie's confidant.

Through all of their family's struggles and triumphs, Carolyn remained steadfast in her desire to see her father's killer apprehended. By 2010 it was almost forty years since that fateful night, but now Carolyn had new technology to use to prod the Montgomery County detectives. She still called regularly, but also used the computer to regularly fire off emails asking the police department not to give up trying to solve J.T.'s murder. It seemed hopeless. Theories about the murder had been making the rounds for years, but no progress in solving the case was made.

CHAPTER TWENTY-ONE

Theories About the Murder

Theory Number One
The Mafia's Mistake

One of the most popular theories about the murder was first expressed in the late 1980's to Carrie and her husband, Ken. A relative told them the story after hearing about Carolyn's ongoing attempts to identify the killer. Carolyn was about to call the Montgomery County police when Carrie said, "Why are you doing that? They already solved it."

Carolyn replied, "What are you talking about?"

Carrie said, "Let me tell you what one of our relatives told Ken and me. We were sitting in the living room of their house. I brought up Grandad and said, "You know, it's such a shame they can't find out who killed him."

Our relative looked at Ken and me and said, "I know who did it. The FBI told me."

We looked at him with expressions that said, "Then tell. We haven't heard this."

He continued, "The FBI looked into it and they found that the person who shot J.T. was supposed to shoot somebody else. They found out it was a guy in the Mafia that did the shooting. He shot J.T. by mistake. Because J.T. is related to Tootsie (a cousin of the Halls who was a known member of the Mafia) then J.T. should be protected from the Mafia. Therefore, they had to kill the guy who killed J.T. and he was found under a bridge."

Carrie asked, "What about the body of the man who was killed?"

Relative replied, "Don't know. They said they think Sheriff Young was supposed to be killed. Not sure why. Maybe his son was involved in illegal activity?"

"So, it was a payback?" Carrie asked.

The relative replied, "Yeah. Mafia man kills J.T. by mistake and since he shouldn't have been killed due to being related to Tootsie, the killer was murdered and his body left under a bridge."

Carrie said, "It's interesting that no one interviewed Tootsie regarding grandpa's murder."

"That is interesting," the relative replied.

Theory Number Two
Money Buys Silence

The second theory that made its rounds regarding the murder was that the killer was the son of a family that lived in the Manor Country Club. The Manor Country Club is prestigious and gorgeous, and the way the golf course sprawled in all directions made it the perfect place for the wealthy to build their mansions. The homes are enormous with huge backyards abutting the golf course and walls of windows facing the golf course. With nothing built behind them, there is the vision that their backyards never end.

It took wealthy people to own this land and build these mansions, and there were teenagers living in this neighborhood who had checkered pasts. Some had histories of run-ins with the law, and others had the reputation as troublemakers. The rumor was that one of these teenagers had decided to rob the house of the Schmidt family house and bring the stolen items across the golf course to the clubhouse parking lot where their car was parked. This juvenile had either taken a family pistol or bought a gun which he was carrying when stopped by the deputy sheriff. He didn't want to be caught, so he pulled out the gun and fired, killing J.T. with the second shot.

This theory assumed that the murderer confessed to his parents, who then used their money and influence to block any meaningful investigation. The deputy sheriff had been hired to patrol Manor Country Club and any surrounding areas originally due to the number of burglaries taking place in the vicinity. Some of the burglaries appeared to be inside jobs. It didn't take too much of a leap of faith to imagine that these inside jobs were carried out by someone familiar with the neighborhood due to living there. The juvenile had made the mistake of getting caught by J.T. and then made the catastrophic error of killing J.T. But no one would ever learn who it was due to the weight that pushed the scale of justice down in the wrong direction, the weight comprised of money and influence.

CHAPTER TWENTY-TWO

2010 to 2021

The most famous cold case in Montgomery County was solved on September twelfth, 2017, when Lloyd Welch pleaded guilty to two counts of first-degrees murder. The facts of the case and how it was finally unraveled are masterfully detailed in Mark Bowden's book, *The Last Stone*. In March of 1975, Sheila and Kate Lyon, ages ten and twelve, disappeared during a trip to Wheaton Plaza, a shopping mall in Montgomery County. An exhaustive search for the girls turned up nothing and the case went cold. Just as in J.T.'s case, the investigation ran out of steam and no progress was made in thirty-eight years.

Then, in 2013, a cold case team of the Montgomery County Police Department reopened the case and found the missing clue that led to the killer. It turned out that one week after the abduction, eighteen year-old Lloyd Welch had gone to the police saying he saw the girls climb into a man's car outside the mall. The police took his testimony and dismissed him as a pothead who had followed the reports of the girls' kidnapping on the news and then came to the police with a fabricated story in order to collect the constantly increasing reward money.

As Bowden says in the first chapter of *The Last Stone*, "The officers missed something about Lloyd Welch that day, something big. Days earlier, Danette Shea, a girl slightly older than Sheila Lyon, who had seen Sheila at the mall that day, had described a man who had been following and staring at Danette and her friends. He had been so obnoxious that one of the girls had taunted him, "Why don't you take a picture? It'll last longer." Shea had described the man as eighteen or nineteen years-old, five foot eleven-to-six-foot, dark brown hair in a shag, medium mustache. A police artist had even produced a sketch which was in the growing file. It looked a lot like Lloyd."

A cold case team was assembled in 2013 which included Katie Leggitt, who was also part of J.T.'s cold case team. They went back and looked at all of the evidence including Welch's testimony and focused on Welch as their suspect. Their incredible use of interrogation techniques and their unrelenting desire to solve the kidnapping, murder, and then burning of these two girls' bodies led to Welch finally confessing and being sentenced. The cold case was closed. But another, older cold case was still unsolved, and it took four more years after the Lyons sisters' case was closed for J.T. Hall's cold case to be reopened.

CHAPTER TWENTY-THREE

Formation of the Deputy Sheriff Hall Cold Case Team

2021 was the fiftieth anniversary of the murder of J.T. Hall. His daughter, Carolyn, now seventy- eight-years-old, had never given up. She continued to bombard the Montgomery County Police Department with requests to reopen the case on the fiftieth anniversary of her father's death. It had now become the oldest cold case in the history of Montgomery County.

Carolyn's calls spurred a retired officer to ask to reopen the case. He was upset by Carolyn's frequent calls and wanted to shut her up. Chris Homrock, who had been part of the Lyon Sisters Cold Case Team was assigned to put together this team.

Homrock picked three women to make up the cold case team. Lisa Killen was a plain-clothes officer in the police department since 2005 who asked for a temporary transfer to the Cold Case Department. She had never before worked a cold case and wanted to have that experience. She had graduated from college where she had played varsity tennis, and then graduated from the Police Academy. Both of her parents were teachers, so she had blazed a new trail in her family by devoting her career to police work. In 2013 she had been promoted to corporal on the Special Assignment team. Lisa was single, but had been dating the same man, a fellow police officer, for ten years. She had a yellow dog named Dakota and loved to read and take walks. No longer a tennis player, her sport now was running. At the time that Lisa made her request for a temporary assignment to the Cold Case Unit, the Hall murder case was reopened on its fiftieth anniversary, and she was assigned to it. She was given the major responsibility of going through the entire file to see if something had been missed.

Detective Katie Leggitt was the second officer chosen for the team. She had made her reputation in the Lyon Sisters case and now was working as a detective on cold cases exclusively. She had previously been a detective in the Division of Child Abuse. One quote of hers from Bowden's book regarding the perpetrators of the sisters' demise stood out for me: "Evil really exists in a different form than I've ever seen before." This was from someone who had made her bones as a detective in the Division of Child Abuse. Because of her seniority and experience, Katie was chosen to oversee Lisa and be a sounding board for any ideas Lisa came up with. Katie was married and had two children and two stepchildren.

Finally, Homrock chose Sarah White to be the third member of the team. Sarah was a detective who was brought onto the team to aid wherever she was needed. These three women were picked to travel back in a time machine to a cold, rainy October night in 1971 and find the person who'd shot Captain Hall in the back of the head, killing him.

CHAPTER TWENTY-FOUR

Work of the Cold Case Team

A box containing all of the information going back to 1971 regarding the deputy sheriff's murder was placed on Lisa Killen's desk. The box was large, and there was a lot of information for Lisa to go through. She took things out individually and went through each of them with a totally clear mind on what had transpired fifty years before. Anything that she had questions about she discussed with Katie and Sarah. Katie oversaw Lisa and travelled with her around the country interviewing people who were connected to the case.

Lisa interviewed the couple who had first come across J.T.'s body in the parking lot and reported it to the receptionist at the club. She travelled around with Katie and interviewed all of the juveniles who made up the 'Coke Machine Gang' and were now men in their sixties. Their recollection of October twenty-third, 1971 was exceptional, and they all told the same story.

As more and more of the evidence was evaluated and re-evaluated, and notes and questions were piling up, Lisa realized she needed a bigger space to conduct the investigation than her small desk in the middle of dozens of desks in the Detective Offices. She commandeered the conference room on the floor and began laying the evidence out there and utilizing the drawing boards to try and find the detail that had been overlooked. Day after day she came across new names and new information to add to her growing notes on the wall, but none of it seemed to lead to a suspect.

One piece of evidence that caught Lisa's eye was a reel-to-reel tape. It was something that Lisa hadn't seen before and did not know how to access. The tape was labelled 'Interview With Richard Hobart'. Hobart had been the name of a family that lived in the Manor Club area. Their son was a teenager at the time of the murder. There was a connection to J.T. Hall because in the notepad that he carried whenever he worked at the country club there was written Richard's name and the license plate number of Richard's parents' car. Could this be the break she was looking for? Could Hobart somehow have slipped up in this interrogation and recalled something vital? She discussed the finding of the tape with her partners, and they decided that since they had no leads up to this point, the next step would be to get the tape digitized so that they could listen to it. Reel- to-reel technology hadn't been used in forty years, so Lisa knew that digitizing it would require a significant amount of work.

Lisa took the reel-to-reel tape labelled 'Interview with Richard Hobart' to a civilian police employee. He had no equipment to change the tape to a CD. Next she took the tape to a video editor who had a store in the area and he was able to convert it to a CD and thumb drive. Lisa was able to listen somewhat, but the recording was not clear or concise, so it was hard to reach any conclusions. She did hear enough, though, to think that the tape was significant. The conversation on the tape talked about the night Deputy Sheriff Hall was shot. Katie Leggitt heard the tape and also felt it was important. She contacted the FBI and they agreed to convert the tape in its current form to a form that they could listen to and comprehend. It took a week, but one week later the detectives were in their conference room/office listening intently to the audio.

CHAPTER TWENTY-FIVE

What the Reel-to-Reel Tape Revealed

The tape was from April fifth, 1973, and was an interview with a man named Larry Becker. Becker had been in prison for robbery but escaped from a work release program and was captured and given more jail time in addition to his original sentence. He said he was volunteering to give information about the murder of Deputy Sheriff James Hall in exchange for a reduction in his sentence. The interview was conducted by Sergeants Miller, Lother, and Roby, none of whom had a connection to the detectives working on the murder case.

Detective- "Larry, do you realize this conversation will be recorded?"

Becker-"Yes."

Detective- "Is the recording made with your consent and is the recording apparatus in plain view?"

Becker- "Yes."

Detective- "You made reference to the shooting of Sheriff Hall. It occurred sometime in 1971. Why do you recall this?"

Becker- "I witnessed it."

Detective- "Go back to that day and tell us what happened."

Becker- "I was with a couple of friends in Flower Mound and I left them at dusk. One guy and another guy with a girl. I knew John and his last name started with an R...like Rizzo. He was white and about one and a half years younger than me. We were walking around the streets on foot. Just before dusk I left them and walked to Carrollton which leads to the Manor Club. I got to a wooded area on club grounds. I saw seven to eight guys hanging around the grill to the right of the clubhouse."

Detective- "How far from you?"

Becker-"Pretty close. Close enough to identify them. Four that I could recognize and three others. It was dark but light enough to see. There were lights around the clubhouse parking lot. Two of them were in contact with a Coke machine. One was Mike Holloway who was sixteen to seventeen years old. I knew him at that time for three to four months. We met at the shopping center and went to his parent's apartment in Belgrade apartments. They lived in the last building next to the woods on the top floor to the right. This building faces Georgia Avenue. He was breaking into the Coke machine and the machine was moving a lot."

Detective- "Did you see any instruments?"

Becker- "Not really. I saw Stevie Gruner who I knew from Aspen Hall and Maggie's Place. He was sixteen years old at the time."

Detective- "How tall are you?"

Becker-"I'm five foot three and a half inches. Stevie was standing off a little way from the Coke machine."

Detective- "Where did he live?"

Becker-"Off Aspen Hill near Grace Road."

Detective- "If you saw photos of them would you know them?"

Becker- "I saw Greg Swarr. White, sixteen to seventeen years old."

Detective- "You were shown a photo of Greg Swarr prior to this interrogation."

Becker- "Swarr was facing a little driveway off the parking lot and he was standing five feet away from the Coke machines. He was standing to the left of the Coke machines. I could show you where people were standing. Greg lives in Aspen Hill. The fourth person was Danny Finch. Sixteen to seventeen years old and five foot six to five foot eight. Danny lives over on Beacon off Parkland Drive. I knew Danny for quite some time. He was standing ten feet away from the Coke machines up near the hedges. The three other people were all white. I've known Greg Swarr since 1971 for at least a year. The other three in back of the Coke machines on the grass I never saw before. They didn't know I saw them. They messed with the Coke machine. Greg walked fast with a gun in his hand. Suddenly he was kneeling down. I heard two shots and saw a man fall; it was the first time I saw this man. I'm pretty sure he had a uniform on. The weather that night was pretty fair, not cold or warm. It was clear. I saw what was going on. Greg kneeling down and stood up fast. Gun in his right hand. Just before I took off, someone said, "Greg, you're crazy." Greg was from here (pointing) to the second desk. About twenty feet from me. The deputy was ten feet farther than Greg. The deputy was standing. Greg got up and the man followed him and I heard two shots. This man was facing off to the right. Greg had a thirty-eight. I heard two shots. One after the other. I saw the man fall and I ran and the rest did the same. I heard, "Greg, you're crazy." I have no doubt it was Greg Swarr who fired the gun. I ran to Aspen Hill Shopping Center and then to Maggie's Place. They also came up to Maggie's."

Detective- "You saw Greg stand up..."

Becker- "He had a gun a little ways from his body. When kneeling, I was not sure if the gun was in his hand or in the beltline. He made a half turn. The Deputy had come around the grill from the pool area. He came around in front of the grill and Greg shot him. The officer said, "What are you doing?" The officer landed in the driveway. The deputy sheriff was wearing a dark outfit of some kind. Suit or something. The lights weren't great but threw a beam of light in that direction. He was reaching for something when he yelled out, "What are you doing?" He may have had a flashlight. I didn't know if it was a flashlight or a light reflecting from the Coke machine. The deputy had just come around the corner of the grill. Fifteen feet from the corner. Bang, bang. Two shots. I saw the man fall. I didn't know he was a deputy at that time. Man was ten, twelve, thirteen feet from the Coke machines. Steve was standing a little away from the Coke machines. Greg was kneeling in front of the Coke machines to see how they were doing."

Becker- "My foster parents live in Manor Club. I've lived with them since 1963-1964. I'm not with them now.

Becker- "I knew there was an officer there. I couldn't see his face. I'd say he was white. Not that small. Came around the corner of the building and Greg stood up and fired two shots and he fell there. He and Greg were facing each other when he was shot. His attention was on Greg and the others doing the Coke machines. Seven guys by the Coke Machines and one gun. I can't say I saw the deputy's gun. He didn't shoot. No one else was around. The country club is closed on Monday night. There was a car around there, but I couldn't say what type. 'Sixty-nine' parked there quite often. Someone who goes to the club a lot. A member, goes so often."

Detective- "Exclusive club with a two-year-old car?"

Becker-"A lot of fixed-up cars there; fifty-seven Chevy. Greg drives his mother's car."

Detective-"How long did it take you to run away from the shooting?"

Becker- "After the sheriff fell, I took off immediately. Five seconds after. The other guys started to run. I'm not sure what directions. The deputy fell at a slant. Came down like this (demonstrates). Hands moved but didn't grab a part of his body. I couldn't tell if it was blood."

Detective-"How long after the shooting did these people show up at Maggie's Place?"

Becker- "One hour after I got there. Not all of the people. Three of the four I named came to Maggie's but not together. Steven, Greg, Dan. They all came on foot. I was there after they left. They were there for five to ten minutes. Nothing I could hear about what happened. They came one hour after me. I ran like this: on the golf course, woods that back up to houses. I ran to Chesterfield and walked to Bel Pre Road. Three blocks from Parkland school and then the shopping center. No one was behind me. I was going to Maggie's. Chesterfield to Bel Pre Road. Past elementary school and went to where Chesterfield sits across Bel Pre and dead ends into another street. Went down Parkland Drive to the shopping center and got to Aspen Hill. Gas station there, Citgo."

Detective- "Why did you cut through yards?"

Becker- "No particular reason."

Detective- "Why didn't you go down Georgia or down Chesterfield?"

Becker- "I wanted to cut through as many places as I could. I didn't want to be seen. I thought the cops were coming up Bel Pre."

Detective- "Did you hear any sirens?'

Becker- "Fire truck sirens. I saw cop cars. No detective cruisers till I got to Aspen Hill. Officer Hill was in uniform. I saw officer Haynes. I never talked to anyone."

Becker- "The next day Greg's sister, Sarah, and a couple of girls I don't know were at Maggie's. She said that she and her brother and

Stevie were fingerprinted. She said they found a gun with fingerprints on it that were Greg Swarr's. Took his fingerprints off the gun."

This is the end of Part One of the 1973 interview with Larry Becker. There were numerous differences between what he said and what the evidence showed. His account was not consistent with where the body was found. He described the sheriff falling in the driveway but he was in the southeast corner of the parking lot. He failed to mention the sheriff had on a bright yellow raincoat. It was a miserable day and Becker described it as clear, not cool or hot. No firearm was recovered. Swarr was never fingerprinted and was never a suspect in this case until this interview.

CHAPTER TWENTY-SIX

What the Reel-to-Reel Revealed (Part Two)

Detective- "Did you ever know Greg to have a gun?"

Becker- "No. I knew him for a year. Mike Hollaway shot thirty-eight before. I never saw him shoot. I never saw any of them with guns."

Detective- "How well did you know these people?"

Becker-"Pretty well. Friends. Hung out at Maggie's with them."

Detective- "You saw a guy shoot someone and then saw him at Maggie's. Why didn't you go over to him and talk to him?"

Becker-"I talked to him about other things like when he was getting his mother's car again. If I had said something and he was picked up, he figured it would be me. He knows Danny Finch's older brother, Jack. I was afraid."

Detective- "Why are you saying it now if you are afraid?"

Becker- "I was never asked before."

Detective- "If you were not in jail would you have said anything?"

Becker-"Yes. If I had gone to the police station the boys would have known something was wrong because they know I hate cops."

Detective- "You didn't say anything because they might accuse you. You're not worried about the same people, bad people?"

Becker- "It does worry me. When my prison sentence is over, I'm never coming back to Montgomery County."

Detective- "You said seven people there. Did the three standing in the grass see the other four by the Coke machines? Did you see any items lying around? Monkey wrench or table top at the club?"

Becker- "No."

Detective- "Your parents live on Chesterfield. Did you hear of any house break-ins?"

Becker- "No."

Detective- "Did anyone talk to you about any burglaries?"

Becker- "No. After that day, Murphy... he, Marshall and Cranston. This was in Aspen Hill. I recognized four people and three more in the grass. Steve was up on grass with two other guys. Mike was standing on the side of the Coke machine. Greg was standing five to ten feet from the Coke machine. The three on the grass moved around in circles. Greg and Holloway and the guy in front of the Coke machines bent down. Trying to get money."

Detective- "Do you know Robert Canaveri, John Bruner?"

Becker- "I do know Robert Canaveri and John Bruner. John is Steve's older brother. I know Norman Perry and Shoemaker. Perry wasn't there."

Detective-"All five of those boys broke into the Coke machine. Five plus four makes nine people there. Who yelled, "You're crazy!"

Becker- "It was faint. Just flat enough to pick up. I didn't know five had broken into Coke Machines. Four I told you about. Holloway lives at home. Greg lives at home. I was staying on the streets or friends' houses or the woods. I stayed in the woods near the church. Rainy nights

I was in that church. Night of the murder I was in the woods. I slept on the ground. Not really cold enough."

Detective- "Did you have much clothing?"

Becker- "Pair of pants, T-shirt, and shirt only clothes. The guys didn't have jackets, maybe sweaters."

Detective- "What was the deputy wearing?"

Becker- "Dark color coat. Dark like county police officer. No doubt it was a dark night. Not short sleeves."

Detective- "How about hat?"

Becker- "Not really sure. Not sure if he had a hat. He was coming from the building. Don't know if same person. Sixty-nine car, no one sitting in."

Detective- "Where would the deputy have fallen in relation to the telephone pole?"

Becker- "Here's the snack bar. He fell down in the driveway itself. Driveway comes down like this (points with hands). I was in front of the club, just walking through."

Detective- "Why go through the hedges?"

Becker- "The hedges were between me and the shooting."

* * * * * * * *

Lisa Killen listened to the tape over and over and had Katie Leggitt join her. There were so many inconsistencies and falsehoods. All of the people Becker named in the interview were not there that night. The four individuals he named were not present. The night of the murder had been rainy and not clear, and the deputy sheriff was wearing a bright yellow raincoat and not a dark suit. The location of J.T.'s body according to Becker after the shooting wasn't even near where the body was actually found.

There were so many discrepancies that in 1973 the detectives who interviewed Becker did nothing. They believed Becker was making a statement to reduce his sentence and knew nothing about the shooting. He was given no reprieve from his original sentence and additional time for the escape. He went back to jail to finish serving his time and the officers filed the reel-to-reel tape in the box that contained the rest of the evidence from the murder.

Lisa Killen realized several things from listening to the interview. First, Larry Becker was a man who placed himself at the scene of the murder and at the very least, was a witness to what had happened. Second, the police had a hold back of evidence from the murder that they hadn't released to the public or press. Lisa again researched all of the articles written at the time of the shooting and afterwards; in none of them was it mentioned that there were two shots fired. One bullet to J.T.'s flashlight and the second to his head. Becker had stated two shots multiple times in the interrogation, something that no one should know unless they had been there that night. After discussion with the cold case team, Lisa decided to make finding Larry Becker and interviewing him the focus of her investigation.

CHAPTER TWENTY-SEVEN
Finding Larry Becker (Smith)

Larry Becker had disappeared! There was no sign of him anywhere Lisa Killen looked. No taxes paid, no state or federal government information. Lisa located the man who was Becker's best friend and had been known as 'The Raven' as a teen-ager, and he said he thought Becker had moved to upstate New York. The trail again went cold.

Next Lisa decided to speak with Larry's brother, Leslie Becker. She used investigative data bases and found Leslie's obituary. "Leslie Becker survived by Larry Smith," read the obituary. The obituary provided details that Larry lived in New York and had a wife named Ruth.

Lisa found Larry David Smith who lived in Little Falls, New York. She found his address in Little Falls. Larry David Smith seemed to match Larry David Becker.

The next step was a deep dive into Larry Smith. Lisa located a Facebook page for Larry Smith, Senior. It mentioned that he was from Little Falls, New York. It stated he attended Robert E. Peary High School in Rockville, Maryland, which Larry Becker attended. On the Facebook page Larry Smith was offering a Pittsburgh Steelers jacket for sale and gave a phone number to call if interested in buying it.

Next, Lisa and Katie decided to go up to Little Falls to do some reconnaissance work. They reached out to the New York State Police to tell them of their plans. They didn't contact small towns or municipalities in New York where someone might know Larry Smith or his family. In the end of May, 2022, Lisa and Katie drove to Little Falls, New York. They were unable to get inside the apartment building where Smith now lived because it was a high rise with restricted access. The receptionist had to be present to let you in, and she wasn't available. They stopped by the New York State Police Barracks on the way back to Maryland. It was a two-day trip; up one day and back the following day.

Lisa and Katie came back and immediately set up monitoring on Smith's phone. They didn't get the content of text messages but were notified of the phone number of who was contacting him. They had to get this approved and signed off on by a judge. Throughout the summer: Larry Smith's cell phone was monitored. There were minimal phone calls with his daughter, Melinda Allen. The next step was to confirm that Larry Smith was Larry Becker, and for this Lisa dug up an old acquaintance of Becker's, John Rizzo.

CHAPTER TWENTY-EIGHT

Initial Phone Calls and Exchanges with Larry Smith

Corporal Lisa Killen got in contact with John Rizzo who was a known associate of Larry David Becker. John Rizzo was named by Larry Becker the person he was hanging out with when he walked to the Manor Country Club. Lisa interviewed Mr. Rizzo and asked for his assistance. He said yes.

John Rizzo was asked to conduct controlled phone calls with Larry Smith. A controlled phone call is a recorded phone call done on behalf of the police department. Rizzo and the police were present for the calls. The two phone calls took place on July eighteenth, 2022 and July twentieth, 2022.

First Phone Call — July 18, 2022

Becker-Smith-"Hello."

Rizzo- "Is this Larry Smith? This is John Rizzo. Did you live in Aspen Hill?"

Becker-Smith- "No, I lived in Glenmont."

Rizzo- "We hung out at Maggie's Place, the church in Aspen Hill. I went to school with your brother, Les. I worked hard trying to track you down. We did burglaries together and even robbed your parent's house."

Becker-Smith-"I can't talk. I have business..."

Rizzo- "I need to talk to you bad."

Becker-Smith-"You got the wrong person, buddy."

Rizzo- "Glenmont is walking distance to Aspen Hill. Weren't you friends with Raven, Ed Hill, me?"

Becker-Smith- "I don't know them."

Rizzo-"Sure sounds like you. We did a lot of crazy shit together in the seventies. I have a feeling it was you and there's a lot of stuff I have to talk to you about. You didn't go by Larry Becker?"

Becker-Smith- "No."

Rizzo-"Know Raven?"

Becker-Smith-"No."

Rizzo-"Ed Cranston?"

Becker-Smith-"No."

Rizzo- "Where'd you go to high school?"

Becker-Smith- "Long time ago."

Rizzo- "Robert E. Peary High School."

Becker-Smith- "No. Could have been Kennedy, I guess. I don't know."

Rizzo- "I'm in trouble dude and I need to get with Larry so I don't get in deeper trouble and Larry doesn't get into trouble. Police brought me to the police station regarding shit I did in the nineteen seventies."

Becker-Smith- "I'm not interested."

Rizzo- "You sure sound like him, dude. We broke into a townhouse in Glenmont."

Becker-Smith-"That's not me."

Rizzo- "Same guys who robbed your parents. I went to jail over that."

Becker-Smith- "I don't know what you're talking about."

Rizzo-"Police came to my door and sooner or later they will come to yours. They played a tape where you gave them my name back when that security guard got shot. You can be honest with me. Why did you give the police my name?"

Becker-Smith- "This call is over and don't call my number again."

* * * * * * * *

Lisa Killen on witness stand during trial: "We thought the phone call had value. He denied who he was and didn't hang up. We asked John Rizzo to send a screenshot to Larry Becker-Smith's cell phone. This was done the next day, July nineteenth, 2022. After this, Larry Smith's cell phone called Rizzo's cell phone two times. We told Rizzo not to answer so we could set up another controlled call."

Second Phone Call — July 19, 2022

Rizzo-"Larry."

Becker-Smith-"What?"

Rizzo-"John Rizzo. We hung out a lot, got locked up for burglary and for armed robbery of your parent's house. Police think you're dead. They played a tape about the incident at Manor Country Club. You told them you were there and I was with you. I need to know what to tell these people."

Becker-Smith- "I was arrested for burglary."

Rizzo-"That's not it. We did sentences for that. They re-opened the case for the fiftieth anniversary. You told them I was with you and you saw the sheriff get shot. They think you're dead. What the fuck happened?"

Becker-Smith-"I didn't talk to the cops at all. I went to the judge and he sentenced me. My brother snitched on me."

Rizzo-"You said your name on tape and that I was there."

Becker-Smith- "Cop supposedly shot. I don't remember the interview at all. I pled guilty and I'm waiting for my lawyer."

Rizzo-"I'm not going down for this. Granddaughter and neighbor see shit. Burglary and armed robbery of a house a year later."

Becker-Smith- "That's the only time I ever pulled anything off."

Rizzo-"Why on tape did you say you were at the scene of the shooting and I was with you? These fuckers are coming after me. I'm not a big fan of pigs."

Becker-Smith- "I didn't know you were there when we did burglary at the townhouse."

Rizzo-"This is a year earlier. You broke into a house and the sheriff surprised you and you gave them my name and told them that I was with you. You're going to force me to give everything I dug up to find out."

Becker-Smith-"Tell them you're not a witness."

Rizzo-"You gave them my name and they're coming after me like I'm guilty. Who was with you that night? If I know how it went down I can get them off my back."

Becker-Smith- "Where was the cop killed?"

Rizzo-"Manor Club."

Becker-Smith- "How long before in jail?"

Rizzo-"I got out of jail due to treatment with the VA. I stayed in treatment places."

Becker-Smith- "I got out of jail in 1980. I went to jail seventy-four, seventy-five for that burglary."

Rizzo- "I went to jail in seventy-two. I was sitting on peat moss bags when pigs drove up and arrested me. You need to give me something. I need to get these fuckers off my back."

Becker-Smith-"I didn't witness any cop getting shot."

Rizzo-"I heard you identify yourself and give them my name. I'm not going down for this. They think you're dead. Give me some facts and maybe they'll close the fucking case. They're going to keep on coming for me. Fiftieth anniversary. They opened this case and are coming for me hard. Are you the one who shot him?"

Becker-Smith- "No."

Rizzo-"If you tell me we can get the whole thing resolved. I will tell you how I found you. If they find out you're alive they're coming to get you."

Becker-Smith-"They know I'm not dead. Raven still alive?"

Rizzo-"Yep."

Becker-Smith- I'm surprised he hasn't gotten ahold of me."

Rizzo-"He told me you were adopted and using the Smith name. I must have called one-hundred Larry Smiths. You said I was with you and you were a few feet away and witnessed it. Why did you give them my name?"

Becker-Smith- "Police tactic. I didn't see a cop getting shot and I wasn't there when it happened. When they come here I'll tell them the same shit."

Rizzo-"If you change your story you'll be in worse shape than me. You said you were there and I was with you. Everybody else is fucking dead."

Becker-Smith-"Only one dead is my brother."

Rizzo-"You said there were two shots."

Becker-Smith-"Tell them you're not a witness. That's bullshit! I was there for a burglary a year later."

Rizzo- "You didn't do any burglaries in Manor Club?"

Becker-Smith-"No, that's where I was living."

Rizzo-"You even told them you did robbery there on tape."

Becker-Smith- "I wasn't there when they robbed my parent's house."

Rizzo- "Les had a gun."

Becker-Smith- "Probably got it from Mark. He got picked up with a whole trunk full of weapons."

Rizzo- "Was Mark part of the incident with the Sheriff?"

Becker-Smith-"He could have been involved, but I wasn't."

Rizzo-"We did burglaries, let's face it. Maybe Mark's idea. I remember sitting in those people's dining room drinking a soda or beer. I need you to help me. Did Mark shoot the sheriff?"

Becker-Smith- "I don't know what he does."

Rizzo-"They have DNA. We're not in the seventies anymore. They're coming at me as an accomplice."

Becker-Smith- "You're a witness, not an accomplice."

Rizzo-"If you don't help me I'll turn you in."

Becker-Smith- "I got caught for burglaries. Others may have snitched on me."

Rizzo- "Were you doing burglaries the night the cop got shot?"

Becker-Smith- "I lived in Aspen Hill."

Rizzo- "We slept at Maggie's Place until one day one of us had an underage girl and they threw us all out."

Becker-Smith- "Those were the good old days."

Rizzo- "What happened that night at Manor Club? Why did you tell them you were there and I was with you?"

Becker-Smith- "I wasn't there."

Rizzo- "We're in the digital age. You can't tie your shoe without someone knowing."

Becker-Smith- "Best thing you can do is say you didn't witness anything."

Rizzo- "They're coming after me. They've got you on tape."

Becker-Smith- "That never happened."

Rizzo- "I'm trying to help you man."

Becker-Smith- "They would have come and found me. (laughs) They suckered you really good."

Rizzo- "They're coming after me if you can't give me something to tell them. I need a story to give them so I can walk away from them like you did."

Becker-Smith- "I never did an interview."

Rizzo-"Damn. Why you gotta lie to me? Why can't you help me? I called one-hundred different Larry Smiths. You said you were from Glenmont."

Becker-Smith- "You wanna know why? I was tracking your cell phone."

Rizzo-"You should know it's me. I'm being honest with you."

Becker-Smith-"Where do you live now?"

Rizzo-"Outside of Baltimore. I've got kids and grandkids. Did you shoot him?"

Becker-Smith- "I never had a fucking gun. I told you four or five times I wasn't there."

Rizzo-"It's on a cassette tape. You were cutting through Manor Club."

Becker-Smith- "None of that shit happened to me."

Rizzo-"You got something to hide?"

Becker-Smith- "I got nothing to hide. You got the truth. I don't lie to people."

Rizzo-"You're a better man than I am. I am the same as in the seventies."

Becker-Smith-"How old are you?"

Rizzo-"I'll be sixty-nine. I was born in fifty-three. I don't want to be seventy and be in jail for something I didn't do. I'm trying to help you."

Becker-Smith- "I told you all I know."

Rizzo-"They don't care about the burglaries. They want to get me for an accessory because you told them on tape I was there."

Becker-Smith-"I didn't do it."

Rizzo-"I'll give them all the information I have so they'll talk to you. If you're not going to help me, I'll talk to them."

Becker-Smith- "They know where I live."

Rizzo- "That's it." Hangs up the phone.

CHAPTER TWENTY-NINE

Life of Becker (Smith) from Birth in Little Falls, New York to Rockville, Maryland and Back to Little Falls

Little Falls, New York is the second smallest city by population in the state of New York. It's known as a leader in the knitting industry and in the marketing of cheese. It bills itself as the "Cheese Capital of the United States". Its most famous native is Charles Lindbergh. It is a white-collar city east of Utica, New York. Although tiny in population, it occupies both sides of the Mohawk River.

Larry David Smith was born in Little Falls, New York in 1952, the second of four children. His most dominant physical characteristic was his slight stature. Always small, he reached a maximum height of five foot three inches. His father was a truck driver who was away working most of the time. His mother was an alcoholic who was apparently gone in her own way most of the time. Larry and his three siblings were taken from their parents and lived in a Foster Home run by a minister.

At the age of seven Larry was adopted along with his two brothers and their sister by the Becker family who lived in Schenectady, New York. It was a difficult process, because the Beckers only wanted one child, the daughter, to be a sister to their recently adopted son, Jimmy. However, the birth mother would not allow the four siblings to be separated, so they could only be adopted as one harmonious unit. Clarence and Catherine Becker agreed to adopt all four children, and the Beckers went from a family of three to a family of seven. The day that he was adopted was the last day that Larry David Smith, now Larry David Becker, had any contact with his biological parents.

The Beckers and their new brood lived in Schenectady, New York and Clarence Becker worked for General Electric. Clarence was a bright, motivated man who subsequently moved the family to Rockville, Maryland for a better job. In Maryland he worked for IBM and became a university professor. Catherine Becker became the music teacher at the local high school. They moved to an area in Rockville called the Manor Club, a group of beautiful large houses and mansions that surrounded the Manor Country Club. The house had a large front yard with two mature trees for the children to climb. It was a brick house with four white columns holding up the roof over the front porch. There was a second story not visible from the front of the house but easily seen on the side of the house with two windows over the garage. Behind the house was forest with dozens of enormous trees covering luscious green grass.

Clarence Becker had definite ideas about the way his children should and shouldn't act. As Larry told the investigators in 2022, "I wouldn't jump when he said jump." Larry always felt his new father liked his siblings better than him. It appeared as though Clarence held up Larry as a bad example of what the other children shouldn't do. At age nine Clarence caught Larry playing with cigarette butts. For punishment he made Larry smoke an entire cigar which Larry proudly was able to accomplish. This eventually led to a smoking addiction which reached its peak later in life when Larry smoked three packs a day. This high smoking rate was only limited by Larry's finances. Clarence was not physically abusive to Larry or his siblings, but when angry with Larry he would throw money at him. His father set strict rules which Larry would continuously and knowingly break. "I didn't conform to everything. I never found out what a seven-year-old conforms to." Larry was closer to his sister, Yvonne, who was one year older than him, than he was to his natural brothers, Leslie and Hollis.

His sister was the one who would get upset with the way their parents treated Larry. The children were:

> Yvonne-one year older than Larry
> Larry
> Leslie
> Hollis
> Jimmy-small baby adopted before the Beckers

A neighbor who lived across the street remembers the children playing outside all of the time and always seeming to be happy and getting along.

At age twelve, Larry was sent for a psychiatric evaluation by his parents. Larry's only recollection from the sessions was that the psychiatrist said Larry's mother was a 'cold bitch'. Whatever the outcome, Larry was soon put in Boys' Training School. It was not a jail, but was run like one for young, wayward boys. The school, located in Maryland, was comprised of big buildings with lots of boys and not a lot of space or time devoted to fun activities.

Larry returned home after completing time at Boys' Training School, but it wouldn't be for long. There continued to be confrontations between Larry and his father, many of which ended with Clarence throwing money at Larry in disgust. It all reached a boiling point one day when Larry was a teen-ager. He and a neighbor were amusing themselves by throwing darts at a bicycle tire until a bullseye caused immediate deflation. Larry's father found out what happened and marched right into Larry's room. There was a model house displayed on the dresser that Larry built himself and took great pride in. Clarence took the model house off the dresser and broke it up piece by piece in front of Larry. Within twenty-four hours Larry was thrown out on the street with nothing except the clothes he was wearing. He was sixteen years old.

CHAPTER THIRTY

Life on the Streets

Larry spent the rest of his adolescence/early adult years growing up on the streets of Montgomery County, Maryland. It encompassed an amazing total of over four years from age sixteen to age twenty. He claims that he did no burglaries until the infamous townhouse burglary in 1972. His only other arrest was when he was apprehended by a store owner in Aspen Hill and accused of burglary after he bought a cupcake. He says he was taken before a judge who laughed at the charges and immediately dismissed them.

Larry often slept at Maggie's, which was the Church of Mary Magdalene and was located not far from the Manor Country Club. Part of Maggie's was dedicated to being a youth hall where teenagers could find a place for shelter and sleep when there were no alternatives. Unfortunately, in the late sixties and seventies, Maggie's served as a meeting place for groups of teenage boys to get to know each other, and then to form groups to perform criminal acts. Larry was the only one who spent nights there consistently, and he slept on the hard, wooden benches. He also slept on the ground of the pet cemetery which was located next to Maggie's when he couldn't get inside. Larry met Bobby Ray Edwards, known as Raven, at Maggie's. Raven became Larry's closest friend.

Larry's friends helped him out getting him food, clothes, and money for cigarettes. He dropped out of high school and turned his attention to surviving on the streets. Although he was not arrested for crimes prior to the 'Townhouse Burglary', he told his daughter, Melinda Allen, that he, his brother Leslie, and two friends did day-time robberies. His love of smoking Eagles Twenty Short Brand cigarettes continuously was always affected by how much money he had.

Larry summed up life on the streets: "We weren't bad kids. I just took a different road than the rest of them. I wasn't on drugs. I smoked cigarettes. When I quit smoking once, my nerves were so bad I had to go to the hospital."

Residents of Manor Country Club saw it differently. There were a lot of crimes committed in the area. When you read the newspapers prior to 1971, they were full of reports of robberies in the Manor Country Club area by unknown perpetrators. This was the reason the country club hired a sheriff to be there looking for young men up to no good. Whether it was breaking into houses, breaking into soda machines, or causing damage to the houses or country club it had to be stopped. The Sheriff's Department was hired to put an end to the lawlessness.

CHAPTER THIRTY-ONE

Townhouse Burglary

In 1972 at the age of twenty Larry committed the burglary that changed the course of his life. He and three other boys robbed a townhouse on what Larry calls "a spur of the moment thing." He later identified two of the boys as Mark Jensen and Raven but says he couldn't remember the other kid's name. The boys picked a townhouse just outside of Aspen Hill in the city of Glen Mont. No one was home at the time, and Larry remembers breaking in and stealing radios and money. He claims they didn't have guns in the execution of the robbery. The plan seemed to go well until one week later when Larry was hanging out at Maggie's. Suddenly the parking lot was filled with police cars and police came inside and arrested Larry. Larry was sure one of the other burglars had snitched since he was the only one arrested and the only one who served jail time.

Around this time Becker's house near Manor Country Club was robbed at gunpoint. Larry claimed he only found out about this burglary while in jail for the townhouse burglary. The robbers knocked on the Becker's door and when Mr. Becker opened it they stuck a gun in his face and said, "We're here to rob you." Larry claimed he never had any idea of who carried the gun or who was involved in this robbery. He felt his parents told the police that he burglarized their house. Larry felt Rizzo was involved in his parent's robbery from the way he told Larry the story.

Leslie Becker didn't do any time for any robberies according to Larry. He thought Leslie might have snitched on him, but he never asked him. "I don't hold grudges except Mark Jensen and that idiot,

Rizzo. I don't scare at all. I didn't confess to it," (the townhouse burglary). It was the last and only bad thing I did."

In August of 1972, Leslie Becker was interviewed by the police. He said, "My brother Larry might know something about that sheriff's death." For some reason, the police couldn't find Larry Becker. The police found Leslie Becker from a tip that an individual had information about the murder. Leslie said he believed Larry had knowledge of the shooting or was involved and knew who owned the gun used.

After being convicted of the burglary of the townhouse, Larry was sent from the courthouse to a minimum security prison to a work release program in Annapolis, Maryland where he was supposed to stay for five years. In 1973 he took off the government-issued prison work shirt. He left it on the ground and ran off. He escaped from the work program by himself. He had been one of the fastest runners in high school and was able to make his escape without much difficulty. He ended up free from prison and got married to Keri Nain with whom he had a daughter. He decided to go to Basic Training in the Military. One day his sergeant came in and told him the Maryland State Police were there looking for him. According to Larry, he was told the military could get him out of his prison sentence if he went into the service. Larry was concerned that if he joined the military the police would still come after him, so he surrendered and was taken back to serve his original sentence and three additional years for escaping. His wife, Keri Nain and his daughter both died in the next few years and weren't a part of Larry's life.

After his capture, on April fifth, 1973, Larry wanted to make a statement to the police in exchange for dropping the additional three years of his prison sentence. He said that he might have some information from the sheriff's murder but wouldn't talk unless given leniency. The prison officials agreed to his request if his information was truthful and helpful. Becker talked to police for three hours. During the interview he said, "When I leave Maryland I'm not coming back." In the interview Becker gave enough false statements that the police felt his whole story was fabricated. They didn't believe him and refused to reduce this sentence. The police concluded that he had no personal history of involvement in the murder. The reel-to-reel interview was incorrectly labelled as the Hobart Interview and filed in the box containing the information regarding Deputy Sheriff Hall's murder.

CHAPTER THIRTY-TWO
Moving Back to Little Falls and Life There

In 1980 at the age of twenty-eight Larry David Becker was released from jail and moved back to his birthplace, Little Falls, New York. He went before a judge, and had his name legally changed back to Smith from Becker. He got married to Ruth and they had two daughters and a son together. He worked in a variety of jobs over the ensuing years, including being a security guard for seven years, working in a shoe factory, working in a make-up factory, and working in a nursing home as a Certified Nursing Assistant. He enjoyed taking care of elderly people. He worked, he said, in order to raise his family. His wife worked in the shoe factory with him, then when she got her Certified Nurse Assistant certification Larry got his also. His last job was also his favorite job, working hospital security.

Larry raised a law-abiding, productive family. His oldest daughter was also a Certified Nurse Assistant at one time and now runs a bed and breakfast. His son works at Walmart and his youngest daughter is a licensed security guard who also helps troubled kids. Larry had grandchildren, too. Over time he developed diabetes, chronic obstructive pulmonary disease, elevated cholesterol, and heart disease.

He began having declining health in his mid-fifties. He was working as a hospital security guard when he was awakened one morning with pain in the middle of his chest and light-headedness. He was rushed to the hospital where he was found to have a heart attack. He had stents put into his coronary arteries and was cleared to return to work. He developed a weird feeling while working a couple of months later and was rushed to the hospital. One of the stents was blocked, and he suffered a second heart attack. Due to his coronary artery disease, congestive heart failure, and chronic obstructive pulmonary disease he went on to permanent disability.

When they were married Larry told his wife Ruth Anne that if she cheated on him he was leaving. He did have to leave her a couple of times, but always came back for the children's sake. Finally, after going on disability, he says he caught Ruth Ann with some guy at the Bingo Hall. He moved out and never went back. He would still see her occasionally but had nothing to do with her.

Larry moved in with his oldest daughter, Melinda Allen, and lived with her for years. She took care of her father completely and watched him closely. He would completely forget something was on the stove and burn it. Sometimes, he would forget to eat. He was gradually less able to take care of himself. Melinda had to drive him everywhere because his eyesight was poor and he sometimes didn't pay attention to the road.

Eventually Larry moved out and moved into a high-rise building in Little Falls for seniors. There was restricted access to the building, and a receptionist had to be present to let visitors in. Melinda kept close tabs on her father, calling or visiting him frequently. He seemed to spend most of his time in his apartment, playing solitaire on the computer. Melinda made sure he took his medications and ate. She cleaned the apartment for him and would bring her children to see their grandfather. Larry never divorced Ruth Ann, saying, "I wasn't paying for a divorce." Other than his children and grandchildren and his computer and television he had minimal contact with the outside world until he received the controlled call from John Rizzo.

CHAPTER THIRTY-THREE

Officers Killen and Leggitt Going to See Larry Smith in Little Falls, New York

After deciding that Larry Becker-Smith was the person they needed to interrogate next, Lisa Killen and Katie Leggitt took a two-day reconnaissance trip from Montgomery County to Little Falls, New York. First they contacted the state police in New York. They found the building where Smith lived but were unable to get inside of it due to restricted access and no receptionist present. They also stopped by the New York State Police Barracks to meet the officers there. The primary officer Lisa had been in contact with wasn't there that day.

After the controlled phone calls made by John Rizzo to Larry Smith in July of 2022, Lisa and Katie felt ready to proceed with meeting Smith in person and interviewing him. At nine a.m. on September first, 2022 the female officers from Montgomery County and two New York state police investigators drove in separate cars to Smith's apartment building. The four officers walked up to the main entrance of the apartment building and were let inside by a property manager. They asked for a room suitable for an interview. The room they were shown would not be private. It was a sensitive tape they would be recording their interview on and would not be free from interference in this room.

They next took the elevator to the ninth floor where Smith lived and knocked on the door. The entire dialogue with Larry Smith was recorded. Door opens.

Investigator Solls-"Are you Larry David Smith?"

Smith-"Yes."

Investigator Solls-"Investigator Solls, State Police. Can I step in?"

Katie-"Sorry so many of us. We're from Maryland. We're looking for some help from you. Do you know Rizzo?"

Smith-"He wasn't there that night."

Officer- "You know him from back then?"

Smith- "He's been calling for three months. Every day. I told him you say what you want to the cops."

Officer- "So he's implicating you?"

Smith-"Yes. He called me four weeks ago. Tried to pass himself off. I know where he lives and looked it up on the computer. I asked him if he knew Raven. He tried to tell me he's in the hospital."

Officer- "He actually is in the hospital."

Smith-"Told me the cops were looking at him for shooting a security guard."

Officer- "We are here. Have grand jury with him and we want information from you to help. We want to bring you back to the State Police Barracks. You are not under arrest. You are free to go."

Smith-"I don't have any useful information."

Officer- "You don't know what's helpful for us. You ran in that circle with those people. Is your memory pretty good?"

Smith-"Mine?"

Officer- "It seems like it's pretty good. We'll take you there and bring you back."

Smith-"That front door locks automatically and I've got my key."

Officer- "Nice little facility."

Smith-"Twenty-seven per cent of what you'd pay. Meals on Wheels comes in."

Officer-"Beautiful view."

Smith- "Two daughters live up here (Little Falls) and gotta son-in-law. I've got all kinds of kids. Each one has a key. Youngest we have living here is fifty years old."

Lisa-"We're out to police barracks."

Larry rode with the two male New York officers to the police barracks. The conversation was recorded and was congenial.

CHAPTER THIRTY-FOUR
Interrogation of Larry Smith

The police barracks in Herkimer County, New York has a small interview room with video equipment inside. The walls are white and there are no windows. There is one brown wooden door.

Smith- "This is smaller than my apartment."

Katie-"Understand that you are not under arrest. We need you to clear up some information. Tell us who you are."

Smith-"I'm from Mars. (laughter) I'm not an alien." (Tells about birth parents, adoption, being thrown out of the Becker's house).

* * * * * * * *

Katie- "My brain is crazy and I forget everything. Raven told us some guy could get people guns. Does that ring a bell with you?"

Smith-"No."

Katie- "How did you choose townhouses? Were people there?"

Smith- "We didn't care. We didn't have guns."

* * * * * * * *

Lisa-"Raven was your best buddy. How did you meet him?"

Smith-"I really don't know. Maybe he came to Maggie's Place. We started palling around. So long ago."

****

Katie- "Rizzo has given us a time."

Smith- "I never knew Rizzo. I never heard his name. Mark Jensen I knew since age sixteen. We always hung around Maggie's. I didn't like him. He had a mouth on him like 'I know everything. Leslie knew him before I did. He brought Rizzo in."

Lisa-"You understand who Raven is?"

Smith- "Yes. I met Raven first. I didn't like Mark; smart mouth, swearing, putting people down. I took an automatic dislike to him. I left him alone because my brother was close friends with him. Rizzo was involved in the group due to Mark. One other, I can't remember name, but Rizzo knows him. They robbed my parents. I had no idea this was going to happen. Mark told me one of the kids tried to rob them. If they thought I'd known about that, they would have arrested me for that, too. My brother told me about robbing my parents."

Lisa-"Who went to your parent's house?"

Smith-"The other kids that Rizzo named. Not Raven. None of my friends. I'm smarter than that to rob my parents."

****

Katie- "Gun involved in that burglary (of parent's house)." When that happened, you were gone from the house. But people you knew did it. Was it Rodney who had the gun?"

Smith-"Could be."

Katie- "You and your brother weren't involved in the burglary of your parents?"

Smith- "I wasn't and I don't think Leslie was. Leslie never went out of his way to fight."

Katie- "Somebody put a gun to your father's face... Did you fight with hands or weapons?"

Smith-"Just hands. Mark Jensen was picked up for having guns in his car I was told after I got out of jail."

Katie- "Were you curious who did it?"

Smith-"I thought Mark did it but Rizzo and the other kid did it. Mark didn't care about too many people and doesn't like too many people...I never had a gun and didn't know how to get one. Mark Jensen was arrested with a forty-five. Only burglary I did was the townhouse. Rizzo did others and tried to say I was with him. Rizzo might have done other burglaries...I don't hold grudges except Mark and this idiot, Rizzo."

* * * * * * * *

Katie- "We need to take a break for bad backs."

Smith- "Can I go smoke a cigarette?"

Katie-"Sure."

They all leave the interview room. Fast forward tape through the break.

Back To Interview Tape

Katie-"I wanted to circle back to Rizzo. When was the first time he called you?"

Smith-"Four to five months ago. I don't remember him at all. He tells me my whole life's story; I don't know where he got it from. He knew we were adopted, that I changed my name, and the rest of the people at home were dead. He said I told the cops about him."

Katie- "Tell me about the security guard."

Smith-"I didn't know there was a security guard and I didn't know anyone got shot."

Katie- "No one said anything about that? Craziest phone call ever."

Smith-"He wanted to know what to say to the police to get him out of it."

Katie- "When he first called did he make connection with you? I would have hung up."

Smith- "I told him you're talking about stuff I don't even know. I wasn't there that night because I wasn't with him. I said as far as I know, no one was killed there."

Katie-"I'm getting confused. You said the night we did burglary that I wasn't aware there was a security guard there. He called you and told you the cop got shot at townhouse?"

Smith-"That's what he said."

Katie-"If you participated in burglary at Manor Club I don't care. You just said, "I wasn't aware of the security guard or cops after the burglary."

Smith- "I never did a burglary at Manor Club."

Katie- "Rizzo put your name in it. When you say there wasn't a cop or security guard at Manor Club that night I can't trust what you're saying."

Smith- "I never knew there was a security guard anywhere."

Katie- "We're talking about the Manor Club. I don't care what you did that night unless you shot the security guard. I need you to tell me the truth. Was there a burglary at Manor Club?"

Smith-"Just my parents. I was just charged for burglary at the townhouse. I don't remember seeing Rizzo there, but he says he, Mark Jensen and I were there. He told me a security guard or cop got shot at the townhouse."

Katie-"Do you think he shot the cop?"

Smith-"I don't know if he did it or that other kid did it. Possible that Mark Jensen did it."

Katie- "You never heard of burglary at Manor Club the night the cop was killed?"

Smith-"Never did burglary there that wasn't caught."

Katie- "You have a very good memory, better than mine. Don't remember burglary?"

Smith-"This is the first time I ever heard about it. I went to the funeral for my adopted father and Rizzo told me about it."

Katie-"We spent more than a year digging into this case. We took shoe prints and DNA. In our travels through the case file, we found an interview with you and the police. You name Rizzo as being with you that day."

Smith- "I was sure I hadn't said anything at all to the cops."

Katie- "You put yourself there as a witness and saw the officer shot."

Smith-"As far as I know, I never spoke to the cops."

Katie- "You're afraid of getting someone else in trouble. Your brother told police you knew who shot the cop. We can play it for you.

You name step by step what happened to the security guard. You were there for the burglary but had nothing to do with murder. I don't want you to get jammed up with murder. We don't give a shit about burglaries at Manor Club. We care about who killed the security guard and you're our number one witness."

Smith- "Well, apparently I don't remember."

Katie- "I believe everything you've said. Your life has been squeaky clean. No way you forget a man getting shot. You saw this bad thing going down, you shot him or you saw someone else shooting him. I believe one hundred percent you didn't shoot the security guard/sheriff. We have to be very consistent with how we do our jobs. I one hundred percent believe you saw; I have no doubt you were there burglarizing one of those houses. You have to be honest with me about what put you there that night. I have a guess the security guard came up and scared someone who accidentally shot him. I don't get a pay raise if someone innocent is punished for what they didn't do. We have your word that you were there that night. I don't believe you weren't involved in the burglary or didn't see a man shot. I do believe you became a very good man. You're saying things that no one else knew because they weren't released to the public. You wouldn't know that unless you saw that. I don't know why the police didn't say we've got a gem in 1973. I believe in my heart it was an accident. You have to know by television shows you watch that police already know the truth before asking questions. Don't insult my intelligence by lying to me. Who were you with doing burglaries that night?"

Smith-"I can't remember that. The Manor Club..."

Katie- "We know you were there. Who else was there?"

Smith-"Only one was me 'cause I went to jail. Rizzo put himself there."

Katie- "Do you remember being there?" I don't want to beat around the bush. Heavy stuff was taken."

"The night security guard was shot. Who was there with you? I know you remember."

Smith-"Have to be the same ones I did townhouse with. Me, Rizzo, Mark Jensen, the other kid, my brother."

Katie- "Why would your brother tell on you if he was there?" I'm trying to establish what you know. I don't think your brother was there unless he was trying to get out of trouble. This is shit going sideways. There are things as a police officer I will never forget. I know from this interview you were there. In your statement you put in a lot of people who weren't there. You're a completely different person now than you were then. Larry has lived a good life and wouldn't want any harm to come to a security guard. I know you were there for burglary. Who else was there?"

Smith-"Rizzo."

Katie- "Because he told you or you remember. What did you get out of that house? Some interesting objects."

Smith-"Some radios. Cash. Nothing big, though."

Katie- "Little table or coins?"

Smith-"Coins is possible."

Katie-"How many of you were there?"

Smith-"Couldn't have been too many of us."

Katie- "Whose idea was it to burglarize the house the night the security guard got shot?"

Smith-"Might have been..."

Katie-"Those people weren't home. I don't care if you did one hundred burglaries. It has nothing to do with my job. I'm not judging you. Don't tell me anything you don't remember. I know the answers to the questions I'm asking you. I think you're in a good place."

Smith-"I don't know."

Katie-"Do you know who shot the security guard? Did you see it?"

Smith- "I don't know."

Katie-"That's like being kind of pregnant. I've done this more than one-half of my life and have been a detective twenty out of twenty-four years. I want to have mutual trust with you. I just want to know the truth. You're struggling with something. Either you did it accidentally or you saw someone who did it. If you didn't, your answer would be automatic. We have one and a half hours of you telling us everything you saw. We've established you were there for the burglary. Were you there for a burglary? Did you have a getaway car?"

Smith-"Yeah, someone had a car."

Katie- "There was a car. How else would you have hauled all that shit away" Did he interrupt the burglary?"

Smith- "I think so."

Katie-"I want to make sure I'm not upsetting you."

Smith-"I know we took off in a hurry. A couple of 'em got in a car and were driving around."

Katie- "Were you bringing stuff back and he had a flashlight and you guys got spooked? What happened? Did you hear sirens? Other juveniles there heard sirens."

Smith-"It was scary. He asked what we were doing. Everybody took off."

Katie- "Do you feel like you're ready to tell me who shot him? I don't want you to stop here, I know you ran but you saw him get shot first. Either you or somebody next to you shot him. I'm feeling what is cost or benefit of you telling me the truth. We already know a lot of the truth. We know you saw it because you said it yourself. This reel-to-reel has been authenticated by the FBI. I took the time to get to know you. I think you're a good guy who has cleaned up his life. I'm not here to mess with that. Imagine how your daughter would feel if you got shot. There's a story here. The security guard wasn't even supposed to be there. I want to know if it was an accident or someone went boom boom!"

Smith-"I know I didn't shoot anybody because I didn't have a gun."

Katie- "Was Rizzo in the military in 1971? I subpoenaed military records that show Rizzo was in the military in 1971."

Smith- "I might have seen who did it. Rizzo, Rodney..."

Katie- "So you saw the whole thing go down?"

Smith-"Yeah."

Katie- "Were you scared?"

Smith-"Yeah."

Katie-"Were you scared to tell the truth? Why?"

Smith-"I don't know."

Katie- "You were at Manor Club with friends. You remember someone flashing a light and saying, "What are you doing?" I want you to trust me. We've been out there. There wasn't a bush there like you say. So, where were you to know these specifics?"

Smith-"Oh boy. I had to be somewhere near. I really did see it."

Katie- "That kid was Raven's brother, Rodney, and he wasn't there that night. He was much younger than you guys. Rizzo wasn't lying. We know you were there doing the burglary. For shooting you use words like probably. You're distancing yourself. I don't believe that you forgot the shooting. What is keeping you from telling me about the shooting? What are you afraid of?"

Smith- "I don't want to go to jail. I know I didn't shoot..."

Katie- "Why would you go to jail if you didn't do the shooting?"

Smith- "'Cause I was there."

Katie- "Not a problem in our county unless you're the one who did the shooting. I know you're holding something back. You either shot or saw who did."

Smith- "Not me. I know I didn't do it."

Katie- "Let's get out of that space. Not having fun there. I think you're a good guy. Why did you just say you don't remember anything?"

Smith- "Natural reaction."

Katie- "I'm struggling with it. What do you remember? We know the answers before you come in here. Why do you remember now doing the burglary, him saying, "What are you doing?" This is the most important part you don't want to forget. Something else is keeping you from telling me who shot this guy. Reflex, accident, fucking malice."

Smith- "Probably an accident. Person who had a gun got scared, turned around and shot him."

Katie- "Do you remember what you said that night regarding how many shots, where the sheriff landed?" Who was left behind on foot besides you? For sure, be sure."

Smith- "Rizzo and Mark Jensen."

Katie- "Was Reven there that night?"

Smith- "No. I'm not afraid of those people. I'm not afraid of anyone."

Katie-"You're afraid of going to jail. Any dreams or nightmares seeing a man get killed doesn't stay with you your whole life?"

Smith- "No. Maybe I blanked it out."

Katie-"If you saw me getting shot outside it bother you?"

Smith-"Yes."

Katie- "Do you think you shot him that night and have blocked it out? It's not Rizzo. Could it have been Raven? You're there and you didn't do it, nothing is going to change against you. Like Mark Jensen. Only thing is if we find out you know or you did it. Maybe an accident."

Smith-"I'm trying to picture where each of those two guys was."

Katie-"It wasn't Rodney who called you. We had to talk to every single person. Raven's brother said he got a strange message from you."

Smith-"He told me I said Raven was there. He wanted to know why I was bringing Raven into all of this."

Katie- "You named Greg Swarr as the shooter in your original statement. He didn't do it so why did you name him? That guy was a dork, a nerd. Why did you name him?"

Smith-"Maybe I saw Raven or Mark and didn't want to tell on them."

Katie- "At that stage in your life would you have told on someone if you saw them shoot someone? Leslie never told you that he said that two times to the police. Did you ever talk to Leslie? Ask what happened that night. You've got to remember who shot this guy. Do cost-benefit analysis again. Just say it."

Smith-"I'd say Raven."

Katie- "Who did you see do it?"

Smith-"I see Raven's hand and the security guy drop to the ground. We were close together. I see his arm up. I didn't know he had a gun. Not to get the heat off of me."

Katie- "Are you sure?"

Smith-"I'm sure it's Raven. I didn't want him to get into trouble. We were close and never snitched on each other."

Katie-"That night you called him did you want to warn him? Did he ever say keep this secret or if you say it's me I'll say it's you? An unspoken pact?"

Smith-"No."

Katie-"I'm not saying it wasn't Raven. Who drove the car?"

Smith-"I don't know."

Katie- "How many in the group?"

Smith-"Probably five of us."

Katie- "Sure it was Raven, no question?"

Smith-"Yeah."

Katie-"Why did he turn around and raise his hand? You had to turn around at the same time."

Smith-"We were walking away from the complex and heard a guy holler. "What are you doing?" and turned around."

Katie shows him a map of the country club and surrounding area. Lisa pulls her chair next to Smith's chair.

Lisa-"This is the house where the burglary happened. This is the golf course. Here is the parking lot. (Lisa drawing) Over here is a semi-circular driveway. Here is a star where the country club is. Walk us through. Draw for me with little dashes where you guys were headed."

Smith-"Towards vehicle. We were on foot. We were coming this way and heard the noise. Almost half-way to the parking lot."

Lisa- "Who is we?"

Smith-"Not Mark. We were carrying some things."

Lisa-"Where did the voice come from that said, "Hey, what are you doing?"

Smith-"Driveway or something next to the house. He shined a light at us and hollered. Raven and I turned around and I saw Raven's hand in the air. Raven was holding something and I figured it had to be a gun."

Lisa-"Did you hear a gunshot or multiple gunshots?"

Smith- "I think I remember one. After that we took off. I went one way and Raven went the other way. I think Raven took off. Mark was the only one in the car."

Lisa-"Raven on left and you're on right. Which way did you go?"

Katie-"Want water or a beer?" (Katie leaves the room)

Smith-"The old man went golfing. My adopted dad. We went for toboggan rides in winter. I don't know exactly where that hill thing was. I went left and Raven went right. I think I went back to Maggie's Place."

Lisa-"Did you see Raven again that evening?"

Smith- "No. Never saw him or Mark."

Lisa-"Did you talk to them about what happened?"

Smith-"Never talked to Mark. I talked to Leslie about it."

Lisa-"There were conversations about the night of the burglary and what went down."

Smith-"Raven had something in his hand and I saw the security guard go down."

Lisa- "Did Raven say anything like, "Oh, shit,"?

Smith-"I don't remember him saying anything."

Lisa-"So you guys robbed a home, took it across the golf course to the parking lot to a vehicle. Security guard came up and shouted..."

Smith-"Like, "what are you guys doing?"

Lisa- "You know it was a gun after gun shot went off. Was he holding it like someone who has a gun?

Lisa-"You and Raven take off and Mark drives off."

Smith-"Mark wasn't in jail. Raven and me."

Lisa- "Did you know the man with a flashlight was a security guard?"

Smith-"No. Raven didn't know."

Lisa-"Do you remember what he was wearing?"

Smith-"He had a powerful flashlight in my eyes."

Lisa-"How much taller was Raven than you?"

Smith-"He was six foot and I was five foot three."

Lisa-"Do you know what happened to the gun?"

Smith-"No."

Lisa-"Do you remember leaving the property?"

Smith-We dropped it when we ran. We went to the house because it looked empty."

Lisa- "People who lived in the house (Schmidt's) thought someone was there right before."

Smith- "We weren't there."

Lisa-"How did you get inside?"

Smith-"Somebody had something to jimmy the door open."

Lisa-"Whose idea was it to break into the house?"

Smith-"We were just looking."

Lisa- "Were you doing it for cash?"

Smith- "I don't think Raven needed money. His family was wealthy. Mark needed money. Items all went into Mark's car."

Lisa- "What would you do with a camera if you stole it?"

Smith-"Sell it to someone who wants a camera."

Katie has returned to the room.

Katie- "Do you need a smoke? You're not being held here."

Smith- "I have pills I need to take."

Katie-"It's three o'clock. Do you want a smoke? You can go whenever you're ready!"

All leave the room
Empty room on screen
Larry David Smith, Lisa, and Katie walk in.

Lisa-"Feeling okay?"

Smith-"Yeah. Told I can drink tea, not coffee.

Lisa now sitting right next to Smith-could touch him.

Lisa-"Thank you for clearing up what happened."

Katie- "I appreciate you're coming into the police station and staying this long. Do you feel we treated you fairly?"

Smith-"Yes. Like on TV. Cop puts hands on prisoner..."

Katie- "I never put my hands on anybody. The family just wants closure."

Smith-"Hard for me. Such good friends."

Lisa- "Forensics. Things were stored. Do you know what trajectory means?"

Smith-"Path of something."

Lisa-"Problem is the autopsy of the security guard. Raven is a tall guy. Impossible for Raven to have shot the guard, too tall. Shot came from a different angle, your height. I need to know, was the shooting accidental? Raven is not responsible for the shooting. Is this accidental or intentional? Was it an accident then?"

Smith-"Yeah, I guess so. I saw Raven's hand go up..."

Lisa-"Raven is not responsible. Did you accidentally shoot the sheriff?"

Smith-Yeah. I didn't intentionally shoot anyone."

Lisa-"Do you feel remorseful about it?"

Smith-"Tell me about it."

Katie- "I saw tears in your eyes. You didn't shoot him because you were having fun. I always felt it was an accident. You didn't come clean. You knew you shot him and it was an accident. Did you tell anyone?"

Smith-"Didn't know he died. Didn't know until one of you told me."

Katie- "What did you think that night when he felt?"

Smith- "I saw him fall."

Katie- "You don't remember two or three shots?"

Smith-"I shot him and ran."

Katie- "You're one-hundred percent sure you shot him and Raven was with you?"

Smith-"Raven probably knows I shot him."

Katie- "What kind of gun and where did you get it?"

Smith-"Forty-five and I got it from Mark Jensen. He gave it to me and I never had a gun before."

Katie- "Where was it during the burglary?"

Smith-"Probably in my waistband."

Katie-"I very much appreciate you. I had a vibe you were a good guy. We offered to let you leave and you stayed. You had to get something off your chest. It's important to me that people feel they were treated with respect. Lisa is the brains and beauty. How do you feel now?"

Smith-"I feel better. Am I going to jail?"

Katie- "You're going home today. I don't lie to people. We've got a lot of stuff to figure out. You don't feel like you're going to hurt yourself?"

Smith-"Oh, no. That's the coward's way."

Katie- "I've never heard anyone say that they didn't feel better. Of course you care. I think you believe me that I'm a student of human nature. Thanks for giving this family closure. I know you need to eat and have stuff to do."

Lisa- "The day the security guard was shot, walk me through that day."

Smith-"Didn't eat breakfast. All hanging out at Maggie's Place. Ate what I could (chuckles). We were thinking what to do; decided to break into homes. Someone hollered at us and I spun around and pulled the trigger. Accident. I didn't mean to kill anyone."

Lisa-"Did you want to help anyone or just wanted to take off?"

Smith-"Ran off. Heard sirens so we took off."

Lisa-"Mark got the gun from where?"

Smith-"Don't know. I had gun twenty to thirty minutes."

Lisa-"Mark gives you a gun the same day the security guard is shot. Did you ask for it?"

Smith- "He had it in his waist band in the back and he handed it to me and I looked at it. Never held a gun before. Don't know if it's a forty-five or a revolver. He said just cock the hammer and pull the trigger. Then we all decided to do burglaries."

Lisa-"Was it already cocked back when you shot the security guard?"

Smith-"I'm pretty sure I just pulled the trigger."

Lisa-"What kind of car?"

Smith-"No."

Lisa-"What color?"

Smith-"I'm color blind. (laughs) Dark car, medium-sized with four doors. Don't know where Mark was staying."

Lisa-"How did you know Mark?"

Smith-"He wasn't there when we all met at Maggie's."

Lisa-"You had known Mark."

Smith- "I'd say...three weeks before I met him at Maggie's Place through Leslie (Larry's brother)."

Lisa- "What would you say to the sheriff's family?"

Smith-"Terrible thing that happened and I'm sorry I shot him. If I could take it back I would. I thought about it for a couple of years then didn't, so I took his word that he died. I didn't know since Rizzo told me."

Katie-"You just thought you shot him and he was okay? You didn't see the news?"

Smith-"I didn't watch the news. My kids know that I did burglary at the townhouse complex. Never told them about shootings."

Katie- "What do you think the kids will say? When we came in here you said you didn't do it. Do you feel you were forced?"

Smith-"No."

Katie-"Do you feel you were respected?"

Smith-"Yes."

Katie- "I have a sinus infection."

Smith-"You can apologize for me."

Katie-"You promise you're not going to hurt yourself?"

Smith-"Yeah."

Katie-"We'll call our boss and give you a number how to reach us. If we want you to come in we'll come to get you. Don't hide from us. Anyone you want to call now, like your kids?"

Smith-"Not tonight."

Lisa-"What did you do with the gun? Do you still have it?"

Smith-"If I threw it somewhere I don't remember. I believe I threw it. I didn't have it at Maggie's Place."

Katie-"You ran like Forrest Gump."

Smith- "I was a long-distance runner. Somewhere between the golf course and Maggie's Place I threw it."

Lisa- "Here's my business card and my information and phone number and email."

Smith says something and Katie laughs. All stand up.

Katie-"If your brother, Leslie was still alive, would you be pissed at him for turning you in?"

Smith- "No. Not now. I don't hold a grudge."

Hear Smith laughing outside the room as the room empties.

CHAPTER THIRTY-FIVE

Talking to Detective Katie Leggitt about Interrogation and Case

Katie Leggitt and Lisa Killen did a brilliant job interviewing Larry David Smith and finally getting him to confess. When I reviewed the beginning and middle of the interview, I could never have imagined where the interview would end. Katie and Lisa had a plan for the interview and how it would go, and they refused to veer away from the plan even as Smith's mind wandered onto different subjects. They always brought him back to the focus of the interview, and gradually wore him down. I asked Katie after the trial if I could contact her about her techniques in conducting a police interview, and she agreed to talk to me. She is a very pleasant woman in her late forties who is medium height with red hair and glasses. She exudes personality and humor but has a demeanor that tells you she's been around as a police detective and seen it all. I went back and read the interrogation techniques used by Katie and her colleagues to solve the Lyon sisters' rape and murder in Mark Bowden's book, *The Last Stone*. Here is my conversation with Detective Katie Leggitt:

Me-"Who put together the cold case team and how did he pick the three women on the team?"

Katie- "I am the only one who is actually a cold case member. Lisa was doing a temporary assignment and Sarah White was assigned to homicide. She does homicide instead of cold case. She wanted to do a cold case. My sergeant was the one who assigned the case. Chris Homrock is his name."

Me- "Was it Lisa working initially and you joined her after she narrowed it down? Or did you go through all the stuff with her, all the material?"

Katie-"I was the senior detective on the shift so my job is to oversee and train the new people who come in or the temps. We don't have a corporal, which is what Lisa is. I'm the lead investigator for lack of a better word. My sergeant does a lot of administrative stuff and I do most of the investigative stuff. When he assigned that case to Lisa, which really had a low solvability, the idea was that I would just be shadowing her because I have several other cases on my desk. It was just to give her an idea of what cold case looked like and that kind of a thing. Periodically, I would pop in. When she first came I told her she'd never been in cold case obviously, so I told her how it goes. You rearrange the case to however it works best for you. You go through the case file. I went through the steps with her of how you do it. She started digging into the case file with Sarah and I would come and go. She was the one; I travelled with her and did interviews because these type of interviews weren't something she had done before. She did the majority of digging and then a couple of times we would have meetings like round tables. I had several other cases that I was working, so I would pop in, get up to date, make sure things were going in the right direction. Which you don't really need with Lisa. She's very competent as you've gathered by now. She did a lot of the digging and the tedious work and I would check in and see what kind of trail we were running that day. It wasn't until we started doing interviews that we thought were of substance that I was heavily involved."

Me- "Who were those interviews with? Were they with anybody who wasn't mentioned in the trial?"

Katie-"No, everyone that was interviewed was mentioned at the trial."

Me-"Any cold case that comes in, are you assigned to it no matter what?"

Katie-"Not really. Things have changed. I have been there for ten years. We have started taking missing persons where it just started out as missing persons that were suspicious circumstances or we believed were dead. Now it's kind of evolved. We do a lot of missing person's work now. At any time, I can have eight cases on my desk. I've got a bunch. You'll work it, then you'll get stuck, and you'll have to wait for something to come up or for an interview or for DNA or any number of things. Cold cases are really not a start to finish case. Generally, like this one, unlike the Lyon sisters which was a case I worked for four straight years. That was a start to finish type of case where we didn't do anything else. But generally, that's not how it goes. We always get interrupted with an acute case of a missing person that could be a murder or something like that. It's not typical for one person to get every case. I'm generally involved to some extent if we have a round table or an interview to be done. I have a history in sex crimes where no one else really has that. So, if it's a rapist or someone that has some kind of sexual proclivity I'm usually the one who's involved in the interviews because I have that training. But no, there are three other full-time people on my shift that are assigned cold cases and they all have their own cases. We do work together."

Me-"Are you in charge of them?"

Katie-"No, no I'm the exact same rank as all of them. I just have more seniority."

Me-"What is your and the department's definition of a cold case?"

* * * * * * * *

Katie- "That's interesting, too (laughs). I think it's any case that the initial investigators have exhausted all the investigative steps. Also, generally as a rule, when people leave homicide their cases go cold meaning they're not there anymore to work them. Or it's something that's been cold for years that they lost any kind of investigative stuff that they could do with it. In the cold cases nowadays, there is so much that's changed in DNA. We have a humongous cold case room that has cold case files in it. Sometimes people will call in and say, "Hey, we never heard anything about our mother's cold case from 1975", and we'll pull it. It can be defined in so many different ways. There's not really us going down and handpicking a case. A lot of times an anniversary is coming up like what happened with the Hall case. The same thing happened with the Lyon sister case. Sometimes the age of the case is such that we know that witnesses are going to start dying so that kicks it up to the top of the list. Things like that. We don't get anything from our homicide unit, and if there's still people on the shift to work the case they keep it. Most of our cases are old unless it's a missing person that results in a death and we'll either keep it or work with homicide."

Me- "What percentage of cold cases that you work are solved?"

Katie- "I don't know. I don't think I would be able to do that. We all kind of dig in and out of each other's cases. In this case my role was to oversee and then basically get a confession."

Me- "Was Lisa working on this cold case full time, that's all she was doing?"

Katie- "Yeah, that's pretty much all she was doing. If we had a missing person case that we had to be all hands-on deck, she would jump in. For the most part, she did not get involved in any other cold case."

Me- "Did you set up the responsibilities for the case after you explained to Lisa how things are done?"

Katie-"Not really. Lisa is so competent. There's no rocket science about police work, especially not cold cases. It's really just showing her the way that I do things which is recreating my own case file so it makes sense to me. Going back to the witness interviews. Just basically explaining textbook stuff to her and then she took off on her own because she's very tenacious and very talented. No one really had to... in terms of things like the phone stings and stuff like that, that's not typically things police do. I would step in and do it and guide her through that. The interrogation: that's not something she had ever done before to that caliber, so that's why I pretty much led that. Other than that, the investigative stuff, if you do one investigation in police work and you're good at it you can really do all investigations."

Me- "Did you have any preconceived notions going into the case? Did you have any ideas about what was going on? I've been looking at this for a year and a half now since Carolyn Philo asked me to write the book. I saw the press conference on the internet and read the book about the Lyon sisters. Any preconceived notions you had about what had happened?"

Katie- "No, I think the idea always among our group was that it was a robbery gone bad. Initially people thought that maybe it was a hit on the other officer or that he was just at the wrong place at the wrong time. But there was never any way to prove that and it just didn't seem probable. I didn't put in a lot of effort or work... I know that a couple of other people on the shift prior to me had dabbled in it a little bit. There were some of the people involved in the soda machines who were notorious throughout the county. I'm sure you heard at the trial they blamed it on this one person for a long, long, time. I didn't really dig into it too much. I had so much else going on at my desk that I stayed in my lane."

Me- "When you were travelling to do these interviews was it all over the country or just in the area of Maryland where you are now?"

Katie- "We went to Utah..."

Me- "Wherever these people were that were there that night or could have been there that night that's where you went. Were these interviews done before you figured out the reel-to-reel or after you had that information?"

Katie- "Both."

Me- "I saw your interrogation technique in the Lyon sister case. Can you give me more details about the philosophies and techniques you use in interrogation?"

Katie-"The funny thing is I don't really have a technique other than my own at this point because I've just been doing it for so long. There is a big difference between interviewing different kinds of people. You don't interrogate a sex offender the same way you interrogate a murderer. So, there's a science behind that. Basically, I found after many years that you get more with sugar than you do with salt. Going in there and trying to establish a rapport and humanizing these people and minimizing, which I'm sure you heard me say on the stand, it's a big thing."

Me- "Tell me more about that."

Katie- "People don't want to come out and say that they're a murderer. It's not something that most people are proud of. You minimize it the best you can which creates a lot of problems in society and I'm sure we saw it play out with the jury and whatever. But the bottom line is it doesn't matter how much you minimize it; an innocent person is not going to confess to taking anybody's life. They didn't do it. There are exceptions to that, of course, such as people that are prolific liars and killers and want to be all over TV. We certainly see that in society. I've never dealt with that. Pretty much anyone that I've ever had confess I've never had an issue with a confession. A confession has always been a confession especially when it's not custodial or there's no tricks being done. The minimizing is a huge part and I really learned my craft when I was dealing with pedophiles because nobody wants to confess to having sex with a kid. You minimize that stuff and that has certainly helped for every case that I have ever worked. It's just minimization and then you kind of ease into it like I did in that interrogation. There's not a protocol I follow. There's a lot of people that go to different schools and different interrogation schools. I pay a lot of attention to body language and to statement analysis. He had cues of deception all through that interview. You could tell when he was lying when he was messing with a bottle. If you were to go back and watch that interrogation now that I've said that to you, you're going to see that when he gets nervous he plays with a bottle he had in his hand. Really a lot of walking and chewing gum. You have to be on top of your game, watching everything that they are saying and doing. What they're doing with their hands, what they're doing with their eyes. So that's the stuff that's interesting to me, the science of a confession. That's more of what I do instead of a style. I just kind of roll with it and see where I'm getting with it. That's hard to explain to a jury or people that don't do it for a living and they think it's junk science. I'm a polygraph examiner. There's so much that I believe in polygraphs. I believe what I get as a result of a polygraph (lie detector machine). That's body language and human behavior."

Me- "Seemed like two different interviews in the interrogation, before and after the smoking break. Initially more just a conversation and after more getting down to brass tacks. Is that kind of... is the person just worn out by then? Tell me about that. It seemed as though there was a change in your focus."

Katie- "There was a break because I knew that he was caving. I wanted to do all of the things again. For instance, I wanted to make sure that I went through that he wasn't in custody again because I knew we were getting ready to get a confession. I wanted to have a natural break where I said, "Do you want something to drink? You're free to go." That kind of stuff because I knew I would get hammered in court. In general, people do not like non-custodial interviews because everyone has this idea from what they see on TV that you have to be read your rights every single time the police deal with somebody which is completely untrue. I wanted to lay it out because I knew a jury would be watching that or at least it would be judged by a defense team at some point. I wanted to have a natural break in that. But I knew I was close, and I knew how we were going to get it. The biggest part of that is Lisa worked so hard on this case, and I've had the case of my career—the Lyon sisters is the case of my career—I'll never be able to top that. I wanted her to be able to get the award and get the confession. We took the break for the reasons I enumerated, but we went out into the hall and I said, "Okay, this is what is going to work and I want you to do it." I wanted her to get the win and to feel the win. That was the rationale behind all of that."

Me- "One of the jurors was a counselor, and she told me the difference between pathological liars and compulsive liars. She said this man is a compulsive liar. Pathological liars are lying for a gain while compulsive liars are doing it to try and please someone. She was concerned that the defendant had stopped his maturing at age seven, and she couldn't tell when he was lying. She felt he was guilty but couldn't figure that out. Did you have that feeling?"

Katie- "No, never. If you listen to the phone sting he sounds like a flat-out criminal. He's talking differently, his demeanor is different. I never thought that this was a premeditated murder like he sat and said, "Tonight I'm going to go kill a sheriff." Not in that sense. But he definitely did a lot of past stuff especially on that phone sting. The guy he presented himself as in that interrogation, he was playing us just as much as we were playing him. He might be an okay guy in real life. He was a kid when this happened. Certainly, everybody changes as they get older and he led a pretty low-key life after that. That was the thing that really impressed me but not in a positive way was listening to him in those phone stings (controlled calls) where he was cussing and the criminal came out in him. He was not a dumb man. He had a memory, and I wasn't lying when I said his memory was better than mine. His memory is far better than mine. He paints this picture like he was the victim of this horrible life but all his other siblings came out fine and didn't have that same kind of experience. I'm not saying that for everybody across the board; even biological kids of biological parents don't have the same experience as their siblings. There is no part of me that buys any part of that crap, honestly. I don't think he has the maturity of a seven-year-old. I was in the room with Lisa. I spent a long time doing an investigation on him and I orchestrated those phone stings and they worked exactly as they were supposed to. He did a lot of digging before we got there in computers and locating people. A seven-year-old couldn't do the things he did. A seven-year-old doesn't know the things he knows. That's potentially the danger in that kind of a jury pool because they have a week of listening to both sides and when you have professionals like that who have a lot of experience but not experience with that particular person, I think it becomes problematic for us. They're seeing just what is presented to them and they don't have the whole picture. In fairness to them, there is so much information thrown at them. Fifty-some years of information thrown at people in five days is a lot."

Me- "A psychologist told me that long-term memory even with dementia isn't affected as much as short-term memory."

Katie-"One hundred percent."

Me- "I thought the State should have brought that out in the trial."

Katie-"Hindsight is twenty-twenty... But the problem is most criminals are liars until they're not. You know what I mean? And if he's lying, why didn't he just keep lying and say he didn't do it? The other part that's really hard for me to dismiss is you can say whatever you want. I put some super power on him and had him worn down, but there is no explanation for why he independently confessed to both of his children with things that we did not tell him or we did not say. Said things like, "I've been waiting for fifty years and I never told anybody, I didn't even tell your mother." None of that came up in our interrogation."

Me- "Why did he confess? Did he think there weren't going to be any consequences?"

Katie- "I think he was just tired, that's very typical. There was nothing strange about the way that that went especially when... I mean, did I wear him down psychologically? Yes. Would that work on an innocent person? Most of the time, no. Not to that extent. Even if it worked with me then why did he go and independently confess to both of his kids afterwards Instead of saying, "Man, this chick got in my head and I don't know. I need help, I need a lawyer." None of that. Something like that happened."

Me-"What are the things about you that you would like to have included in the book? I read what was written about you in The Last Stone like your polygraph expertise. What would you like me to say about you?"

Katie-"I'm not much of a horn-tooter." I don't like a lot of attention, honestly. I'm getting ready at some point in the near future to retire. My kids and my husband are my priority. I like to live a normal life and travel. My husband has retired once and has a second career that he'll retire from."

Me- "Was he in law enforcement also?"

Katie-"He was."

Me- "How old are your kids?"

Katie- "I have two stepchildren that are thirty-one and nineteen, and then my kids are almost sixteen and twelve."

Me- "Would you recommend a career as a detective or as a police officer to your children?"

Katie- (laughs) "Not a police officer, I think. My son is convinced he's going to be a major league baseball player so we don't even talk about careers much. He's a left-handed pitcher so he's a hot commodity now. My daughter and son are both very proud of me but my daughter even more because she was a little bit older for the Lyon sister case. She's more focused because she's a girl.

She, I think, as much as she would never say it, I think she very much idolizes me and what my husband and I both did for a career. Police officer, patrol officer, there's just too many people that hate police. It's dangerous and the laws don't support us. No, I would hate it actually. I would never sleep. Now if she could go into a Federal agency. We joke all the time and say she should go into the CIA because she's got ice in her veins. Be the lioness. She's very smart and she's very athletic and the sky is the limit for what she can do if she puts her mind to it. She loves to argue. I'd rather she be a lawyer."

Katie- "I actually wanted to be a lawyer. I went to the University of Maryland at College Park and realized very quickly that I did not like the library, which is problematic for someone being a lawyer. It's funny because now I spend all of my days reading and researching and doing all of the things I would have done as a lawyer. I love to argue which is probably why I'm so good at interrogating. I would prefer my kids to do other things."

Me- "You've answered all of my questions. I appreciate your time. Thank you very much."

CHAPTER THIRTY-SIX

Arrest of Larry Smith

After the interview was completed, Larry Smith was given a ride back to his apartment by the New York State Police. He asked the officer to drop him off a little farther down the road because he didn't want the neighbors talking. Lisa Killen typed up a statement of charges and e-mailed them to her supervising detective who sent them to the commissioner who issued a warrant. Katie presented the charges to the New York State Police since they had to make the arrest because Smith was in their jurisdiction.

The arrest warrant came down at six p.m. that night. Officer Jason Nellis of the New York State Police Department verified that the warrant was good. Investigator Nellis drove with another officer to Smith's apartment and knocked on the door.

Smith answered, "Who is it?"

The officers identified themselves and gave their reason for being there.

"Fuck," Smith said before the door opened, "I figured you guys would be back."

The officers put him in handcuffs and then took him down to their car. They drove him to the police barracks and treated Smith as a 'fugitive from justice'. There was a bond hearing which was done by video with the court. Then Smith was transported to jail.

CHAPTER THIRTY-SEVEN

Phone Call to Carolyn Philo about Solving Murder of Her Father

Bob and Carolyn Philo lived in Far North McKinney in an adult housing community. McKinney is a suburb north of Dallas, Richardson, and Plano. Their community catered exclusively to adults with a wide variety of perks. One of the perks was the Amenities Center where one afternoon Carolyn was gathered with her friends playing Bunco.

Bunco is a dice game with twelve or more players, divided into groups of four. Each group tries to score points while taking turns rolling three dice in a series of six rounds. A 'Bunco' is achieved when a player rolls three-of-a-kind and all three numbers match the round number which is decided at the beginning of the round. It is a very social game and Carolyn and her friends had refreshments to go along with their socializing.

Bob and Carolyn had met with Corporal Lisa Killen prior to that 'Bunco Day' and she had shown them a powerpoint presentation. The presentation showed that the cold case team was getting close to solving the murder of Deputy Sheriff J.T. Hall. While at Bunco, a call from a number in Montgomery County, Maryland showed up on Carolyn's phone, but she chose to ignore it. When a second call from the same number appeared a few minutes later, Carolyn excused herself from the game and went outside the Amenities Center to answer it.

It was one of the senior police officers from the Montgomery County Police Department on the line.

"Is this Carolyn Hall Philo?"

"It is."

"This is Lieutenant Jones with the Montgomery County Police Department. I've got good news for you. We've got the guy who killed your father. I just got off the phone with the cold case detectives, Lisa and Katie, and he's in jail in Herkimer County, New York awaiting extradition to Montgomery County. Lisa Killen will call you tomorrow with more details."

Carolyn started to cry as she put down her cell phone. She walked back inside the Amenities Center and her friends could see she was crying.

"Carolyn, Carolyn, what's wrong?" they shouted. "Are you alright? Sit down."

Carolyn sat down and managed a smile in between all of the tears. "After fifty years," she said, "they've arrested the man who killed my father."

There wasn't a dry eye in the Amenities Center.

CHAPTER THIRTY-EIGHT
Press Conference
September 7, 2022

BAM!!! KABLAM!!! OOOFFF!!! HERE WE GO!!!

This press conference is where I started my involvement in the Deputy Sheriff J.T. Hall Murder Case. Carolyn Philo had just told me the story in my office and asked me to write a book on the case. She told me to watch this press conference to understand better what had happened and what was going to transpire.

* * * * * * *

Press Conference

At the podium is the police chief, Marcus Jones. He is an African American man in his sixties of medium height and build. He is bald and wears glasses. There is a white man to his right. The police chief reads from notes.

Police Chief-"Cold case detectives reviewed files, recordings and interviews. During the course of their investigation, Leggitt and Killen narrowed in on one person, Larry David Becker. He had been interviewed by investigators in 1973 but had not been labelled a suspect. Leggitt and Killen determined... Becker began using the last name Smith and had been living in Little Falls, New York for over forty years. Leggitt and Killen travelled to New York and on September first of this year they Interviewed Smith. During that interview Smith admitted to shooting Captain Hall. Larry David Smith was arrested and has been charged with murder. He has waived his extradition and is expected to be back in Maryland this week to face charges. I want to talk about the fabulous work of Detective Leggitt, Corporal Killen, and cold case detective Sarah White. These ladies have put forth a tremendous amount of effort. They have been dedicated and committed to finding justice as we have never shown that we have given up on finding justice for this case."

"They have persevered in a manner that demonstrates the high quality of Montgomery County Police enforcement and I am so very proud of their efforts. We are all very proud of the efforts they have put forth and to obtain a confession from someone who committed a crime fifty-one years ago is a tremendous accomplishment."

"At the time of his death, Captain Hall was married to his wife of thirty-three years, Anna," (Pauses) "To come full circle, to bring this kind of home for me it's personal. It's personal in a different kind of way. Captain Hall's nephew, Frank Hall, Corporal Frank Hall, who retired from the Montgomery County Police, was my training corporal when I first started here thirty-six years ago."

"In closing, I want to say to the Hall family that we are pleased to bring justice to your grandfather, to your father, and to your uncle. I want to thank partnering agencies that helped us bring this case to a close: the Layton City Police Department in Layton, Utah, the FBI Behavioral Analysis Unit, ATF of Albany, and the New York State Police Trooper D, Herkimer. At this time, I want to bring forth Sheriff Popkin to say a few words."

Taller white man standing next to Chief Jones moves to the lectern. White hair on sides and bald on top. Puts on glasses. White uniform.

"Good afternoon everybody. My name is Darren Popkin. I am Sheriff of Montgomery County. On behalf of the entire Sheriff's office, certainly the Hall family, and all of Montgomery County's law enforcement, I want to express my incredible gratitude to Chief Jones and the Cold Case Unit for solving this fifty-one-year-old murder case. As the murder of Montgomery County Sheriff's Office Captain James Hall was the only and oldest unsolved homicide of a law officer in Montgomery County, this brings a tremendous sense of relief. On October twenty-third, 1971, Jim Hall, or J.T. as he was known, was working security-related part-time work at Manor Country club as an off-duty deputy sheriff to supplement his income for his family as many officers do now and did back then as well. But sadly, that night at age fifty-three Jim was ambushed, rushed to the hospital, but passed away a few days later at Montgomery General Hospital. Having grown up in Aspen Hill very close to where this homicide occurred, I remember the shock and sadness in the community when Jim was taken from us. Every year since I've been on, close to forty years, during Police Memorial Week, the Hall family, Carolyn. Carrie, Bob, Frank and others travel from across the country and locally to meet with Chief Jones and I to honor and recognize and remember Jim's ultimate sacrifice at the Montgomery County Safety Memorial. Next year in May of 2023 when we gather again for Police Memorial Week at the Montgomery County Public Safety Memorial perhaps Jim will be resting a little more peacefully. Thank you."

Carolyn Philo comes up to the microphone.

"My family, please come up." She motions with both hands to come up. "They have been so strong with me and my brother." Brother, Melvin, stands next to her. He is the same height as Carolyn with receding grey hair.

"We're so happy. I just want to thank the Cold Case Unit. My heart goes out to them. I want to thank the Sheriff's Department and the Police Department. We love you. We will never forget you. I just knew somebody was out there. I don't want anyone to forget: if you are missing a loved one, if someone is hurt please don't give up. Please keep after the police department, the Sheriff's Department. They are here to help you. They really do. We found that out."

Carolyn steps back from the microphone and looks over at her brother, Melvin. He takes her place at the microphone. He is wearing a grey suit with no tie but with a sweater and shirt.

"I never thought this case would be solved. It has been. And anybody out there that wants to be bad just remember that." (Laughter)

Carolyn says thank you as the family leaves the podium.

The State's Attorney walks up to the microphone. He has long grey hair which is shaggy in the back with a moustache and goatee. He is wearing a dark suit with a white shirt and purple tie. He has no notes.

"My name is John McCarthy. I am the State's Attorney for Montgomery County. I'm honored to be here with the Hall family today and I like your words (pointing at Melvin). You're going to do something bad, watch out, we're going to get you ultimately. This is a great day for the Hall family to have this man arrested and charged. You suffered a long time without your dad, your brother, uncle, cousin. Thank you again. It's a great honor to be here with you. I'm really not surprised to be here, though. I've been at this awhile myself. I actually lived on Carrollton road for thirty years. This was the street I lived on. I came there after this happened. But I have known the men and women of this police department for a long time. And the fact that you have people like Katie Leggitt, Lisa Killen, and Sarah White that do this kind of work all of the time, it doesn't surprise me. We are blessed here in Montgomery County with a magnificent police department. It was not lost on me that they opened this investigation in celebration of the fiftieth anniversary of the death. This department is now celebrating their one hundredth anniversary. So, we have two things to celebrate: one hundred years of magnificent work by the men and women of the department and the fact that these wonderful, tremendous detectives solved this case."

"You know, Katie Leggitt was also involved in the Lyon sister case which everybody in this room knows about the Lyon sisters. Great work. Lisa Killen. I'm looking at her mom and dad. I've been friends with them before you were here. Then Sarah, thank you for the work that you've done here."

"Mr. Smith, also known as Larry Becker, grew up pretty close by. He lived on Farraday with his adopted parents. Not too far away from where this murder actually took place. Wasn't living there when this happened, but he was living nearby. He will be extradited as the chief said. He's going to be back soon. Probably by the end of the week. I would anticipate that you will have a bond review in the district court for this man who's coming back. He faces first degree murder. A life sentence that he faces. Obviously, he is not a young man at this point in time with the passage of time. But he'll be back at a bond review probably on Monday in the afternoon in the district court. We would anticipate that this matter would be forwarded to the grand jury for their consideration. They would return an indictment at some time in the upcoming months. Four to six months from now we'll begin the process of trying to hold him accountable for this horrific act. So, chief, you have a lot to be proud of and I think the people of this community have a lot to be proud of and again, thank you, thank you, thank you to the Hall family. I knew you as members of the police department. I'm sure this was a huge loss not just for the family, but for the community when you lost your loved one. Thank you very much for meeting with us." (He steps back and Chief Jones steps to the microphone.)

"Thank you Mr. McCarthy. A special thank you to Mr. McCarthy as well as to Sheriff Popkin and to all of our good friends with the Montgomery County Sheriff's Department. Again, this is about a law enforcement brother that's been lost. This shows you the impact that we never forget. In all serious crimes, particularly as it relates to homicide and rape, these are crimes that are forever to be prosecuted. We never forget, and we work very hard and diligently to establish what we can evidence-wise in order to be able to solve these cases and bring closure for the victims' families. Because these families suffer over time because of the loss of their loved one. I'm really appreciative of the Hall family being here today. I'm very grateful for you all to be here. I did want to make some statement so that the press would have this information as well. And speaking about Sheriff Hall's wife, Anna, unfortunately she passed away in 2005. But he left behind a great legacy. He will be proud to know that his children made their own careers in law enforcement and even married police officers. As you met Carolyn Hall Philo, she was twenty-eight-years-old at the time of her father's death and she married Bob Philo. Bob is a retired Montgomery County Police Officer. He was a K-9 officer as well as a detective and unfortunately Bob couldn't be with us today but we're very grateful for his service. Carolyn Philo is also here with her daughter, Carrie Philo Crutcher, Sheriff Hall's granddaughter, and she was eight years old at the time of his death. You met Melvin. Melvin Hall was thirty-two when he lost his father and he went on to become a Montgomery County Police Officer. He's here with his wife, Judy, and their younger son Brian who's a retired lieutenant from the Fairfax County Police Department. Brian was three years old when he lost his grandfather. As I mentioned earlier, Sheriff Hall's nephew, my field training officer, I will always remember him as my FTO, my good friend Corporal Frank Hall. Another nephew of Captain Hall and one of my former shift mates in Germantown Town Special Assignment Team, retired officer John Custer. We are again appreciative of you and your families being here."

"In closing again, I want to say I am grateful for the service of the men and women of the Montgomery County Police, particularly our major crimes division. The leadership of retired Captain Rosario as well as Lieutenant Sanger and others. Sergeant Homrock. For all of their phenomenal work on the cold case unit. At this point in time, I'll turn it back over to Mrs. Goff."

(A young black woman comes to the microphone).

"Okay, we're gonna allow time for questions and answers and for the representatives from our major crimes division to answer any of your questions."

Question-"Had did Leggitt and Killen get focused on this guy?"

Retired Captain Rubin Rosario-"How they got focused on this particular individual is probably something I can't say, but what I can say is how they got focused on this case in the first place. As was mentioned earlier today, it was the fifty-year anniversary. I was, at the time, the captain of the division. Detective Sergeant Chris Homrock, who leads the cold case unit, came to my office and said, "Hey, it's the fifty-year anniversary. We need to get focused again on this case. We had done other things in the past to bring attention and to try and develop leads. But he brought it out that it was cold and we should get back to it. As I've had with many of the detective sergeants in the unit we had a staffing conversation. If you guys remember last year at the end of the year we had a lot of homicides so we were stretched thin as a division. Almost by a blessing from God we got a temporary assignment request from Detective Killen who's the person responsible for getting onto this particular suspect. We worked with the executive staff of the Rockville district to get her to come over to the division. She is excellent and had prior experience with the Major Crimes Division and we knew would be dedicated and hard-working and would run this case through. So, we added Detective Katie Leggitt who's an experienced cold case investigator also responsible for getting us onto this particular individual. We also stole one of Lieutenant Drew's best investigators who is Detective Sara White. That sort of trifecta, that triangle, if you will, took primary lead in this case."

"I can tell you this. They kicked me out of my conference room. I had to have meetings with fifteen to twenty people at a time in my office. It was humiliating but worth it. They put together a timeline on the wall going through every inch of every case file. They did interviews, they went over old interviews. They spoke to previous investigators who spent a lot of time and effort on this case who deserve recognition as well."

Reporter-"How many cold cases are out there and how long generally does it take to get this kind of an end result?"

Captain-"Well, I can say that's a brilliant question. I wish I could answer it. I don't know the exact number. It is the oldest and coldest case unsolved in Montgomery County. It was the only ongoing law enforcement related homicide which we're super proud to close that."

CHAPTER THIRTY-NINE
Enter Covington and Burling LLP

Kevin B. Collins
Covington and Burling LLP
Washington, D.C.

My only questions are how and when did your firm get hired to represent Mr. Becker-Smith.

Thank you,
Michael F. Weisberg, M.D.

Michael F. Weisberg, M.D.

Given the complexities of the case, the workload that would be needed to defend the case, and the limited resources of the office of the public defender in Rockville, the District Public Defender for Montgomery County asked us in early 2023 to handle the case as specifically assigned public defenders. We thereafter entered our appearances in February, 2023

Kevin B. Collins
Covington and Burling LLP
Washington, D.C.

Covington and Burling is an American Multinational Law Firm headquartered in Washington, D.C., which advises clients in transactional, litigation, regulatory and public policy matters. The firm has additional offices in Beijing, Brussels, Frankfort, Dubai, Johannesburg, London, Los Angeles, New York, Palo Alto, San Francisco, Seoul, Shanghai, and Boston. The firm was founded in 1919.

Covington and Burling is ranked among the world's top thirty international arbitration practices. It employs twelve hundred attorneys and is ranked twenty-seventh in the United States based on size. Its gross revenue was over 1.5 billion dollars in 2022.

Since its founding, Covington and Burling has demonstrated a strong commitment to public service. The firm is frequently recognized for pro bono service, including twelve times being ranked the number one pro bono practice in the United States by the American Lawyer magazine. Much of the pro bono work is involved in meeting local needs, serving economically disadvantaged individuals and families in their surrounding communities. The American Lawyer magazine has ranked Covington's pro bono practice among the nation's top ten for thirty-one of the past thirty- four years. Law 360 has honored Covington as a pro bono firm of the year for their work on a range of issues, including securing the release of Guantanamo Bay detainees, defending civil rights and combatting racial profiling, reforming the criminal justice system, and representing prisoners on death row.

According to authorities I spoke with affiliated with the Montgomery County judicial system, it is not unusual for Covington and Burling to take pro bono cases in Montgomery County. It is easy to travel to Rockville by Metro Rail or car from Washington, D.C., and pro bono cases here afford their younger associates experience in trial settings.

CHAPTER FORTY
Meet the Defense

Kevin B. Collins was the lead defense attorney for Covington and Burling Law Firm representing Larry David Smith. Mr. Collins, a partner in the firm, has participated in more than sixty trials and is a fellow of the American College of Trial Lawyers. He graduated from the Worcester Polytechnic Institute with a B.S.M.E. in mechanical engineering in 1987. He got his law degree from the University of Baltimore School of Law where he graduated Magna cum laude and was the associate editor of the law review. He went on to get an L.L. M. in 2007 from Temple University. He maintains an active pro bono trial practice representing indigent defendants in criminal proceedings in various state and federal courts. He has served as lead counsel in more than forty criminal jury trials.

Accompanying Mr. Collins to court and making out the rest of the defense team were three associates from Covington and Burling. All three appeared to be in their twenties and thirties and all were male. There were also two paralegals helping the defense, both women.

The first order of business for the defense team was to get Larry David Smith's confession thrown out. They claimed his Miranda Rights had been violated and the confession was obtained illegally by Officers Killen and Leggitt. The judge set the hearings on the motion for October fourth, 2023.

CHAPTER FORTY-ONE

Becker (Smith) and the Miranda Hearing
October 2023

After placing the suspect under arrest, the officer will say something similar to, "You have the right to remain silent. Anything you say can and will be used against you in a court of law. You have a right to an attorney. If you cannot afford an attorney, one will be appointed for you. You have the right to have an attorney present during any questions." These statements constitute Miranda Rights.

Without a Miranda warning, what the arrestee says in response to custodial questioning can't be used for most purposes as evidence at trial.

Police must read you your Miranda Rights when arresting you or holding you for custodial interrogation (even if you haven't been charged). Police and prosecutors must continue to respect your Miranda Rights throughout an investigation.

The Miranda Rule only applies if the suspect being questioned is in police custody and not before that time. Until a questioning session begins and the suspect is in police custody, police are not required to provide a Miranda warning.

While Miranda warnings are extremely important, an officer's failure to read them in and of itself does not result in a dismissal of criminal charges. Simply put, Miranda warnings themselves are not constitutional rights; rather, they are safeguards against the Fifth Amendment privilege against self-incrimination.

Two conditions must be met before police are required to issue the Miranda warning. First, the suspect must be under police custody. Second, the suspect must be under interrogation.

There was no physical evidence linking Larry Smith to the murder of J.T. Hall. There was no DNA evidence to tie Larry Smith to the murder of J.T. Hall. There were no eyewitnesses who saw Larry Smith kill J.T. Hall. The only evidence was Smith's own confession, and his defense team from Covington and Burling challenged whether that confession should be admissible in a court of law. The judge set the date of the first hearing for admissibility of the confession for October fourth, 2023. I was unable to go to the hearing, but Bob and Carolyn Philo went to the hearing and Bob provided the following summary of the judge's decision after the hearings were over:

Bob- "The judge told everybody that when she heard all the testimony she was going to take a break to review her notes and then she'd come back. She returned. Her summation, her finding of facts went on and on. She went back over everything. So and so testified to this and I find that this was more believable. In any case, it was brilliant from this standpoint: if they file an appeal and say that her ruling was not supported by the evidence she laid it all out completely. Start to finish. Then at the end she said, "I find that he was not in custody, Miranda Rights were not necessary under the circumstances. He was capable of asking to leave, standing up for himself."

"She said he went out to smoke and could have gotten an Uber or a taxi cab. She said he wasn't under arrest."

Bob- "The defense was arguing that even though he went outside that he had no way of getting home (laughs). Kind of a silly argument, quite frankly, because he's across the street and he could stick his thumb out or keep walking."

Me- "What the State had to prove was that he was capable of making decisions and that he was free to go whenever he wanted. With these two things, you don't have to have Miranda Rights. Is that correct?"

Bob- "Yes."

Bob-"The State overcame any assumption that he was in custody, even though he was at a police station. The Defense was trying to say he was intimidated by the fact that the officers had guns and badges. One of them had her gun in her purse and the other said it was either in her purse or in her backpack. Their badges were beneath their clothing and not visible."

CHAPTER FORTY-TWO
Day One of the Trial
Monday, January 8, 2024

I've always enjoyed looking at buildings. Some of them I appreciate for their beauty like the Louvre in Paris or the Mort Meyerson Symphony Hall in Dallas. Some I appreciate for their historical significance. When I spent ten days in January of 2024 covering the murder trial I was able to spend one Sunday with my son, Brent, who lives in Washington, D.C. I took the Metro rail from Rockville, Maryland to D.C. and spent the day walking thirty-thousand steps with Brent looking at the history of our country. I still have tremendous pride looking at the Capitol, the White House, all of the monuments, and the buildings which house various agencies like the State Department. Some of these buildings are architecturally appealing, but no matter what they look like they appeal to me because of their place in our nation's history and their symbolism as to what America stands for.

The Montgomery County Circuit Court Building is not architecturally or historically interesting to me. It is a seven-story rectangular building made of white and grey terrazzo stone. It has a very large entrance hallway with multiple security guards with x-ray machines who make you wait in lines to check in and out of the building. Every part of your body and whatever backpack, purse, or other object you bring into the courthouse is scanned entirely. Most days the lines to get in are small; on snow days when the court house opens later (say ten a.m.) it can take half an hour in the freezing snow to breach the entrance.

* * * * * * *

January eighth is my parent's anniversary, and for some reason I made it a point that day to tell everyone I talked to that fact. I told them it would have been their sixty-eighth anniversary, but my father died July fifth, 2023 at the age of ninety-seven. (My mother died at the age of ninety-three while I was writing this book). Everyone had the same response, whether it was the Philo or Hall families or the two paralegals working for the defense. They all consoled me on the loss of my father but congratulated me on my exceptional genetics and how they foretold a long life for me. I think that I kept bringing up the anniversary because I wanted to remember my father, Fred Weisberg, and somehow relive my relationship with him. Of all the men in my life, excluding my two sons, I will always love and revere my father the most. He was number one. He taught me so much: how to be a man, how to treat others, and most importantly, the value of hard work. He worked from the age of six until a heart condition forced him to stop at age eighty-three, and never complained about the difficulty of what he did or how hard it was at times supporting his family.

Yet I will always have conflicting emotions about my father. There were so many things he said and did that were hurtful to me that I never called him on or understood. He truly believed that by shouting the loudest he won every argument, so most of our arguments ended when he reached that certain degree of loudness. He made me feel little and unimportant at times, as though my only worth came from making my mother and my sister happy. Anything of value that he and my mother accumulated in their lifetimes (no money, but pieces of furniture, jewelry, and the one painting they ever bought) were given to my sister as if she was the only child. A true story is that after I had moved my parents to Dallas and found them a senior living place to stay, they offered to sell me their only painting for seventy-five hundred dollars.

Michael Weisberg

They had bought the painting of a vase of flowers forty years before for the extravagant sum of one thousand dollars. The painting was the only one they had, and the pretty, colorful flowers were really the only thing of beauty in their otherwise bare-walled apartment. I thanked them for their offer but said no, keep it and I will continue to support you financially. Two weeks later when I visited them the area where the lovely painting had been hanging was bare white wall. I asked them what happened to the painting and was told my sister had decided the painting would look better in her house than in their apartment, so she and her husband just took it off the wall and carried it home without a whimper from my parents about paying for it.

There were so many things I wanted to argue about with my father, so many mistakes that he made that I wanted to point out to him, so many times that he made me feel invisible. But by the time I realized how much these things meant to me and how they had influenced/stunted my growth, he was in his late eighties and nineties, and I didn't want to upset him. I just bit my tongue and listened to what he had to say, did everything to prolong his life and preserve his dignity, and then mourned him when he died. A son's relationship with his father is an incredibly important part of how he develops, and Larry Becker Smith's lack of a relationship with his birth father and adversarial relationship with his adopted father certainly influenced the person he became.

* * * * * * * *

The trial took place in courtroom 6 B on the sixth floor of the Montgomery County Courthouse.

The jurors' chairs were tall green chairs. Our gallery chairs were red studio chairs and there were seventy of them. The back walls of the courtroom were painted grey, and the front walls were comprised of more decorative fluted light wood panels. Behind the prosecutors' desk on the floor were stacked various pieces of evidence. The picture of J.T. Hall on the floor was easily recognizable even though the picture was lying on its side. Next to the judge's seat was a flagpole flying the Maryland state flag.

There were already people in the courtroom when I arrived. I picked out an aisle seat in the third row behind the jury and lay my over-the-shoulder briefcase/backpack on the seat next to me. My wife had bought this briefcase/backpack for me to cover my first trial. I had batteries, notebooks, pens, a tape recorder, newspaper articles about the murder and other written information in the briefcase/backpack.

Donna, the Assistant State's Attorney in charge of prosecuting the case, was there with her assistant attorney, John Grochowski. Donna wore a white blouse with a black jacket and long skirt that went well below her knees. She had black glasses on. Her hair was brown with blonde streaks. Around her neck she wore a necklace as well as an identification lanyard. John was a stocky, bald man of medium height who appeared to be in his late thirties or early forties.

I glanced around the courtroom and greeted Carolyn's three cousins who were sitting in front of me: Frank, Becky, and John Michael. The courtroom itself was circular with the gallery coming off of it in somewhat of a rectangle. There were two sides of chairs in the gallery separated by a walkway.

There were four defense attorneys in the courtroom, two at the defense table and two sitting in the front row on the other side of the gallery. Three were white men and one appeared to be a man of Indian descent. The oldest defense attorney, Kevin Collins, was in his late fifties and balding. The other three attorneys were in their late twenties to thirties. All wore dark suits.

Since nothing was going on, I decided to take some pictures of the courtroom with my iPhone camera. I smiled at one of the deputy sheriffs who I recognized from Law Enforcement Memorial Week and then I began taking pictures. Within seconds I felt the presence of someone next to me. It was the tall, powerfully built deputy sheriff I'd just acknowledged. He didn't bother saying hello and didn't smile.

"Delete all of the pictures you've taken right now. If you take any further pictures I will confiscate your phone and you will be escorted out of the courthouse."

My face turned red. "No pictures are allowed?" I stammered.

"The Judge does not allow any photography in her courtroom."

I quickly deleted the photographs I had taken, turned my phone off and put it back in my pants pocket.

Carolyn and Bob came in with Carolyn's brother, Melvin, and sat in the front row on my side, just behind the jury. On my side the seating was:

Melvin-Bob-Carolyn

Frank-Becky-John Michael

Deputy Sheriff who had me delete my pictures-my briefcase/backpack-Me

"All rise," the bailiff announced.

The judge, Cheryl Lee McCally, walked in and took her seat.

"You may be seated."

Judge McCally appeared to be in her late fifties with blonde hair and a gold hair pin on the right side. She wore a black robe. She called the court to order and then called all six attorneys to her bench. Any time there was a meeting of the judge and attorneys at the bench, the judge flipped a switch and white noise played over the jury box and gallery so that we could hear nothing of what was said. This meeting lasted twenty minutes. I looked around the courtroom while the meeting was going on. There were two men sitting to the judge's left with computers in front of them. One was the bailiff and the other was an aide to the judge.

The judge gave instructions to the witnesses in the courtroom before excusing them to the lobby. "Don't discuss testimony. If you do, your testimony will be struck from the record." The witnesses left the courtroom. There were now twenty-two people in the courtroom.

"We are ready for the jury," the judge proclaimed.

At nine forty-five in the morning the jury walked in. There were fourteen jurors, eight men and six women. There was one Asian man and one Indian man and the rest were Caucasian. There were two alternate jurors who sat in smaller chairs to my right of the jury box. One was a small man with gray hair and the other was a woman in her thirties with long brown hair and wearing blue jeans. The jury was sworn in. The judge had the bailiff hand out pads and pencils to the jury for note taking. Then she gave the jurors a lecture on proper behavior of a juror. Finally, she called for opening statements. Donna Fenton stood up and addressed the jury:

Donna- "One phone call. That's all it can take to change your life and the lives of those you love. That's what happened to J.T. Hall and his family. The call was to ask him to cover a security guard shift. He was having dinner with his family. He donned his police uniform, one last time holstered his weapon, and left for one last shift. October twenty-third, 1971, J.T. was 53 years old.

"J.T. arrived at his work shift as the security guard at Manor Country Club at seven pm. The country club was a large property built in the late sixties. In the 1970's the Montgomery County Sheriff's office

Michael Weisberg

was responsible for patrolling the area. Jim Young asked Captain Hall to work that night. Captain Hall asked his wife, Anna, and she said okay. Dark, stormy, rainy night. Captain Hall was shot in the back of the head. Three days later he died."

(Shows slide of Captain Hall)

Donna- "Born in 1918. Part-tine job as a police officer. Special deputy who worked evening shifts four to five nights a week. During the day he was a mechanic for DC Transit Company and worked on buses. Sheriff Hall kissed his wife, daughter, and grandchildren goodbye for the last time."

"Ten-fifty pm. The receptionist at Manor Country Club called in. Told a couple found Sheriff Hall lying injured at the country club. Sheriff Hall lying face down in a pool of blood by a couple who left an event at the country club. Called for emerging help. Five teenagers pulled into the country club. They immediately saw Sheriff Hall and they reported Sheriff Hall lying in blood."

"Mr. Trisgrad, part of the couple, said J.T. Hall was struggling to breathe. He was shot behind the ear and the bullet lodged behind his forehead. He was taken to Montgomery County Hospital where he died on October twenty-sixth, 1971.

"His family waited days, weeks, months, years, decades."

"2021 the case was reopened."

"The police began the investigation that night. The police received another call from the Manor Club area at ten fifty pm. Roger and Diane Schmidt returned to their home (Donna shows a map to the jury of the country club parking lot and Schmidt home). They moved into that home one month before. They found they locked themselves out of their house. They had painted their daughter's room and left the window open (on the second floor). Mrs. Schmidt climbed up a neighbor's ladder and into her daughter's room. She realized the house was ransacked. The patio door was pried open. Piles of things were next to the patio door. Office Jerry Boone who is now retired and living in Florida drew a sketch."

"The police felt the people who robbed the Schmidts were taking property across the golf course. The property was found next to the pump house. The Schmidts found their property. A diamond engagement ring was taken and not recovered. Items by their back door and in the parking lot. Making trips back and forth. Come upon by Sheriff Hall."

"Two fourteen-year-old boys and two fifteen year-old boys told the officers they were at the country club trying to break into the Coke machines. They were unsuccessful. They heard sirens and left. They left a screw driver behind and went back to get it when they saw Sheriff Hall. The police eliminated the boys as suspects based on timing, and the tool marks at the break-in at the Schmidt's house were not made by any tool the boys had. All of the fingerprints at the Schmidt's house were theirs or their friends. The police thought the burglars were wearing gloves."

"In 1972 Leslie Becker was interviewed by the police. He grew up on the corner of Faraday and Chatterfield (part of Manor Country Club). Leslie Becker had an older brother, Larry Becker. Larry Becker is Larry Smith. In 1972 Leslie said my brother, Larry, might know something about that sheriff's death. The authorities couldn't find Larry Becker."

"In 1973 Larry Becker was in jail for burglary and escaped from the work release program. (After being recaptured) he went to the prison officials and said, "I might have information from the sheriff's murder. I won't talk unless you get rid of any penalty from the escape charge." The police said yes."

"April fifth, 1973, Larry Becker talked to police. He was walking through from Flower Valley to Aspen Hill and saw seven to eight boys around soda machines (at Manor Country Club) and one shot Sheriff Hall near the soda machines. It was a clear, cool night. Said sheriff was wearing a dark uniform; it was a full-length bright yellow raincoat. Becker said it was not raining and omitted the rain coat."

"Police confronted him and he maintained this is what he saw. Larry said during the interview, "When I leave Maryland I'm not coming back." He was not heard from again until 2022."

"The investigation went on and police investigated every lead. 1973, 1976, 1979, 1984. Police tried to do DNA tests on cigarettes; worthless."

"2021. The fifty-year anniversary of the murder. Corporal Lisa Killen doing temporary cold case effort. Assigned this case and she dove in. She went through boxes with a fresh set of eyes. She found all of the evidence and clothing including glasses of Sheriff Hall. Corporal Killen found all of the old police reports. She set out to find the Coke machine boys and Norman Shoemaker who was the driver of their car. His father, a police officer, wouldn't let him be interviewed. 2021- Corporal Killen interviewed him and same story."

"She found two men, Bobby Ray Edwards "The Raven" and John Rizzo. She found in the case file an old reel to reel tape labelled "Interview Richard Hobart". She had no means to play the tape. She went to Police Information Technology, a shop in Rockville, and finally went to the FBI Forensic Audio Enhancement. They transferred the tape to a Maxell reel to reel and then to a CD."

"She heard the 1973 interview with Larry Becker, a three hour interview. It was mislabeled. Corporal Killen said he knew details not released to the public. He's at least a witness and said we need to find Larry Becker."

"Larry Becker had disappeared. No taxes. Went back to the "Raven". He thought Becker had moved to upstate New York. Lisa found an obituary for Leslie Becker, Larry's brother. It said he was survived by a brother, Larry Smith, of New York. She found a Larry Smith on Facebook. He was Larry Smith Senior and he had gone to Robert E. Peary High School in Rockville, Maryland. The individual was selling a Steelers' jacket and there was a phone number."

"Lisa turned to John Rizzo, the younger brother of a group that hung out. She arranged a phone sting, a recorded conversation that police can do in an investigation. Mr. Rizzo made a call to the number (listed on Facebook). First Larry Smith denies being Larry Becker. Rizzo sends a message to Smith's phone. The police want to talk about Sheriff Hall's murder. We need to talk. After the text, Larry Smith texted and said. "I'm with my granddaughter and I'll call you tomorrow." Second call was made and it was clear Larry Smith was Larry Becker."

"August of 2022, Lisa and Katie Leggett drove up to New York. September first of 2022 the two detectives (Lisa and Katie) and two New York Police Officers went to the apartment. Tiny one bedroom apartment. He said, "I knew you'd be coming.""

"Four hour interview. He admitted to robbing the Schmidts. First said it was Raven. Then he confessed to shooting and killing J.T. Hall. Told detectives he knew he'd hit the man. He thanked the detectives and asked them to tell the family how sorry he was. The detectives had a decision to make. Smith was driven back to his apartment by New York Police."

* * * * * * *

"He called his daughter, Melinda Allen, and confessed. "I've got something to tell you. I guess I killed someone. I've been holding it in for fifty years." He, his brother, and two friends were doing daytime robberies and a security guard flashed a flashlight and he had a gun in his hand. He never told anyone."

"That evening detectives got permission to charge Smith. First thing he said to New York officers, "I knew you'd be back." He confessed for a third time to his son, Larry Junior. He told his son he confessed to everything: robbery gone wrong that involved a security guard. The defendant was extradited from New York to Maryland. He said his children were cleaning up his apartment and he would not be back."

"Question of the defendant not being capable of making a statement to the police. Man living alone, taking care of his health and finances. He agreed to go speak to the officers. Fingerprints matched Larry Becker's. Man living in New York for forty-five years was Larry Becker. Not one, two, but three confessions. No fingerprints, DNA. The defendant's own words broke the case open. Now we know what happened. You, too, will all know what happened and will find the defendant guilty."

* * * * * * * *

Ten minute break. I haven't seen Larry Smith yet. Evidence is blocking my seated view and I dare not stand up. I note one female juror is wearing a mask. Courtroom fills back up as Defense rises for their opening statement.

Defense Attorney-"On the night of October twenty-third, 1971, J.T. Hall was working security at Manor Country Club when he was shot. Police thoroughly investigated the case. No one was charged in the murder. Case lingered. Increased pressure as time went by and clues became more and more sparse. These detectives put on blinders and committed themselves to finding someone they could charge. Larry

Smith is a seventy-two-year-old peaceful citizen. Earlier in life he was adopted with his siblings by the Beckers. By age fourteen to fifteen he was no longer welcome in their house."

"In 1972 Larry Becker was arrested for breaking into a townhouse. He moved back to New York in 1980 and changed his name back to Smith. In his mid-fifties he suffered from declining health. Multiple heart attacks and COPD and his health declined. Now he is permanently disabled."

(The defense attorney giving the opening statement was one of the three younger attorneys. He had brown hair, glasses, and a blue suit and blue tie. He was holding his notes as he spoke.)

"The State has no DNA, fingerprints, or evidence from the crime scene. No one on the witness stand can tell you Mr. Smith was even near the country club. The State will ask you to find him guilty based on a series of events the police gave him and said were true. Mr. Smith's statement is false. Absolutely no other evidence. The standard required to find him guilty is the State must prove beyond reasonable doubt he is guilty. Smith is innocent now and at the end of the trial. There is no forensic evidence linking Smith to the crime scene. This case is not like other cases. The State doesn't have any fingerprints or DNA. They don't have a murder weapon or evidence that Smith had a weapon."

"It was a busy night at the country club. Members of the club, neighbors, and young men all interviewed. None saw Mr. Smith. The sheriff was killed in 1971 and Smith was arrested in 1972 (for a townhouse burglary). He escaped in 1973 and after being recaptured, spoke to the police about the murder in 1973. The State says Smith will disclose details that were not public. The opposite is true. Smith was not at the shooting so he gets many facts wrong. The officers concluded he had no personal involvement in the shooting. Smith wasn't alone, but no eyewitnesses to support Smith were at the scene of the crime. No one will say he was there or shot Hall."

"The State and police haven't ruled out other suspects. Good suspects never ruled out. One had a history of violence towards the police. J.T. Hall had his name in his notepad."

"Mr. Smith's vulnerability. In his seventies. He was a nursing assistant and then a security guard. His daughter will say he had multiple heart attacks in his fifties. He moved in with his daughter and then left and she had to check on him regularly. He sat in his apartment playing solitaire on his computer."

"On September first of 2022, four police officers showed up. He said he never shot anyone. He agrees to go with the police officers. The officers take him in the back of a police car. He is seated in the back corner of the investigation room. Blank walls and no windows. Four hours. At the start the officers are friendly and tell him they are not there to mess up his life. The officers' questions become more aggressive and they challenge the truthfulness of his recollections. Things start to get confusing. The events of the townhouse burglary are confused with the Manor Country Club. At one point Smith thinks the townhouse burglary is where someone was shot. He thought what he said in 1973 made him guilty. He can't go to Maryland alone. He can't drive. They told him that admitting to the shooting was not a big deal."

"After four hours they asked yet again if he shot Hall by accident and he responded, "Yeah, I guess so.""

"He then repeated that statement to his daughter. Half-hearted portion of what the officers told him to say."

"Evidence shows two shots fired at Sheriff Hall, not one which Smith said. The details are not from Mr. Smith's memory. The information elicited from him is false."

* * * * * * * *

"Instead of relying on his own recollection, Mr. Smith more likely relied on what he was told might be true by what the detectives said. Mr. Smith agreed to their narrative claims."

"This is not justice for Mr. Smith or for Sheriff Hall. This is a cold case murder of a law enforcement officer. Your job is not to bring closure for J.T. and his family. There are three principles:

-Innocent until proven guilty
-State has burden to prove guilty
-Must be guilty beyond reasonable doubt"

"This case is only simple if you don't look closely at the details. The State would have you conclude that the statement of a cognitively impaired seventy-year-old from fifty years before is enough to convict him. Larry Smith is presumed innocent unless each and every one of you is convinced. At the end of the trial, we will ask that the State has not proven its case beyond reasonable doubt and Smith is not guilty." He sits down.

Donna stands. "Call Carolyn Hall Philo as first witness." Donna asked Carolyn questions about her father and the type of man and father he was. He was a loving, wonderful father who worked several jobs to provide for his family including as a special deputy sheriff. Carolyn identified her father in photographs as well as identifying his pipe in a photograph.

Carolyn told the story from her standpoint of what happened on that fateful night. She said her father was dressed in his sheriff's uniform with his long, yellow raincoat over his arm. Carolyn described the rest of the evening and then being awakened by a phone call at eleven pm which informed them her father had been shot. They picked up

Carolyn's mother and went to the hospital. J.T. died three days later and was buried at Washington National Cemetery three days after his death.

Carolyn- "For years I would call and ask what is going on? I thought if I was alive the person who killed my dad was alive."

Carolyn told about her life, and how Bob left law enforcement to practice law and then they moved to Texas. She talked about being told by Corporal Killen on the fiftieth anniversary of J.T.'s murder that there was activity in the case and then told how she was informed by phone by another police officer that an arrest had been made.

Donna entered all of the clothes J.T. wore on the night he was murdered into evidence. When she entered J.T.'s glasses, Carolyn started crying. "Those are my dad's glasses." She continued to cry as they entered J.T's pipe into evidence. "Oh, my goodness, Daddy's pipe. Always had that with him."

For the first time in the trial with some of the evidence on the floor moved, I got a glimpse of Smith. He had a beard, moustache, and wore glasses. He appeared very short, maybe five feet tall. The defense had no questions, so Carolyn stepped down.

After a brief recess, Donna called Smith's daughter, Melinda Allen, to the stand. She was forty- three-years-old and petite with long brown hair pushed over to one side. She wore glasses. I looked over at Mr. Smith and got a better look at him. His beard was gray and neatly trimmed. His glasses were red and he had short gray hair. He wore a blue suit.

Melinda Allen testified that she had a sister and a brother, but her sister passed away. Her mother and father (Larry Smith) were separated. She gave her assessment of her father's health and overall constitution. Then she talked about her father's phone call to her after being interviewed by the detectives.

Melinda Allen- "He told me that he had gotten back from trooper barracks and had been interviewed about something that occurred fifty years ago. He was worried and scared about how I was going to react. His voice was shaking. He said they came to talk to him about a robbery. Nothing about a security guard. There was a security guard, but not specific place."

The lawyers approached the bench and the courtroom was filled with white noise. After the brief break, Donna gave Melinda a paper to read and asked her to read lines three through twelve to herself to see if that refreshed her memory about what her father said to her.

"I don't remember all of it. I remember he was there with others doing daytime robberies and his brother was there."

Donna tried to press Melinda on her father's phone confession to her about shooting the security guard, but Melinda couldn't remember even when her typed testimony was presented to her to review. Melinda denied being told about a gun by her father.

Donna- "Page eight, lines one and three. How he was feeling to be telling you this."

Melinda- "He was relieved to get it off his chest regarding robberies."

Donna- "Read lines three through eleven again."

Melinda- "He did a bunch of daytime robberies..."

Donna- "This paragraph goes beyond daytime robberies."

Melinda- "I told you he said he'd committed daytime robberies."

Donna- "These lines talk about an action taken."

Melinda- "I don't remember anything else."

Donna- "You don't recall being told he'd never told anyone over the last fifty years what he told you?"

"Did he say he told your mother?"

Melinda- "He didn't say anything about my mother."

Donna kept asking Melinda about specific lines in her statement which Melinda could not recall.

Donna- "No further questions pending playing of the interview."

Recess for lunch

I went down to the cafeteria for lunch with the Philos and Halls. The cafeteria was huge and had all different types of food. I settled on Chinese food and filled my plate with chicken fried rice and an egg roll. I grabbed a Diet Coke also. I didn't realize that the cafeteria charged you by how much your tray weighed, so I was surprised when the cashier weighed my food and told me my bill was over seventeen dollars. I paid it and sat down and ate my expensive and somewhat mediocre- tasting lunch.

Court Resumed

Court resumed at one thirty-five pm. Smith's daughter, Melinda, came back to the witness stand and Donna Fenton said, "State's exhibit number twelve, audio recording of the call between Smith and daughter to be admitted."

Recording

Larry Smith- "I've been holding this in for fifty years. I guess I killed someone. Myself, Leslie, and two others were doing robberies and a security man came out from Manor Country Club. He flashed a flashlight at us and I had a friend's gun in my hand and I shot him. I needed to get everything off my chest. I'm relieved to get it off my chest."

* * * * * * *

Donna- "Do you remember telling the trooper whether or not you felt your father had told the truth?"

Melinda- "I don't recall talking to the troopers."

Donna has Melinda read the highlighted part of the page to herself.

Donna- "You told the troopers that if he didn't do it, he wouldn't say he did it. Why did you tell the troopers that meant only the robberies? If he didn't do it, he wouldn't admit it."

Donna asks for a bench conference with the other attorneys and the judge. I look over at Larry Smith who is staring straight ahead. He has a large dark mark on the left side of his face just below his left eye.

Attorneys return to their places and white noise stops

Donna- "Isn't it there? If he didn't do it, he wouldn't say he did it. He was in tears when talking."

Donna sat down and one of the young defense attorneys got up. He recounted how Melinda had learned of the events that led Larry Smith to call his daughter and then discussed the call. "Your father called after the interrogation. He said I guess I killed someone. You don't remember. When you talked to investigators did you feel the statement was truthful?"

Melinda- "No."

State- "Objection."

Judge-"Sustained."

White noise as the lawyers approach the bench. Asian juror in back row flipping his pencil skillfully through each finger of his right hand.

The defense went on to query Melinda about her father's overall condition the past few years and how involved she's been in his care. After a brief cross examination by the State, the witness was excused.

The State next called Larry Smith Junior, the defendant's son, to the stand. Donna's assistant, John Grochowski, got up to interview him. John wore a suit and a yellow tie. Larry Smith Junior was short, bald, and had a moustache and long goatee. He wore glasses and a checkered blue shirt. He was forty years old. Larry Smith Junior had talked with his father in jail within a couple of days of his arrest. Larry Junior's account was similar to Melinda's. He talked about being told of robberies by his father. His father told him he knew it was something that was going to catch up with him. Larry Junior also refused to corroborate being told about a killing. The defense cross-examined and asked the son to recount what he said about his father's condition previously. He said his father is slipping from health issues and memory issues the past few years. The witness stepped down.

The State next called Diane Schmidt to the stand. Fifty-two years ago, it was her home on the Manor Country Club golf course that had been burglarized the same night J.T. Hall was murdered. She was an attractive, fit woman who looked younger than her age. She had gray hair parted in the middle and wore large earrings and a colorful jacket. Mrs. Schmidt told the story of how on returning from a trip to the mountains on the evening of October twenty-third, 1971, she and her husband found their home ransacked and burglarized. They called the police who said it would be a while until an officer got there because they had another problem at Manor Country Club. Within five minutes there were four to five police cars in their driveway.

Mrs. Schmidt testified that the most sentimental item missing was her wedding ring, which was never recovered. The most expensive item taken was their flatware sterling silver set left in the bushes. She and her husband were driven by the police to the country club parking lot where more of their possessions were found. Included in the items stolen was a Formica coffee table, liquor, candles, brand new sheets still in their wrapping, and a ceramic jack-o-lantern.

After Mrs. Schmidt was finished testifying, her husband, Roger, took the stand. He was very athletic-looking and wore a blue jacket and checkered shirt. He related that he and his wife had been married for fifty-four years and had lived in the same house in Manor Country Club for fifty- two years. He gave the same accounting of that fateful evening as his wife.

Slides were shown of photographs taken in the house that night. There was a bar in the basement and alcohol had been moved to a chair. Suitcases were lying on the bed and dressers were open. Roger again went over the list of items taken and reiterated that they weren't home when the burglary happened and didn't see someone taking things. The defense had no questions.

Donna called retired police officer Jerry Boone as the next witness for the State. Officer Boone appeared by Zoom on a screen set up in the courtroom. He was now living in Tampa, Florida. We could only see his head and shoulders. He wore glasses and a white tee shirt. Officer Boone had worked for twenty-four years for the Montgomery County Police Department in patrol, narcotics, and detective divisions. He was directed to the homicide at the Manor Country Club the evening of October twenty-third and stayed through the early morning hours of October twenty-fourth. He found out the victim was a police officer when he arrived at eleven fifteen pm. The victim had already been transported by ambulance to the hospital when he arrived. It was a dark, dreary night and the lighting on the parking lot was dim. Other police officers were already there, but Boone was the crime scene detective. Boone gave the dimensions of the parking lot: two hundred and ten yards by one hundred and fifty yards and said there was one vehicle parked there. On the ground there was blood and a flashlight. A weapon had already been collected and preserved by Officer Joe Sargent. They took sketches of the scene and marked evidence with a crayon. He did a cursory look and decided to come back by daylight. He came back at eight am and reviewed the police report, scene sketch, and sketch of the surrounding streets and neighborhoods. The items collected were turned over to Sergeant Sweat. They found a bullet ten feet north west of the deceased's head. A flashlight which had a bullet pass through it was twenty feet away from Sheriff Hall. A gun was close to the leg of Sheriff Hall and concealed by his clothing. The gun was discovered when Sheriff Hall's body was moved. The lone vehicle was Sheriff Hall's car. The stolen property was outside of the paved area, twenty-two feet from the parking lot and one hundred and forty-four feet from Sheriff Hall. The property was all household items.

The scene was documented by photographs taken by Officer Martin Taylor. There were also a series of aerial photographs taken the morning after the murder. These showed the parking lot's location, parts of the fairway, and the location of the home on Beverly Road that had been burglarized.

* * * * * * * *

Donna- "Did you attend the autopsy?"

Officer Boone-"I did. The autopsy was conducted on October twenty-seventh, 1971 in the State Medical Examiner's Office in Baltimore, Maryland by Dr. Ronald Kornblum. The autopsy report came back as a Caucasian male in mid-forties. Gunshot wound back of head and abrasions to face and hands from falling to the pavement. Collected bullet from autopsy from inside the skull. Entrance three inches behind the left ear and stopped near the right eye. Cause of death: gunshot wound to the head."

A Second Shot

The last thing Donna asked Officer Boone about was the use of an officer and K-9 dog to try and trace where the murderer had fled. There were dotted lines on the aerial map of the area showing the track of the officer and dog. The track began at the location of the discarded property just off the parking lot. The first portion went to Carrollton Road and then to Beverly Road right past the Schmidt's house. The scent stopped here. The officer and dog went to the Schmidt's house and picked up a fresh scent which tracked back to where the stolen property was next to the golf course.

The defense attorney reconfirmed that there were two bullets fired at Sheriff Hall and that he was shot in the back of the head.

The State's Attorney called Norman Shoemaker as the next witness. He looked approximately seventy years old and was bald with a gray moustache and goatee. He was about five foot nine inches, stocky, and dressed totally in black. Mr. Shoemaker lived in South Carolina now, but grew up in Rockville, Maryland and lived there most of his life. He attended Robert E. Peary High School. He lived with his parents and took care of them when they got older. He had two younger brothers. His family lived four miles from Manor Country Club and he caddied at the golf course there starting at age fifteen.

Mr. Shoemaker remembered the night Sheriff Hall was shot. He was driving around smoking pot with three friends. They decided to break into soda machines at the Manor Country Club using a screwdriver and a tire iron. They were unable to break in but continued trying until after ten to fifteen minutes they heard sirens. They were parked in the parking lot and Shoemaker was able to point to the spot where their car was parked. The soda machines were off to the side. Shoemaker said he only saw parked cars and no police officers. When the boys heard the sirens they ran to their car, jumped in, and headed east to the service road. They saw fire trucks go by with sirens wailing, so they turned around and went back to the country club. They'd been gone a total of ten minutes.

It looked like someone dropped a big trash bag in the parking lot when they returned. They got out of their car and it was the sheriff in a yellow raincoat. He had fallen towards the soda machines. His head was at a forty-five degree angle. There was a puddle of blood around him. The boys ran into the clubhouse and had the receptionist call the police, who arrived within ten minutes. It was pouring down rain and cold and the parking lot was dimly lit. After talking to the police, all of the boys went home.

Mr. Shoemaker talked to the police again the next day, he said. His father was a Montgomery County police officer. Norman spoke a little bit the first time, but he didn't know what to say. His father was aware he was speaking to the police. He never had a firearm until five years later at the age of twenty. Much later he spoke to the police again. The police always said. "Why don't you admit you did it?" He had nothing to do with the murder of Sheriff Hall. He felt like he was harassed by the police. He felt wrongfully blamed for the crime.

The Defense cross-examined and asked Norman Shoemaker if he knew Larry Becker or Larry Smith; he didn't. Smith was not with him at the Manor Country Club on the night of the murder.

The State's Attorney next called Gregory Swarr to the witness stand. He was tall with white hair and a white moustache. He wore a white shirt. His date of birth was February second, 1955, making him sixty-nine-years-old.

Mr. Swarr grew up in Canada and moved to Montgomery County at the age of ten. He went to high school at Robert E. Peary High School, which no longer exists. He did not graduate, choosing to join the Military in 1972. In high school, cars were his passion. He did not know Larry Becker. A friend of Swarr's joined the military so he did also. The war in Vietnam was winding down and the draft ended. His house growing up was in front of Peary High School. As a teenager he hung out at Hot Shoppes in Aspen Hills and he also hung out at Maggie's Place.

In October of 1971 he became aware of the shooting of a police officer. He had nothing to do with the shooting of J.T. In 2022 he was contacted by Detective Lisa Killen and he found out his name came up in connection with the police officer's shooting. In 1973 in an interview while in prison, Larry Becker named Gregory Swarr as the shooter of J.T. Hall. Swarr maintained his innocence and was not with the group of boys breaking into the soda machines that night. After the Defense asked Swarr if he knew Larry Becker/Smith and he said no, he was excused.

The State next called Robert Canevari as a witness. He was born April thirtieth, 1956 and was now sixty-seven years old. He wore an earring in his left ear. He spent three years in the Army and married at age twenty-four. He was a retired postal worker who lived In Virginia working part-time for a Nissan dealership.

Mr. Canevari also attended Peary High School. He graduated and went into the Army where he served for three years in the military police. Then he lived in Gaithersburg, Maryland for a year before marrying and moving to Blacksburg, Virginia,

On October twenty-third of 1971 he was living in Montgomery County and was fifteen years old. He was hanging out at Hot Shoppes Junior in Aspen Hill. He got in a car with three friends and another boy. They left Hot Shoppes that night and went to an apartment complex and broke into the driers in the laundry room. They took the money and drove to the Manor Country Club to break into the Coke machines. They tried to break into the Coke machines but were unable to. The machines were outdoors. Canevari thought they used a crowbar unsuccessfully. The boys heard sirens and stopped. They went back to their car and drove to a dead end road behind the country club. Canevari didn't notice anything in the country club parking lot as they were leaving. He thinks they were gone twenty to thirty minutes when they realized the crow bar was still on top of the Coke Machines. They returned to the country club and found Sheriff Hall lying face down in the parking lot, struggling to breathe. Canevari stayed with Sheriff Hall, turning his head to the side to try and help him breathe. The others went into the country club to call for help. Canevari saw no people besides Sheriff Hall who was wearing a security outfit. He saw blood around Hall's head. His friends returned from the club house and they waited for the police and medical people to arrive; it took ten minutes. The ambulance arrived and took Sheriff Hall to the hospital. Canevari talked to the police that night and told them about the group's night activities, excluding the part about breaking into the Coke machines.

After Sheriff Hall died, the police came to Canevari's high school and got him out of class to talk to him. He told the truth about the attempted break in and was charged with destruction of property and larceny. He pled guilty. He also testified that the five boys remained together the entire time and had no firearms. There were no household items or tables inside the car. Canevari didn't know Larry Becker and he didn't live near the country club. He had no idea the case had been cold for fifty years since he didn't live in the area. After being contacted by Lisa Killen, he drove back to Rockville voluntarily and walked the parking lot and surrounding area with Lisa and another female detective. He was asked to walk through where the Coke machines were, where they parked, and where they found Sheriff Hall. The defense's only question was if Larry Becker was with them and Canevari replied no.

The State called Corporal Lisa Killen, the police officer who had spear-headed the cold case effort. She was in her nineteenth year working for the Montgomery County Police Department. Her job was with the First District Special Assignment Team. She worked as a plainclothes officer in high crime areas. She testified:

Lisa- "I was on temporary assignment with the cold case unit. Montgomery County police encourage officers to explore where they want their career to go. I applied in the fall of 2021 and was assigned as one of the lead detectives on the fiftieth anniversary (of the Hall murder). Sergeant Chris Homrock assigned me."

"First I went through every piece of paper in the case file. I looked through it for countless hours. The murder occurred in October of 1971, and over the decades it was reviewed several times. Before 2021, in 2018 cigarette butts at the Manor Country Club were tested for DNA and there was insufficient DNA. There was a homicide at Manor Country Club. Officers arrived at 22:45 and observed J.T. Hall suffering from a gunshot wound. He was in the southeast corner of the parking lot."

"There was no 911 then; it started in 1974. The country club called the local police station. Calls were not recorded. The receptionist at the country club called. Robert Trisgrad and his girlfriend were walking through the parking lot, found the body, and went into the country club for help. Five boys were also there, fourteen to sixteen years old. They were driving through the parking lot and found Sheriff Hall. On the scene when the police officers arrived were the receptionist, Trisgrad and his girlfriend, and the five boys."

"The officer was in grave condition but alive. He was transported by Kensington Fire Rescue Department to the hospital. That evening the officers searched the immediate area around J.T. They found a gun and a flashlight with a bullet hole. The bullet was also found. They also found personal property discarded near the bushes. Officer Hall's firearm had not been fired."

"The police were also summoned to the Schmidt home for a burglary. The house is nine hundred feet from where J.T. was shot."

The prosecutor gave Lisa a large map and had her show the location of the burglary, where the items were found, and where J.T.'s body was found. She used a green marker to mark where the soda machines were.

Lisa- "The items were one hundred to one hundred and fifty feet from his body. The officers investigated the burglary that night and it was part of the case file. The officers found the back door of the house had been opened by a crowbar and the house was ransacked and property stolen. Items found included a step stool, sheets, candles, a ceramic jack-o-lantern, and jewelry items. They had JT's vehicle towed to the police station for processing. They seized his clothing and found his notepad."

The judge felt it was late enough in the day to adjourn court, so everyone left.

CHAPTER FORTY-THREE

Trial Day Two
Tuesday, January 9, 2024

The defense team's two paralegals were already in the courtroom when I arrived for day two. The one in charge was African American and appeared to be in her early forties. The other paralegal was Caucasian and younger, probably in her early thirties. They scurried around the courtroom making sure that everything was set up for their lawyers. The two State's attorneys and all four defense lawyers were already there, as was Sheriff Uy who greeted me with a smile. There were a total of fifteen people in the courtroom when the jury was brought in and seated.

The assistant State's attorney, John, called Lisa Killen back to the stand for direct examination. She began by talking about the notepad retrieved from the breast pocket of Sheriff Hall:

Lisa-"There were various notes and vehicle information written down. Richard Hobart's name and home address were written on the pad. A canvas was done in the immediate area, canine tracking was done, the residence was photographed and fingerprints were taken including around the body. Soil samples were taken. They found a shoe print at the canine track. The crime scene was secured from public interference with tape."

"The next morning there was a search and aerial search. They used helicopters or airplanes. They found in the parking lot near the body two General Motors' keys, a screwdriver, and a man's smoking pipe.

They didn't know who it belonged to, and there were no General Motors' vehicles in the area."

Corporal Killen stepped down to point out things on a large aerial photograph taken of the crime scene on October twenty-fourth, 1971- one day after the shooting.

Number One-Country Club

Number Two-Hall's vehicle

Number Three-Victim located Number Four-Discarded property- near pump house (watering system for golf course)

Number Five-Burglarized home

She also pointed out where the soda machines were located. Lisa got back into her seat in the witness stand and resumed talking:

Lisa-"October twenty-fourth, 1971, the day after the shooting. Sheriff is in the hospital and still alive. Officers discovered the soda machines were tampered with. The coin slots were broken into. The damage marks on the soda machines were different from the damage marks breaking into the Schmidt's residence. They drained the pond on the golf course to look for a weapon, but no gun was found. The focus of the investigation was on the five young boys. Nothing came of the shoe print; it was in a sand trap so it couldn't be casted. It measured eleven and a half inches long. The significance of the soil samples was different elements-sulfur, etc.- if the shoes or clothing contained dirt it could be compared with ground samples. There was a need to find a shoe quickly. Nothing came of the soil samples."

"The five boys were interviewed and their stories were consistent and they alibied one another. There was no dispute in the fact the five boys stayed with each other. The boys were willing to be interviewed and eliminated as suspects. Mr. Trisgrad and his girlfriend were interviewed and removed as suspects; they remained on the scene and went for help. The officers continued to investigate the physical evidence. Fingerprints found at the Schmidt's residence were from a friend of the family who was a known visitor to the house and not a suspect."

"On October twenty-sixth Sheriff Hall died. The five boys were brought back in and four of the five were interviewed. Their statements were consistent with prior statements. All physical evidence had been processed. The investigators knew they needed witness accounts or someone else coming forward. On March sixth, 1972, Richard Hobart appeared at the police department. He was interviewed and investigated and eliminated as a suspect. His name had been in the sheriff's notepad. In the summer of 1972, the police received a tip that an individual had information on the murder. His name was Leslie Becker, and he was the brother of Larry Becker. The information..."

There was an objection by the defense followed by a meeting of the lawyers at the bench. After the meeting, the Judge spoke, "Lisa Killen's information is background information. Leslie Becker said he believed Larry had knowledge of the shooting or was involved and knew who owned the gun used. This interview was conducted on August ninth, 1972."

Lisa resumed her testimony: "April fifth, 1973 the police interviewed Larry Becker. He had escaped while being held on a burglary charge. He wanted to make a statement in exchange for leniency. The officers listened to him and he was interviewed. Flash forward to 2021. I was not aware of the interview. It had been there since I first took the case."

Lisa reported how the interview had been mislabeled Richard Hobart Interview and then detailed the arduous task it had been to convert the reel-to-reel tape to a DVD format. David Snyder, who worked for the FBI, did the work and completed a report and attached it. The interview was played.

The tape stopped and the State's attorney asked Lisa, "We heard Becker give his rendition. What was not accurate?"

Lisa- "Not consistent with where the body was found. Deputy sheriff fell in the driveway but he was in the southeast corner of the parking lot. He failed to mention he had a bright yellow rain jacket.

Miserable day and he describes it as clear, not cool or hot. No firearm recovered. Swarr was not fingerprinted and there were no suspects in this case until this interview."

The State now played part two of the interview with Larry Becker from 1973 with Detective Killen still on the witness stand.

Larry denied knowing that Greg or any of the other boys at the Coke machines had a gun. He explained why he didn't go over to Greg at Maggie's after the shooting due to fear of Greg thinking he was a snitch. The police continued to pepper Larry with questions until the end of the interview. Detective Killen was asked to flesh out multiple people on the tape who Larry had mentioned:

Lisa- "John Rizzo. Larry hung out with him. We followed up with Mr. Rizzo and he was in the military at this time in another state."

"Greg Swarr. I spoke with him. He was unaware of anything to do with the sheriff."

"Holloway. Same as Mr. Swarr. No information and no idea what I was talking about."

"Brunner and Finch were not interviewed. All of the people Larry Becker named in his interview were not there. The four individuals he named were not present."

"In 1973 the interviewing officers did nothing. They believed he was making a statement for his escape charge and knew nothing about the shooting. He was not given any benefit towards his sentencing."

Lisa stepped down and the State called Dr. Stephanie Dean to the stand. Doctor Dean is the Chief Medical Examiner of the state of Maryland. She performs autopsies to determine cause and manner of death. She had been contacted to review the autopsy on J.T. Hall from 1971. She found the autopsy reports and photos and reviewed them. She read from the report: "Dr. Kornblum noted height five feet ten inches and weight one hundred and seventy-three pounds. There was evidence of a gunshot wound to the head. The entrance wound was right behind the left ear. No exit wound. Examined the brain, skull, scalp. Stippling is from close range discharge of a firearm. Particles can also exit from the gun. They can be dispersed on the skin as soot or if unburned, as little red dots. There was no evidence of stippling on Officer Hall."

"The internal exam identified the bullet entered the back left side and injured the brain and then recovered. The size of the gunshot entrance is one quarter inch in diameter with abrasion/scrape of surrounding skin. Scalp, skull, brain injured. The bullet was given to the police after recovery. The bullet went from back to front, left to right, and slightly upward. There was also a small contusion to the right side of the forehead, a left hand scrape and a right knee scrape. Internal exam was done. In the lungs was pneumonia or lung infection, Manner and cause of death: gunshot wound to the head; homicide. Injury to the brain which was penetrating. The brain is enclosed in the skull which can't expand. The brain swells and herniates downward to where the head connects to the spinal cord. I used photos to make my own conclusion."

Donna turns on the projector which shows images on the screen.

Dr. Dean- "First photo is the back of his head. See gunshot entrance wound behind the left ear. Second photo is called ID photo. Shows his face. On his forehead there is a contusion or bruise. My opinion of cause of death is the same as Dr. Kornblum's: gunshot wound to head and homicide."

The Medical Examiner stepped down and the next witness was Detective Vincent Sylvester who was a fugitive detective with the Montgomery County Police Department. If someone is arrested out of state, his department takes custody of them and brings them back to Maryland. He described in great detail how he and two colleagues flew up to New York, picked up Larry Smith, and brought him back to Maryland. The entire ride was recorded by a covert recording device in the backpack between the officer and the prisoner. After taking time with the lawyers to decide whether or not to allow this recording to be played, the judge allowed it to be played in the courtroom. Larry talked about his cigarette addiction and they stopped one time on the ride from the detention center to the airport for gas and for Larry to smoke a cigarette. Larry told his life story about his childhood and being adopted and then his fall-out with his adoptive parents. He did describe himself as a "smart-ass teenager" and said he liked New York better than Maryland because it was "too easy to get in trouble in Maryland especially when you live on the streets." The tape ended and after a short break, the detective was back on the witness stand. The State's attorney asked if Larry Smith was always responsive to questions, if they had concerns about the mental status of the defendant, and the Defense objected. There was a meeting of the lawyers at the bench and when it was over the State's attorney asked, "Was there anything you noted that you turned over to the Montgomery County Correctional Facility?'

"No. He was pleasant and responsive on the flight and another recording was made."

"Was that communication similar?'

"Yes, it was.

"No further questions."

The Defense asked, "Did Mr. Smith tell you he went to jail for burglary?"

"Yes."

"Do you know any details?"

"I know it was in the Aspen Hill area and that's all."

"No further questions"

* * * * * * *

Detective Lisa Killen was called back to the witness stand.

State's Attorney-"During your investigation did you become aware of where Larry Smith lived in the seventies with his family?"

Lisa- "Yes, he was living in the Manor area with his family." Lisa puts a pin on the Becker home. "I listened to the interview in 1973 with a different view. It was significant for me. A self-admitted witness placed himself at the crime scene. Other things were accurate. Pieces of information withheld from the public. Details withheld."

State- "What details?"

Defense- "Objection."

Attorneys meet at the bench. Meeting ends.

State- "Based on your review of media articles related to this case."

Lisa-"Yes, and information withheld from the public. In the 1973 interview he stated he heard two shots, both shots didn't hit the man, gun was a thirty-eight, a flashlight was out, and he admits to fleeing the scene. None of the people he named were breaking into the machines. The first person I wanted to speak with was Leslie Becker, his brother. I used investigative databases and found the obituary; Leslie Becker was deceased. Leslie Becker was survived by Larry Smith in the obituary. The obituary provided details that Larry lived in New York and had a wife, Ruth. I located a Larry David Smith that lived in Little Falls, New York. I found his address in Little Falls. Larry David Smith matched Larry David Becker. It was the same relative."

"The next step was a deep dive into Larry David Smith. I located his Facebook page. Larry Smith Senior mentioned he was from Little Falls, New York. Stated he attended Robert E. Peary High School, which Larry Becker attended. He was offering a Pittsburgh Steelers' jacket and gave a phone number if anyone wanted to purchase it."

"The next action: we wanted to approach an investigation. We reached out to the New York State Police. We travelled to New York on a logistical trip to get a lay of the land and to check out the apartment building where Larry Smith lived. I went with Detective Katie Leggitt at the end of May, 2022. We went up one day and back the next. We came back and obtained a pin register on his phone number. We don't get the content of text messages but know the phone number of who is contacting him. We had to get this signed by a judge and sent to the cell phone company. We monitored his phone throughout the summer."

"Next we got in contact with John Rizzo, a known associate of Larry Smith's. We wanted to confirm that Larry David Becker was the same as Larry David Smith. John Rizzo was mentioned by Larry Smith as the person he was hanging out with when he walked to Manor Country Club. I had conducted an interview with Mr. Rizzo. I asked for his assistance and he said yes. We asked John Rizzo to conduct a controlled phone call with Larry Smith. This is a recorded call done on behalf of the police department with Rizzo and the police present. Two calls were made, July eighteenth and July twentieth of 2022."

"In the first call Larry Smith denied knowing Rizzo. In the second call Smith admitted to being Larry Becker and they relived shared experiences. However, Becker-Smith denied ever being at the Manor Country Club that night, ever having a gun, or ever talking to the police about events that night at Manor Country Club."

The judge adjourned the court for the day.

CHAPTER FORTY-FOUR
Trial Day Three
January 10, 2024

The morning trial started with a discussion that fingerprint analysis had been done comparing the fingerprints of Larry Becker when he was in custody in 1973 and Larry Smith when he was in custody in 2022, The fingerprints matched.

The State then called New York State Police Investigator Chad Solls, who went with Killen and Leggitt when they went to Larry Smith's apartment. The tape was played which recorded their interactions with Mr. Smith and then the ride to the State Police Barracks. Smith was told he was free to go and he was not under arrest. In the car Smith denied knowing John Rizzo. During the interview with Smith, Investigator Solls was in his office down the hall. He said Mr. Smith went to the bathroom and went outside to smoke cigarettes. Investigator Solls had to let him back in twice. Solls said there was no fence around the barracks and once outside you could go anywhere you wanted. The interview in the barracks lasted three hours. A different investigator, Thomas Nitti, took Smith back to his apartment after the interview. Nothing on this trip was recorded.

The State next called Investigator Jason Nellis of the New York State Police Department. After being identified and giving his job description, Nellis began:

"On September first of 2022 I came in for my shift. I was told about the investigation with Montgomery County. I didn't participate. The warrant came down at six pm. I verified that the warrant was good. It was a warrant for Larry Smith and they sent confirmation. I had to go get the individual with another officer. We went to his apartment and knocked on the door. Mr. Smith asked who it was. We told him and he said, "Fuck," before the door opened. He said, "I figured you guys would be back." He was dressed in a shirt and tie. We told him he had to come with us. We put him in handcuffs, took him down to our car, and drove back to the barracks. We consider him a fugitive from justice. The bond hearing was done by video. He appeared to understand the bond hearing. Then we transported him to jail."

New York State Trooper Susannah Rose was the next witness. She had been Lisa Killen's contact person in the New York State Police Department, helping arrange things. She began discussing her conversations with the defendant's daughter, Melinda Allen, and son, Larry Junior. She was asked if Mrs. Allen commented to her and immediately there was a meeting at the bench.

During all of the testimony Larry Smith sat impassively at the defense table. He either looked down or forward. The Asian male juror had one pencil twirling across his right hand and another pencil over his right ear. During conferences at the bench, the defendant drummed his fingers on the table. Did the white noise have a beat that I was missing?

After the meeting at the bench, Donna Fenton resumed questioning for the State:

Donna- "Was this recorded? What did Mrs. Allen tell you that her father told her?"

Rose- "Guess I killed somebody."

"Don't guess," she said.

"I killed someone."

"He was with two other individuals when the officer came out with a flashlight and he shot him," she said. "She said he had a gun in his hand and he had to get something off his chest. She said, "I do know that if he didn't do it, he wouldn't say he did it."

State Trooper Rose also spoke with Leslie Smith's son the same day. The defense had no questions.

* * * * * * * *

After a thirty minute break, the state called Bobby Ray Edwards, nickname "Raven," to the stand. Bobby Ray was seventy years old and graduated from Robert E. Peary High School in 1971. He had white hair in a ponytail and a white moustache. He knew Larry Becker.

Raven- "We were just hanging out. I met him at Maggie's Place, the old Episcopal Church where they had arts and crafts and other things. I last saw Larry in 1975."

State- "Can you identify him in the courtroom now?"

Raven- "No. I know where the Manor Country Club was. I didn't know where Larry lived. I heard about the murder at the Manor Country Club. I had nothing to do with the murder or burglary at the Manor Country Club."

State- "Did you become aware Larry Becker left Maryland?"

Raven- "Yes, he went to upstate New York. I moved to Connecticut. Larry dyed his hair blonde. No contact since we moved. I missed his call in the summer of 2022 when he left a voicemail. I passed it on to the police. I told the police everything I knew about the murder of Sheriff Hall. I told the police about the voice message from Larry Becker."

The voice message is played in court: "Bobby Ray Edwards, looking for nickname, Raven. Please give me a call. This is Larry (gives phone number)." State's attorney sits down.

Defense Attorney-"In the early 1970's you hung out with Mr. Smith.""

Raven- "We'd hang out and then not see each other for a few months. My brother helped him find his biological parents. I was not at Manor Country Club the night Sheriff Hall was shot. I never heard about Mr. Smith shooting someone at Manor Country Club."

* * * * * * *

Lisa Killen is back on the witness stand.

State's Attorney- "Corporal Killen you testified yesterday your investigation revealed what was and wasn't part of what was released to the public."

Lisa- "Yes. These are newspaper articles on the shooting of Sheriff Hall."

State- "Not a date on one of them."

Meeting at the bench with white noise. Meeting adjourns.

Lisa-"Calls made to Rodney Edwards, brother of Bobby Ray Edwards by Mr. Smith. Pin register after the second controlled call to Rizzo." (A pin register or dialed number recorder (DNR) is a device that records all numbers called from a particular line)." Larry Smith called the Raven. The Raven left a copy of the voicemail. Raven was an associate of Larry Smith and he wasn't involved in the murder. I received the voice mail on July twentieth, 2022."

Lisa then recounted the first visit she and Katie Leggitt made to Little Falls and then briefly went over the events leading to the interview at Police Barracks in New York. The video was played and had good quality audio and video in the courtroom. The first part of the video was played and then there was a break for lunch.

* * * * * * * *

After lunch the State's Attorney called John Joseph Rizzo as a witness by Zoom. John was seventy years old. He wore a white Tee shirt and glasses. He was a retired audio engineer and did side stuff. He was living in Glen Rock, Pennsylvania and that is where he was appearing from on Zoom. He was not married now but had three children and six grandchildren. He had a gruff, smoker's voice.

Rizzo was familiar with Larry Becker having met him through his brother in late spring or early summer of 1972. Rizzo had enlisted in the United States Navy on March fourteenth of 1971, and in October of 1971 he was in the Navy. A photo was shown of Rizzo at age eighteen and he quipped, "It looks a lot like me."

Rizzo was familiar with the homicide of Sheriff Hall. He'd seen the news stories and his brother worked the desk for the Montgomery County Police. He had been contacted by Detective Lisa Killen who went to Pennsylvania to interview him. He agreed to assist with the investigation and try to contact Mr. Becker-Smith. He made the phone sting from the major crime offices.

Rizzo tried six times to speak with Smith. He couldn't remember how often they actually spoke. Rizzo was in a room with the detectives from the major crimes division and had been told to get information about Larry Smith living in the Aspen Hills area. Rizzo admitted to not being completely honest. "I tried to use what he knew about me and the lies he told me and make the two seem valid."

The first call Smith refused to admit to being the person Rizzo knew. But by the end of the phone calls Smith knew that Rizzo knew who he was. Rizzo tried to get Smith to tell why he used Rizzo's name as a witness in the interrogation. Rizzo said he had nothing else to do with the investigation or murder. He was not at Manor Country Club on October twenty-third, 1971. He did not see who shot the sheriff. In 1973 Larry Becker-Smith named him as a witness, but he had not been contacted until 2022.

The Zoom appearance of John Rizzo was over. The video interrogation of Smith by Detectives Killen and Leggitt resumed with Detective Killen on the witness stand. The entire courtroom sat silent, mesmerized, looking at the video playing on the large screen in the courtroom. The time grew late, and court was adjourned with the decisive part of the video still to come.

CHAPTER FORTY-FIVE

Trial Day Four
January 11, 2024

Thursday morning the judge arrived in the courtroom at nine thirty-five am. After a meeting with the lawyers at the bench, the jury came in and then Corporal Lisa Killen took her place in the witness stand. The video resumed playing with forty minutes left. When the video was over the court recessed. When court reconvened, Lisa Killen was again called to the witness stand.

State's Attorney- "I want you to clarify. What did the officers do after the first interview in 1973?"

Lisa-"They interviewed him again and took him to the scene of the murder."

State- "What caliber bullet was used? In 1973 Smith said 38 caliber and in 2022 he said 45 caliber."

Lisa-"32 caliber. No promises, threats, inducements. He answered questions appropriately and was talkative and chatty. He was arrested four and a half to five hours after the interview. We had no idea how long things would take. Nothing was used to induce him. No extra pressure to solve this case. We are very consistent in how we do our jobs. Robbing a bank same way as a homicide. Only difference in this case was the victim was not able to provide a statement. No negative repercussions on me or my career."

State- "No further questions."

Defense Attorney-"Good morning. The shooting occurred in 1971 and was investigated multiple times. A number of officers investigated the case. It was reopened in 2021, the fiftieth anniversary. Certain evidence has been destroyed: bullet and flashlight."

Lisa-"In 1971 they were sent to the FBI for forensic evidence."

Defense- "You read officers' reports and relied on their evaluation. Multiple gunshots were heard. There were people present at the country club the night he was shot. None of the people reported seeing Mr. Smith. April fourth, 1973-recording of Mr. Smith's interview with the police. He also spoke to the police April fifth and April sixth. He admitted being there and disclosed non-public information. You didn't ask the original detective what information was not disclosed in 1971. You determined from newspaper clippings found in the case file what was withheld. It had never been said by the department what was to be withheld. (The defense attorney holds up a cork board with newspaper clippings attached). Seven newspaper clippings found in the case file, all within a month of the shooting. Eighteen months after Sheriff Hall was shot, Smith was interviewed by police. There were rumors going around about the sheriff's death."

Lisa- "I read the police report that didn't say anything about the shots. Mr. Smith mentioning a 38 caliber gun was significant because a 32 caliber bullet will fit in a 38 caliber gun. Two shots fired would not have been disclosed. The flashlight was not part of public information. Smith said in 1973 he saw a flashlight; he thought lights were illuminated in the area where the sheriff was shot."

Defense- "In 1973 Mr. Smith said no rain. Mr. Smith didn't know clothes, yellow raincoat. Mr. Smith said the sheriff was facing the shooter. Mr. Smith said the sheriff was ten to fifteen feet away from the Coke machines and his body was found one hundred feet southeast of the soda machines. Mr. Smith had an unrelated escape charge and agreed to talk to police for leniency if he provided truthful information. The officers said Mr. Smith's account did not go along with the facts of the case."

The State objected and I looked around the courtroom while the attorneys met at the bench. There were thirty-two people in court including the judge, jury, attorneys, assistants, and spectators. The defense resumed:

Defense-"You reviewed a lot of police reports including April of 1973. You relied on that report as part of your investigation. It was the opinion of the writer of that report that Mr. Smith's remarks weren't factual and he was lying. The writer of the report was Sergeant Roby. Do you know there were three people who interviewed Mr. Smith? Officers Roby, Lothar, and Miller. It was their opinion that he was lying. These were the detectives in the room in 1973."

Lisa-"O.W. Sweat was the lead detective. I can't say if these officers were involved in the case. Where they were or what they did I don't know."

Defense- "These detectives said he had no knowledge. You went to Mr. Smith's apartment with Kattie Leggitt and two New York police officers. Detective Leggitt said you were looking into the case and needed some help from Smith."

Lisa-"Yes."

Defense-"Mr. Smith was taken to the police station. Had to get things wrapped up today. He was told needed to clear up some information. You talked to Mr. Smith about conversations with John Rizzo."

Lisa-"Yes."

Defense- "At this time the defense wants to play a clip from the interview with Mr. Smith from the New York interview."

(Male member of the jury instantly shows the defense attorney how to get the clip to play).

Interview tape-Smith's voice-"I didn't do burglary or whatever there. I did burglary I went to jail for...As far as I know never a cop or guard killed. The burglary I did was the one I was sent to jail for."

Defense- "Mr. Smith says as far as I know, no cop or security guard killed. Leggitt asks what burglary are you talking about? He says the one I was sent to jail for."

Lisa- "She was talking about burglaries at the Manor Club. She was asking solely about burglaries at the Manor Club."

Defense- "He says no one killed. Leggitt asks, "What burglary?" He says, "The one I got sent to jail for." The Schmidt's house is not a townhouse. Leslie Becker, Larry Smith, Mark Jensen were all in jail at the same time."

Defense attorney plays tape:

Lisa-"Know what trajectory means?"

Smith-"Path of something."

Lisa- "Able to place the path of the bullet with the body. Raven was tall. Impossible for Raven to shoot the security guard due to his height. Shot came from someone your height."

Tape stopped.

Defense- "You didn't clear Raven because of his height."

Lisa-"Right."

Defense attorney plays tape.

Lisa- "This is the only time I'm going to ask you this. You are a good guy. Did you accidentally shoot the sheriff? Raven is not responsible. The shooting came from someone your height."

Smith- "I never shot anyone intentionally."

Lisa- "Are you saying you shot the sheriff?"

Smith- "I guess so."

Defense attorney turns the tape off.

Defense- "In this clip you ask three times if Mr. Smith shot the sheriff. He said, "I guess I did if Raven didn't do it."

Defense attorney plays another clip.

Katie Leggitt- "Do you remember anything you got out of that house? Ton of things they seized."

Smith- "Maybe some radios, cash. I can't think of anything big."

Katie- "You don't remember a table?"

Smith- "Coinage is possible."

Tape stopped.

Defense- "He said might have taken radios and no radios taken. Formica table taken and he didn't recall a table."

Plays another clip.

Smith- "Went up and started taking things from the house. Someone shouted. I spun around and a flashlight hit me in the eyes. I got nervous and I pulled the trigger."

Tape stopped.

Defense- "The shot that killed Sheriff Hall hit him in the back of the head. Mr. Smith said he fired one time, a forty-five caliber bullet. No forty-five caliber bullets found. You don't have the gun." Pauses. "Norman Shoemaker was a suspect. He broke into the Coke machines. You said he was seen with a firearm earlier in the day."

Objection by the State. Bench conference. Conference ends.

Defense- "Corporal Killen, you said someone reported seeing Mr. Shoemaker with a firearm and shooting a gun."

Lisa-"That is correct."

Defense- "Was Shoemaker the main suspect?"

Lisa- "He was a person of interest."

Defense- "Shoemaker's father did not allow him to talk to police."

Lisa- "Report states on advice of his father in 1971 he didn't speak to police."

Defense- "You didn't talk to all five boys. Richard Hobart's name was in the sheriff's notepad along with his parent's home address. You said Richard Hobart spoke to police in early 1972. He heard he was a suspect. No audio recording. He died in 1976. Police concluded that he was cleared. No DNA evidence of burglary or shooting of Mr. Hall. No fingerprint evidence at the scene. Shoe print found on golf course in sand trap."

Lisa-"Done in sand so can't get exact size."

Defense- "Trying to find Larry Becker..."

Lisa- "I didn't know when he changed his last name."

Defense- "He only changed his last name, not his first or middle. Becker is the name of adopted family.

"The name change occurred several years after the shooting and imprisonment"

Lisa- "I found Larry Smith through the name in Leslie Becker's obituary. I found his Facebook account that said high school in Maryland. We put a pin order on his phone but didn't track personal messages between Smith and his daughter or Facebook messages."

Defense had no further questions, so the State's Attorney got up for redirect. Question asked.

Lisa- "A thirty-two caliber bullet fits into a thirty-eight caliber handgun and can be fired."

State- "The defense asked what details made you think he was at the crime scene. He said he was. He describes a revolver, thirty-eight caliber. He says two shots and one didn't hit him. In news articles they mentioned people breaking into Coke machines but not who these people were."

Lisa-"The second burglary in the Glen Mont townhouse occurred in 1972 and the first one in the Manor country club. I think he was talking about the one in Glen Mont because he was arrested."

State-"I am aware of the trajectory of the bullet from the autopsy. The first bullet hit the flashlight because if not, that would have been the end of the sheriff. Taking radios. Engagement ring never recovered. So could radios have never been recovered?"

Lisa-"Yes."

State- "Did you tell Mr. Smith how the house was broken into?"

Lisa- "No. He said someone had a "Jimmy "which could have been used to pry open doors,"

State- "Someone saw Norman Shoemaker with a gun that day?"

Lisa- "No further leads and those boys were cleared as suspects."

State- "Would Sheriff Hall often work in the Manor area?"

Lisa-"Yes. Notes and license tag numbers in that notepad. Mr. Hobart was interviewed by police and he was eliminated as a suspect."

State- "Did Mr. Smith provide information on multiple things consistent with the crime scene?"

Lisa- "Yes."

State- "You have spoken to lead investigators. You have spoken to Boone and Sweat. Neither was present at the time of the interview in 1973. Any legal records of name change from what you found?"

Lisa-"No."

State-"How can you fire a thirty-two caliber bullet out of a thirty-eight caliber gun?"

Lisa- "You can, but not the reverse. A smaller caliber bullet can fire from a larger gun."

Lunch Break

After the lunch break the State called Detective Katherine (Katie) Leggett. Detective Leggett said she had been a police detective for twenty-five years and on the Cold Case unit for ten years. She was also on the Special Victims Unit for eleven years. In the fall of 2021, she was selected to assist Lisa Killen in the investigation into the homicide of Sheriff J.T. Hall. Detective Leggett described how early on she mainly served as a sounding board for Corporal Killen until the discovery and conversion of the mislabeled reel-to-reel tape.

Katie- "The tape had significance because he put himself at the scene of the shooting. Lisa did the majority of the ground work, found the obituary for Leslie Becker and tracked Larry Smith down."

Detective Leggett reviewed the first reconnaissance trip she had taken with Corporal Killen, and then testified about the second trip.

Katie- "On September first of 2022 we drove to State Police Barracks in Herkimer, New York. We met with two investigators and then the four of us went to Larry Smith's apartment. It was a secure building and the building manager had to buzz us in. We tried to find a location in the apartment building to interrogate, but there wasn't one. I was dressed in street clothes with my weapon in my hand bag. I don't remember seeing weapons on the New York officers."

"We knocked on the door of Smith's apartment and asked if we could come in. He said yes. The apartment was small but well-kept. To the left was a small kitchen area and the rest was an open room with a computer and bed. Everything was recorded by audio. We asked him to come to the station and he agreed. There were no promises, threats, or inducements. At the apartment we told him he was not under arrest. At the Police Barracks we went to the Interview Room. The entire interview was recorded."

State-"What was the first thing you said to Mr. Smith?"

Katie- "I don't remember. I told the defendant he was free to leave."

State- "How long was the interview?"

Katie- "Three hours and forty-five minutes."

State- "Did he appear to be sober?"

Katie- "Yes. I was a patrol officer first, and I had no concerns about his sobriety level. No concerns about mental health issues. He appropriately answered. Not ill. Never complained of illnesses, discomfort. I offered him a Nutrigrain bar and water."

"We eventually turned the conversation to why we were there. He never asked to stop or asked for an attorney. He had a memory of the event. He started saying he had no knowledge of it and ended saying he shot the sheriff. I used an alternative theory, more socially acceptable, that it was an accident. Eventually he said he shot the sheriff. There were no threats or promises."

"There were two breaks in the interview. The first break he asked to go smoke and then he came back. The second break at three pm he smoked and used the bathroom. He had to leave the premises of the state police barracks and he returned willingly."

"There was no physical contact before, during, or after the interview. The interview was non-adversarial. We asked him how he was treated and he said fairly and not forced. No yelling. Congenial."

State-"You told the defendant after the interview he wasn't going to be arrested or go to jail that day."

Katie- "I didn't think he was going to be arrested that day."

* * * * * * * *

After the interview the results went up the police chain of command. They had to have a conversation with the State's Attorney. They had to author an arrest warrant and send it to a colleague in Montgomery County who would take it to a court commissioner. Detective Killen wrote the arrest warrant. The warrant was secured in Maryland and Smith was arrested five hours later. Detective Leggett ended her examination by the State by saying she was trained on alternative theories. She utilized minimization; taking something and making it appear less serious. The state's attorney sat down and the defense attorney got up.

Defense Attorney-"Mr. Smith was brought to the police barracks room which was a small room with no windows and the door shut. Your guns were not visible but you identified yourselves as the police. Mr. Smith brought up the phone stings from a Mr. John Rizzo. You told him you knew he had kids and grandkids. You told Mr. Smith he's a very great man and raised a good family and lived an honest, good life and you didn't want to dirty that up. This is a transcript of the interview. Page one hundred and seventy-one, line six: You became a great man, raised a good family, and lived a good life. Don't want to mess that up."

"You told Mr. Smith he has a very good memory and less than one per cent chance he doesn't remember every part of the shooting because it is so traumatic. You told Mr. Smith the sheriff was not a police officer. You said you were re-submitting evidence because you didn't have DNA technology at that time."

Objection and meeting at the bench. After meeting:

Defense-"Detective Leggett, turn to page one hundred and seventy of the transcript line ten: But we have a story what you said you saw very clearly. We've gotten DNA and fingerprints off it."

"During the interview you mentioned a reel-to-reel tape from the 1970's and he said he had no recollection. You said you could play it for him. Turn to page one hundred and sixty-nine, line eight." Defense attorney reads from the transcript: "I've had a year to think about this. The officer scared somebody and they accidentally shot him." Puts transcript down and directly addresses Detective Leggett, "Was this the first time you testified that someone was scared by J.T. Hall? You said the shooting was an accident ten times. You told Mr. Smith accidents are not punished as murder."

Katie-"Yes."

Defense sits down and the state's attorney gets up.

State- "You never said any fingerprints or DNA of Mr. Smiths were recovered."

Katie- "Yes."

State- "It is legal to tell lies. Mr. Smith never asked to have the interview from 1973 played."

Katie- "No, he didn't."

State- "When you said the defendant had a good memory he was able to recall great detail."

Katie- "That's right."

State- "The State rests its case."

Recess

After the recess one of the defense attorneys rose. "The Defense moves for acquittal. The State's evidence is not sufficient for first degree murder or felony murder. With regard to both charges there is insufficient evidence that Larry David Smith killed Sheriff Hall. The State failed to show forensic evidence that Larry Smith was present for the burglary or murder. No witnesses. The evidence of confession is not sufficient. They failed to show the statements were reliable."

"Second, the first degree murder charge means willful, deliberate and premeditated killing. Statements by Mr. Smith don't support a willful or premeditated murder. "I got nervous and pulled the trigger," is not legally sufficient evidence for this charge. The defense attorney sat down.

State's attorney got up. "We have a statement by the defendant that he was at the scene of the murder. Three voluntary confessions. He told his daughter he killed someone. Two shots fired means premeditation. He fired a second shot. Regarding count two, felony murder. He placed himself at the burglary and told how it was done. The state's attorney sat down.

The Judge spoke, "Mr. Smith is charged with murder: premeditated; premeditated malice or forethought. Count two-Felony murder-murder while committing a burglary. A break in is a misdemeanor. Burglary is breaking and entering to commit a felony or to take something. When the Schmidts got home they had to get a ladder. Home was ransacked; like someone was coming back for things. Same night - burglary and murder, and the home backs up to the golf course. This gives the burglar the ability to break in undetected. Belongings were found near the country club. An engagement ring was never seen again or recovered. This suggests burglary. First degree murder and accomplice liability. Carrying out of felony where death results is accomplice liability. Larry David Smith gave a statement in 1973; he sought out the police. He told police he wanted full immunity and a lesser sentence. They brought in one of the prosecutors at that time. They walked to the crime scene of the shooting. Mr. Becker was a self-admitted witness to the shooting. He answered countless questions about the crime scene. New information-flashlight, going through the bushes."

"The case stayed dormant for some time. Any lead or tip was investigated and cleared other people. In 2021, the fiftieth anniversary, the Cold Case Unit reopened the case and went through the entire file. Through that process they ended up looking at other things. 1973- Smith said he was with John Rizzo which is impossible because Rizzo was in the Navy in San Diego."

"Move to 2021. Identified Larry David Smith as a person of interest. They did a great amount of background work. The autopsy showed a 32 caliber bullet which can be fired from a 38 caliber weapon. Law enforcement has investigated it all. In 1973 Becker gave an observation of what Sheriff Hall was wearing that night which was the complete opposite of what he was wearing. The culmination of the 2021 investigation was Smith's confession. Up until the time he confessed he attempted to name Rizzo and deflect away from Raven. He has supplied information that has proven correct. Confession is not sufficient. There has to be corroboration of evidence and there is."

"As to count one: Burden of proof to look at evidence in light favorable to the State. 1973, 2021, phone sting. The State has met its needs. He armed himself to go to the burglary and shot Sheriff Hall. Prima facie evidence level the State has met its objective."

"Also, the second count has been met by the State. The Defense's motion of acquittal is denied."

Kevin Collins, Senior Defense Attorney- "Mr. Smith won't testify. He wishes to invoke his Fifth Amendment privilege."

Judge (to Smith)- "Regarding your Fifth Amendment right have you had enough time to think about it?"

Smith-"Yes."

Judge-"Understand you are invoking your Fifth Amendment privileges not to testify. The State cannot say you have invoked your Fifth Amendment privilege."

* * * * * * * *

The courtroom is recessed briefly and then fills back up as the jury is brought back in.

Defense attorney stands up. "The defense calls Dr. Michael O'Connell."

Dr. O'Connell walks to the witness stand. He appears to be in his fifties with a full head of hair. He wears a gray suit with a light green tie. He is a forensic psychologist; he specializes in the application of psychology to the law. He has a PhD in Psychology and is a board certified forensic psychologist.

Dr. O'Connell- "I administer tests to answer questions that were asked."

Defense- "Are you familiar with Larry David Smith?"

Dr. O'Connell- "Yes. In the spring of 2023, I met him. I was initially asked to assess his competency to stand trial, his ability to work with attorneys and understand. I felt he was competent to stand trial. I was asked to assess his psychological state during interrogation. I reviewed many things: the defendant, his daughter, charges, recorded statements between Mr. Smith and the detectives at his apartment, the interrogation and the interrogation from 1973. I reviewed sting calls and medical records. I met with him on two occasions in 2023 for approximately two hours. First interview of clinical history. Second interview about interrogation. I did a variety of tests. I spoke to his daughter two times. It was a multi-source evaluation. I felt his daughter was an important source of evaluation. Mr. Smith tends to downplay things. He has a genetic history of alcoholism and heart disease. His daughter said he was abused but he denied it. Multiple medical problems: diabetes, COPD, elevated cholesterol, two heart attacks. Severe congestive heart failure. I'm interested in that affecting cognitive function. His congestive heart failure is described as severe. I went through his mental health history: thinking, problems with memory..."

State-"Objection."

Judge-"Sustained."

Meeting at the Bench

Defense-"Dr. O'Connell, were there any discrepancies between what Larry Smith said and his daughter said?"

Dr. O'Connell- "He would downplay things."

Meeting at the Bench

Defense- "Talk about testing. Why test?"

Dr. O'Connell- "Multiple sources of data. We test his memory with the Wechsler Memory Scale. This is his ability to remember things he heard or saw. Verbal: I read him a story and ask him to repeat the story and repeat it again in twenty minutes. He scored in extremely low range. After twenty minutes he got three out of forty details. Visual: I show him a design and have him draw it immediately and then twenty minutes later. He had low range in the beginning and then zero out of forty details at twenty minutes. Extremely low range. At or below the second percentile."

Defense- "You saw the video of the interrogation. He recalls details from the past."

Dr. O'Connell- "Not inconsistent with the tests. It's more the laying down of new memories. I tested the Johnson Susceptibility Scale. I read him a story and had him repeat it. He recorded seven and a half out of forty details. I asked him questions about the story and some have no basis. I would tell him in a firm voice, "You made mistakes" and his score was at the low end of average range. I've been giving that test for many years. Some questions are yes or no and others you'd ask blue or red and he said yes. I did the Wechsler Adult Scale for Intelligence. This looks at reasoning, judgement, vocabulary, working memory, and processing speed. His overall score was in the low average range. His IQ was eighty-three which is the thirteenth percentile. Verbal range-eighty seven which is low average. Non-verbal-eighty-six which is the eighteenth percentile. Working memory-seventy-seven which is borderline range in the sixth percentile."

"We test for personality function with the Personality Function Instrument: three hundred and forty-four items as applied to the subject. The test has validity scales; how a person approached the test. If the subject passes these, get into clinical items. The subject may be unable to produce a valid instrument. One validity scale looks for unusual responses. Items similar throughout the test such as sad all the time, depressed at all times. Inconsistency of responses can mean having difficulty paying attention or responding. Malingering is someone making up symptoms. It is unethical not to consider a criminal defendant malingering. I test malingering by testing across sources of data. There were specific measures of malingering I used. Mr. Smith passed both tests. He is not malingering and is retrospective. What he was like in 2022 may not be what he is like now."

"With regards to mental disorder, two conditions: One, Major Neurocognitive Disorder. This is a decline in cognitive abilities that has been assessed and impacts daily function. Two, Unspecified Depression. This consists of low self-esteem worsening cognitive abilities. I think congestive heart failure affects his Depression."

Defense- "What are symptoms of a Major Neurocognitive Disorder?"

Dr. O'Connell- "Memory. During the police interview need to be completely clear. Have to be able to process what is going on. He can be confused and overwhelmed. Depression can manifest during the police interview. Depressed subjects can't advocate or assert for themselves. They give up."

"The standard way to examine how someone does during interrogation involves evaluating the patient and the interview. Techniques can cause pressure on the defendant. You don't have to have a mental disorder to struggle during interrogation."

"His daughter's testimony is consistent with his evaluation. He is not asserting himself. Nothing in his son's testimony changed my conclusions."

"The records of the transport of Mr. Smith to the police barracks in 2022 are consistent with the tendency to downplay the difficulties he's had. Officer asked if there were problems with lungs and he said no. Nothing in the trip to the airport altered my analysis. He remembered the two heart attacks a couple of months apart. His daughter said they were a couple of years apart."

Defense attorney sits down

State's Attorney-"Mr. Smith was confused in interview about chronic obstructive pulmonary disease?"

Dr. O'Connell-"Yes."

State-"You met with the defendant four hours total. One interview was two hours. The first meeting you felt he was competent. You passed on that information. You were asked to go back and look at the interrogation from 2022. In the spring of 2023, he was competent. When we looked back to 2022 you interviewed the defendant twice and administered tests. How long did the tests take?"

Dr. O'Connell- "Ninety minutes and spoke to him for thirty minutes."

State- "You had reviewed the video interrogation, information from testing, and completed a report and submitted it to your client. A whole barrage of information you had not received. At the start of your testimony, you said you asked for all documents relevant to the trial. You never asked for the 1973 interview once you learned that had occurred. Information that would reference other information that you would want to see. Great deal of other information you didn't see. Melinda Allen's interview with New York police where she said he had confessed: "He told me him, his brother, two friends and a guard flashed flashlight in his hand. I'm going to prison."

"You also didn't know Ms. Allen said if he didn't do it, he wouldn't admit to doing it. You also didn't speak to Larry Smith Junior."

"Also, you had not listened to the pre-interview in Smith's apartment, his transport to the police station, any of the sting calls, audio recordings of transport to and from the airport. Also not reviewed: notes in the arrest of the defendant. After a prior proceeding in this case, you reviewed all of these items."

"During your interview he told you his family history, where he was born, foster care, never abused although his daughter said he was abused. He was able to tell you about his health history!"

Dr. O'Connell- "I asked him about his medication, but he couldn't name them."

State- "He was able to give history of marriages and children."

Dr. O'Connell- "I have reason to doubt the accuracy of what he said."

State-"Issues as a teenager discussed. You talked to him about his interview with the police. He didn't remember some details. He told you he recently stopped driving because he nodded off. You testified that the defendant recanted his confession to the police. Fourteen page single space report. No where does it say he recanted his statement to you."

Dr. O'Connell- "During competency he said he didn't do the offense. I asked him why he confessed."

State- "Where is that in your report?"

Dr. O'Connell-"I asked why he confessed and he was unsure why he did so. He told me he's pleading not guilty."

State- "If he told you I did not do this would this be important to record, yes or no?"

Dr. O'Connell- "Yes."

State- "You listened to Ms. Allen's testimony in court this morning."

Donna Fenton sits down and the Defense attorney gets up for redirect.

Defense- "She asked you about audio recordings in 1973, sting calls, drive to the police station, drive to the airport. You have now reviewed these. Do any of the police officers have a degree in forensic psychology?"

Dr. O'Connell- "After listening to all of this my opinion hasn't changed. Mr. Smith told me in competency evaluation he didn't do it. This was in June, 2023.

Defense- "You're free to go. The defense rests."

State's Attorney - "The State calls Dr. Christine Tellefsen."

Doctor Tellefsen is a General and Forensic Psychiatrist. She spent the first part of her testimony going over her credentials and explaining what a Forensic Psychiatrist is. A Forensic Psychiatrist works at the intersection of Psychiatry and the law. She is board certified in General and Forensic Psychiatry. She made the point that psychiatrists are physicians and psychologists have PhD's. Psychologists focus on testing. Psychiatrists look at the whole person.

In early 2023 Dr. Tellefsen was asked to review the report by Dr. O'Connell and asked to take on this case. She was asked to look at the transcript and video of Mr. Smith by police in light of what Dr.

O'Connell had written. She requested more and more information and received all reports and interviews pertaining to the case.

Doctor- "September twenty-sixth, 2023 I requested permission to talk to Mr. Smith. I wasn't allowed to ask him about his confession."

State- "Your impressions about his cognitive abilities."

Doctor- "No diagnosis. I don't agree with Dr. O'Connell's diagnoses. I was able to converse with Mr. Smith. Very pleasant, congenial, polite. He was able to relate details of his life. He had been convicted of a crime after this happened. Fifty years later he knew the names and places of the Department of Corrections. He had a psychiatry evaluation and an IQ test prior to his conviction in 1972. He engaged with his attorney. I asked him about changing his name. He looked at his lawyer and asked if it was okay to answer that. It showed that he could break rhythm and think about it. He was able to shift the conversation."

"Regarding his day to day functioning, he had a fairly regimented life. He was in an apartment by himself, paid his bills, took his medications, was going on the Internet and enjoyed Facebook. He had attempted to pay bills electronically and switched to pay in cash. He was able to line up his bottles on the counter and take his medications. He was enjoying his life. He made his own meals. He was friendly, pleasant, a little bit guarded. Spontaneous. He had worked in a nursing home and had to sit for an exam to get his license."

State- "Did he lose his train of thought?"

Doctor- "No."

State- "Did he give appropriate answers?"

Doctor- "Yes."

State- "Did he drift off?"

Doctor- "No."

State- "Did he repeat himself?"

Doctor- "No."

State- "Dr. O'Connell's diagnosis was Major Neurocognitive Disorder which is Dementia."

Doctor- "His IQ hasn't changed much in fifty years. His performance now is similar to the 1970's. No evidence of dementia such as repeating himself, losing track of the conversation. I didn't see that."

State- "What about Depression?"

Doctor- "No depression. Nothing wrong with his mood. In Detention Center for murder and many people would be depressed. He is not being treated for depression."

State- "Did you do any further testing on Mr. Smith?"

Doctor- "No tests were done by me. Dr. O'Connell had already done them. I relied on the results of his tests."

State-"Did Mr. Smith have a psychiatric disorder?"

Doctor-"No."

State- "No further questions."

Defense- "You interviewed Mr. Smith on September twenty-sixth, 2023 for seventy minutes. You did not speak to anyone else. No family or friends. No testing was done by you. You asked Mr. Smith about medications and his family history. You reviewed Dr. O'Connell's report before you interviewed him and you looked at all the tests he did. You didn't conduct any neuro-psych testing."

Doctor- "Yes."

Defense- "You agreed and relied on Dr. O'Connell's testing. He tested his memory and he scored in the extremely low range, below average. You offered an opinion on Mr. Smith's cognition. IQ was previously eighty-seven and now eighty-three. He had two heart attacks twenty years ago and has a significant heart condition. He was able to get Social Security Disability from the government. You reviewed the interviews with Mr. Smith's children. His son said Mr. Smith is slipping a little bit, which is what Mr. Smith told the detectives. You assessed his demeanor, speech, mood. You conducted all of this one year later without police in the room, no one interrogating Mr. Smith. This is a very different situation."

Doctor-"Yes."

Defense- "No further questions."

State's Attorney- Dr. O'Connell said current IQ is eighty-four and back in the seventies it was eighty-seven. Is this a normal decline for fifty years?"

Doctor-"Yes."

State- "Nothing further."

* * * * * * * *

The Judge spoke to the Jury: "The jury must be fair and impartial and base their decision on the evidence in the courtroom. No one can talk with anyone else. No independent research. Tomorrow you will hear closing arguments, I will give you instructions, and the case will be yours."

CHAPTER FORTY-SIX

Trial Day Five
January 12, 2024

The Judge's Instructions

The day started off with the judge speaking about the missing evidence in the case: the bullet and the flashlight. After letting the defense and state attorneys weigh in on the topic the judge started her instructions to the jury:

"Under these circumstances I must give the jury proper instructions on this topic. Two pieces of physical evidence collected by the police are no longer available: the bullet fragment and Sheriff Hall's flashlight. These two pieces of evidence were under control of the State through the Montgomery County Police Department but were not produced for trial. Let me say this and then you can all have your heads exploding. I'm saying the defense can say we don't have that evidence so that's your reasonable doubt. The state will say it's not important. If the absence of these items is not sufficiently explained, you have to go along with the defense."

"In this case in order to convict the defendant of the felony murder of Sheriff Hall the state must present evidence proving beyond reasonable doubt:

Defendant committed primary burglary as primary act or accomplice

Crime of murder was done while escaping primary burglary

"It is not necessary that the defendant knew his accomplice would commit an additional crime."

"The theory of felony murder is that murder occurred along with the underlying felony. Facts, I agree, have been generated. In 2022 he admitted to participating in the primary burglary of the Schmidt's home after breaking in. Primary burglary is a felony. He was looking for money or other things he'd need. Premeditation comes in because these individuals committed a primary felony. We know the burglary occurred through evidence and the defendant's statement.

Objection by the Defense to this instruction is noted."

"Three pieces of evidence are no longer available:

1. Thirty-two caliber bullet fragment from the scene

2. Thirty-two caliber bullet fragment from the autopsy

3. Sheriff Hall's flashlight from the scene

These items were in control of the state, and not produced for trial. If the evidence is not accounted for, I have explained, you have to decide this evidence would have been favorable to the defense."

"I am going to instruct you in the law of the state of Maryland as it applies to this case. You will have copies. The instructions I give are binding on you. Comments I make regarding facts are not binding. Larry David Smith is presumed to be innocent of charges unless you are convinced beyond reasonable doubt that he is guilty. The state must prove each and every element beyond a reasonable doubt. The state doesn't have to prove beyond reasonable doubt if you are convinced it is true."

"Your verdict must be unanimous. Decide fairly and impartially. Do not be swayed by sympathy, fairness, public opinion. Only decide from the facts in court. While deliberating no electronic devices. Do not communicate about the case. Consider the possibility of implicit bias and try not to use that."

"Evidence in this trial has shown Larry Smith has been incarcerated. This cannot factor into your decisions. Consider testimony and physical evidence."

"You may draw reasonable conclusions from common sense and your own experiences. No conclusions from the judge's statements. Rely on your own memory of the evidence."

"Three stipulations of fact:

-not in dispute

-proven

-no argument to truth of testimony."

"Three pieces of physical evidence no longer available:

1. Thirty-two caliber bullet fragment from autopsy

2. Thirty-two caliber bullet fragment from crime scene

3. Flashlight from the crime scene."

"If you find the absence of physical evidence is not adequately explained, you must go with the defense."

"An example of direct evidence is looking outside and seeing it is raining. An example of circumstantial evidence is a person who comes in with a raincoat and dripping water. Both have the same weight."

"Guilt beyond reasonable doubt. The defendant is charged with murder and felony murder. Consider each separately and give a verdict on each. You may apply your own common sense and life experiences. Consider factors: witnesses' behavior on the stand, question if witness is telling the truth, accuracy of witnesses' memory, whether witnesses' testimony is consistent, whether testimony in court is different from prior statements."

"You have been told what an expert witness is."

"The weight of the evidence doesn't depend on the number of witnesses called."

"Larry Becker aka Larry Smith has a constitutional right not to testify which can't be discussed in deliberations."

"The state must prove the statement to the police was voluntary. If you decide the police used inducement or promises to get that statement you must exclude the statement. Decide if the statement was voluntary. Consider if the defendant was subjected to force. Consider who and where interrogated. If voluntary, give it the weight it deserves. If not voluntary, disregard."

"Melinda Allen and Larry Smith Junior testified. Before the trial they made statements. You can consider these statements to be at the trial."

"Flight may be considered guilt. Decide by:

1. Evidence of flight

2. If flight equals guilt"

"Presence at a crime or witnessing a crime doesn't make a person guilty of the crime. Presence is a fact that can be used to determine guilt."

"In determining intent, consider the facts and the statements by the defendant."

"First degree, premeditated murder of another person with premeditation. State must prove Larry Smith caused the death of Sheriff Hall and was willful, deliberate, and premeditated. Pre- meditated means intent to kill before murder."

"Second degree murder doesn't require premeditation or deliberation. Must prove cause of death of J.T. Hall engaged in conduct to kill or cause bodily harm and death."

"First degree felony murder: don't need to prove intent. The defendant committed a burglary and the defendant or another killed Sheriff Hall while committing a first degree burglary. First degree burglary is breaking and entering someone's dwelling. Can break open a window or a door, Entry means foot in the house. Dwelling is where someone sleeps."

"Accomplice liability: guilty of above crimes. Must prove crime occurred and the defendant aided in the commission of the crime. The presence of the defendant at the crime is not enough to prove he was an accomplice. He can also be found guilty of a crime he did not intend to commit. The state must prove he or accomplice killed J.T."

The opposing counsels approached the bench, and when they left, the judge finished her remarks.

"Counsel pointed out one error. The defendant may also be found guilty of a crime he did not participate in if it was proven he consulted. Example: first degree burglary and accomplice committed murder while committing first degree burglary. Each side will now have one hour for closing remarks."

CHAPTER FORTY-SEVEN

Closing Remarks by the State's Attorneys

State's Attorney- "I'm going to go through the details and explain this case in a linear fashion. Smith and Becker are the same. Three crimes charged: First degree murder, second degree murder, felony murder - someone killed in the commission of another crime."

"The day the crime occurred. What you heard related to the investigation. That evening at the Manor Country Club. The Schmidt residence backs up to the golf course. The defendant used a crowbar to open their door. Parked in the parking lot. Crossed through the fairway and stole multiple items, not all recovered. In the process carried items to the bushes next to the pump house. Kids were breaking into soda machines at the same time. The kids left the soda machines and that's when Sheriff Hall was killed."

"Sheriff Hall comes to the location and sees the missing items. He says, "What are you doing?" The defendant shoots twice. The first shot hits the flashlight and the second shot behind the left ear. The gun had to be cocked to re-fire. In the time to cock, Sheriff Hall tries ducking to safety and the second bullet hits him behind the left ear. In 1973 the defendant says he ran away that night and later he says he ran away."

"The first witness, Carolyn Hall Philo, was his daughter. She was together with her husband and kids at Sheriff Hall's home for a spaghetti dinner. Jim Young called and asked Sheriff Hall to take his shift. Sheriff Hall puts on his uniform, grabs his rain jacket, and goes to work. Later that night they get a phone call. J.T. was hurt and he passed away three days later. She went back to her father's hospital bed and said goodbye."

Soda Machine Kids

"Five boys aged fourteen to sixteen years old. At the Manor Country Club breaking into soda machines. Heard sirens-fire trucks. Left and returned ten to twenty-five minutes later. They saw something on the parking lot. We heard from two of them."

Norman Shoemaker

"Was felt to be the main suspect for a long time and it affected his life. He seemed to be the ring leader. He tried to break open the machines. Saw Sheriff Hall lying in the parking lot. They ran to the clubhouse to get help. The first firearm he owned was a shotgun five years later."

Robert Canevari

"He was with friends and they stole from clothes driers first. They went to the Manor Club to break into the soda machines. He stayed with Sheriff Hall and turned Sheriff Hall's head to the side. The first time he said he was just there, but the second time he admitted to breaking into the soda machines."

Detective Jerry Boone

"One of the lead detectives in the homicide division. He went to the scene of the murder and found the sheriff's gun and items from the burglary. He located the flashlight and the bullet, a thirty- two caliber bullet. He found a screwdriver. He had the pond of the golf course drained looking for a weapon."

Roger and Diane Schmidt

"Recent child. Went to the mountains. Recently moved to their house in Manor Club. Garage door opener not working so got a ladder from neighbor, Mr. Anderson, and went through open upstairs window. Saw their house had been ransacked. They called the police and were told it was going to be a while, but they were there in ten minutes. They did identify property that had been taken."

Doctor Stephanie Dean

"Medical Examiner. The defendant was killed by a bullet to the brain. There was an upward angle of the bullet. It was a homicide."

Investigation

"The 'Soda Machine Boys' were cleared. They all alibied each other and stayed on the scene. Also cleared because the tools used to break into the soda machines did not match the tools used to break into the house. Richard Triesgrad and his girlfriend cleared. Old leads dried up and the case goes cold."

1972-Leslie Becker-Brother

"Provides three names to officers including the name of his brother. Says Larry Becker knows about the gun. Officers didn't talk to Larry Becker. One year later Larry Becker goes to the police and says he has information about the shooting."

Larry Becker Interview-1973

"Burglary and escape. Wants leniency on escape charge. Serving time for burglary and escaped. He puts himself at the scene of the homicide. Then the rambling tale. Trying to calculate answers. Truths and untruths. Location of the body is inaccurate. Weather is inaccurate."

Where's Larry?

"Released from jail. Moves to New York state. Goes by a different name. No paper trail regarding name. Dr. Teollefsen met the defendant in jail and couldn't ask about the case or crime. He looked to the attorney when she asked about name change. Only time he looked at attorney. Dyes his hair."

2018-DNA Testing

"Not enough DNA on cigarette butts."

2021- Fiftieth Anniversary

"Corporal Lisa Killen assigned to the case. Evidence reviewed. Reel to reel mystery-was mislabeled Richard Hobart. Never look at old interview. FBI gets her form she can listen to. She found in interview: Larry Smith puts himself at scene. Details not released to the public. All newspaper articles around shooting: none mentioned two shots, none mentioned flashlight hit, names of boys at soda machines."

"Larry blames people at the soda machines. He names a bunch of random names. He says a thirty-eight caliber gun which can shoot a thirty-two caliber bullet. He names Greg Swarr as the shooter. Swarr was cleared. Why truth and lies? Larry wanted leniency but not to put himself in the crosshairs of the investigation. He lies about what the sheriff is wearing and the weather. He tries to back it up by naming a friend with him, John Rizzo, who was in the military at the time of the murder."

"Lisa decides she needs to talk to Leslie Becker and finds an obituary for Leslie and sees brother, Larry. Lisa goes to New York. She monitors Smith's phone calls. She has John Rizzo do phone calls. The first phone call he denies he's Larry Becker because he is hiding. In the second sting call Larry is dodging, he is nervous. When Rizzo says he will go to the police Larry says he will give information to the police so that they will come after Rizzo. Larry Smith calls Bobby Ray Edwards, the 'Raven', but the phone call is not answered."

Return to Little Falls, New York

"Corporal Killen and Detective Leggett. Where to interview? Larry Becker admits to burglary. He says pried door open. Gives information independent of the crime. Angle of bullet. Says, "I guess I shot him." Says, "It feels good to get this off my chest," and "Thank you for helping me." Apologize to Sheriff Hall's family for me. Telling him not going to be arrested that day took place after confession."

Melinda Allen-Daughter

"Call from Dad: "You're going to be really disappointed in me. I've been holding this in for fifty years. I guess I killed someone." She replies, "No guessing." He says, "I killed someone. Doing daytime robberies and security guard flashed a flashlight and I killed him. I guess I'm going to prison." She knows if he didn't do it he wouldn't say he did it. She was not completely honest. She said he was not able to care for himself. She said they talked on the phone daily, and they talked less than five times in a sixty day period."

Larry Smith Junior

"Visited father in jail, Again confesses to son: "Over fifty years ago. I knew it was going to catch up to me." Robbery and murder of security guard."

The Following are the Charges:

1. "Homicide- First degree premeditated murder. The intentional killing of another person. Premeditated means thought about killing. He fired two shots. In his own words the gun needs to

be cocked. The time it takes to cock the gun and fire the second bullet is premeditation. Smith confessed to murder."

2. "Second degree murder-this is not premeditated. You can probably harm someone with your actions."

3. "First degree felony murder-this is murder that occurs in the commission of a felony- burglary. The defendant may be found guilty if he committed the crime of first degree burglary and the murder was committed by an accomplice in trying to escape. The state has proven felony murder. Accomplice liability means guilty of crimes as an accomplice."

Confession

"The confession is not voluntary. He says he was interrogated by ruthless police officers. They looked for a place in his apartment building to have the interview but couldn't find one. Before they left the location, Detective Leggett says okay for him to leave at any time. He says he watches police shows. It is false that they forced a confession. There are two elements to consider: the mental and the physical state of the defendant."

Dr. Michael O'Connell came and testified

"He met with the defendant two times and has concerns. You have heard conversations Larry Smith has had with others. In the first part of his confession Larry talks about multiple things. Dr. O'Connell talks about his concerns and about the tests he performed. Before writing his report he listened to the interview of the confession and talked to Larry and his daughter. He did not consider a lot of things. He was hired to find problems to get the confession thrown out."

"Dr. Tellefsen reviewed all of the evidence and said she disagreed. His IQ dropped three points in fifty years. Dr. O'Connell is a hired gun. Dr. Tellefsen said no depression. She said anyone in jail charged with murder is worried. She used more materials and is more experienced. She said nothing about Smith's mental capacity which affected his interview with the officers. Why is Smith guilty beyond a reasonable doubt?. Deception-hiding in New York. He knew intimate details of the crime. He put himself at the scene. He confessed three times, to the officers, to his daughter, and to his son. At no point did he recant his confession."

"Sheriff Hall's family has been missing J.T. Hall for fifty years. Hold the party responsible who killed him. Smith was living in New York and doing whatever he pleased while J.T. was dead. Give the family closure." Sits down and the Judge announces fifteen minute recess.

CHAPTER FORTY-EIGHT
Defense Closing Argument

The closing argument was the only time in the entire trial that the senior attorney for the defense, partner Kevin Collins, addressed the jury other than saying Larry Smith would exercise his Fifth Amendment right not to testify.

Defense- "The murder of Sheriff Hall was a despicable, heinous crime done by a coward. Larry David Smith did not do that crime. Everyone is entitled to justice Anyone must have sympathy for the Hall family."

"The murder of a law enforcement officer killed while on duty must be considered fairly and impartially without bias or prejudice. There can be no sympathy."

"Rule number one- Mr. Smith is presumed innocent"

"Rule number two- State has burden to prove guilt"

"Rule number three- Guilt beyond a reasonable doubt"

"Rule number four- An attorney's argument is not evidence"

"Reasonable doubt means you are willing to act upon such belief without reservation. If you think perhaps guilty or probably guilty that is not beyond reasonable doubt. The closing argument of the State's attorney is rash speculation. Mr. Grochowski's closing mentioned many times this probably happened."

State- "Objection."

Michael Weisberg

Meeting of Counsel with the Judge

Defense- "The evidence: there is no DNA, no fingerprint evidence, no gun, bullets, flashlight. No physical evidence is connected to Mr. Smith. The reports and sketches the day after the crime of the crime scene and Officer Boone's report show no connection to Mr. Smith. The State attorney's words are just speculation. No witnesses saw Larry Smith. Lary Boone never saw people. There is no forensic or eyewitness evidence. Only Mr. Smith's statement connects him to the crime. You have to decide on weight and reliability. It is your decision on what are the true, undisputed facts:

> Two shots fired
> Shot back of the head
> Body found in parking lot
> Broken into soda machines
> Names of kids at soda machines

"In his 1973 interview Larry reached out to the State and the State told him if you give accurate information they would reduce his sentence. In the 1973 interview Mr. Smith got a number of the basic facts wrong: clothes, weather, where the body was found. Initially the State said it was absurd; now they're saying it's the key turning point. The officers' conclusion in 1973 was that there is no way this testimony is related to the facts as they occurred. He was lying to get leniency. A law enforcement officer had been killed. Larry Smith got it all wrong because he wasn't there."

"Fifty years later Corporal Killen reopens the investigation. Reads newspaper articles. She doesn't know if there were more articles. She tries to guess what was held back and what wasn't. She guesses that some of the details Mr. Smith said weren't made public. There is no record of what was/wasn't withheld. She starts with a false baseline as to the only information out there. Rumors were circulating at the time. John

Rizzo's mother told him about it including Maggie's Place where Larry Smith lived. Why did the officers conclude that the interview in 1973 had no bearing on the case? Why didn't the officers do more? Why didn't the State contact other people Mr. Smith named? Because he was lying."

July 2022 "Sting Calls"
"Mr. Smith moves to New York and lives there over forty years and has a family
Calls him Mr. Russo, not Rizzo
He has no recollection until the second call who Mr. Rizzo was
He provides details that the police will seize on in the interrogation

Interrogation

"Larry Smith was told the officers were just there to clear up information. They said they were on his side. He readily admits to the burglary of the townhouse in 1972 that he went to jail for. He knows nothing about Manor House. He didn't know a security guard was shot at the burglary at the townhouse. The detectives, Killen and Leggett, turn up the pressure. They tell him they know he was at Manor Club. They have DNA, fingerprints, and shoe prints. Corporal Killen starts off on the wrong foot by not knowing what evidence was withheld. They said they found an audio recording of Mr. Smith talking to the police. He has no recollection of it. He doesn't remember it. Leggett says memory is like pregnancy, you don't forget it. Mr. Smith says if you have it on tape I must have been there."

"Officer Leggett says shooting an accident ten times and says accidents are not murder. She says he is a great man and she's not there to mess that up. He says Raven is the shooter. Leggett says State called Raven and he said no involvement in shooting. The officers tell Mr. Smith the shot came from someone of his height. All of the details were fed to him by the detectives. He finally accepts their narrative. He says, "Yes, I guess so if Raven didn't do it."

"It is not surprising that a seventy-one year-old with cognitive deficiency would do this. On September first of 2022 Mr. Smith said he fired one shot accidentally. Said he shot the officer in front which is false. It was the first time he fired a handgun. He is making this stuff up."

"In the confusion Smith says they took radios. The Schmidts said no radios were taken. Smith keeps referring back to the townhouse burglary. Smith says radios and cash were taken. The State didn't provide any evidence of this, they just showed statements that he adopted from the detectives. On cross examination he parrots back what Leggett fed him. These detectives didn't come for Mr. Smith's memory. They fed memories to him."

"Dr. O'Connell said Mr. Smith had an extremely low range for memory and there was no malingering. His conclusions were Major Neurocognitive Disorder and Unspecified Depressive Disorder."

"Mr. Smith lived a lawful life for forty years and then someone comes into his life and plants seeds. The State says he's a brilliant liar and on the other hand is telling the truth. Dr. Tellefsen agreed with Dr. O'Connell's testing. She did no testing. She didn't speak with anyone who lived with him. She spoke to him for a little more than an hour. The State says the interrogation is valid because others in the car ride with him felt he spoke appropriately."

"What about Mr. Smith's other statements? Four hours later there is a knock on his apartment door. He hears the knock and says, "Oh, fuck." The conversation with his daughter was the same day he talked to the officers. The next day he talked to his son. The story was fresh in his mind after the detectives planted the seeds. This is not reliable evidence. This is not proof beyond a reasonable doubt."

"One week later you heard the tape of Mr. Smith being transferred. He was still confused about events. He did not know what he agreed to. On September ninth, 2022, he still has no understanding who was shot, when, and where. The reliability of saying this was a confession because detectives fed a seventy-one year-old facts doesn't make it competent evidence."

"Mr. Larry Smith had an awful adolescence. He lived in the woods and at Maggie's Place. No wonder he wanted to change his name."

"Evidence must be so overwhelming you would act with certainty on it, beyond reasonable doubt. If he was in hiding, why did he have a profile on Facebook? He had a family."

"The State is now pursuing a theory it never developed at trial. Larry David Smith was an accomplice. The State never provides who were his accomplices."

"The State must prove their case beyond any reasonable doubt. You don't all have to have reasonable doubt. The State overreaches and asks you to speculate. Corporal Killen says possible radios were stolen, but at the townhouse burglary in 1972 radios were stolen. Speculation is not a substitute for competent evidence."

"The new State Theory: Larry wasn't the shooter. Who else was there? The State hasn't given any evidence. Now they want you to reach a verdict on the theory that someone else was involved. They want you to convict on all contradictory evidence. Reject this half-baked theory. Verdict is from the Latin word "indicium" which means find the truth. Can you reasonably believe that fact happened? Half of the story Smith says you know didn't happen."

"You get the last word. You are the sole judge of the evidence. Focus on evidence that matters. What Mr. Smith said, confusion, cognitive issues. Eight days later he parrots back information about the burglary at the townhouse where a security guard is shot. Mr. Smith is not guilty."

CHAPTER FORTY-NINE

The State's Rebuttal and End of the Trial

Donna (State's Attorney)- "The confession is reliable. By the defense saying it is not reliable is misleading. It is more important than DNA, fingerprints, because it came from his mouth: "I shot that man" comes directly from him."

"In 1973 he put himself at the scene of the crime. He thought he was smarter than everyone. I can spin this in a way that will get these cops off my back. Lies peppered with truths. When talking about 1973 he gave lies with facts."

"The investigators in 1973 felt his story was not consistent with the facts. Where the body was found. Defendant said he and Raven carry stuff across the golf course and Mark Jensen in the car. I saw he had a flashlight. A man of the defendant's stature shot upward. In 1973. The story was not consistent with the facts and gave Mr. Smith no benefit. He served his time and poof!"

"In 2021 Corporal Killen realized the significance of the tape. A detail Smith provided saying he'd been with John Rizzo was impossible since Rizzo was in California. Smith names boys at the soda machines, but none of the names are accurate. We know the police were called to the Schmidt's residence at ten-thirty that night."

"In 2021, the Cold Case Team needed to go and re-examine everything in this case. They closed the loops. They got the tape and listened to it."

The John Rizzo Phone Calls

1. Larry Becker Smith denies knowing who John Rizzo is during first call

2. Smith calls Rizzo back. He wants to know what John Rizzo knows

3. The second call-Rizzo says they think you're dead. Help me help you.

The defendant was not biting. He is street smart and savvy. He tells Rizzo he will give information on him."

"Larry Smith calls Raven who turns the tape over to the police. Smith doesn't want to name Raven. He says he was with Rizzo. Then he turns it to Rizzo and Mark Jensen. He relates all of those details. He said Mark Jensen gave him a gun."

"It is absurd to say the detectives fed him. Numerous trips had been made between the Schmidt home and the parking lot. Sheets, blankets, jewelry. The house was ransacked. Who needed sheets to sleep with? The defendant did. The canine tracked the individual's path. After shooting the sheriff, he and Raven went to the home and then Maggie's Place."

"There is no difference between a confession and DNA evidence. You have to look at the totality of everything."

"In September of 2022 the defendant was capable of making a voluntary statement. For years he had been taking care of himself. His daughter lied to you. We know they didn't talk every day. Maybe saw each other every day, but that was not stated in the interview with Detective Rose. His daughter challenged him and he answered, "I did it. I never told anyone. I was doing daytime robberies and the sheriff came out." He had his friend's gun. His daughter wouldn't admit it (here in court) because it's a hard situation for her. He never told her mother or anyone. His daughter knows him best: "He would not say he did it if he didn't do it."

"We played the interviews to show you how with it Larry Smith is. He relates facts of life, where he lived, his marriage."

"His own words: "You never forget shooting someone." He ended up thanking them for relieving this burden. When the police returned to arrest him he said, "I knew you'd be back."

"Nine days later there was no confusion at the time of the interview. He was not talking about the townhouse burglary."

"Dr. O'Connell in his first two hours with the defendant found him competent. Dr. O'Connell didn't look at everything. He didn't look at Mr. Smith's daughter's statement. Sympathy or what could happen if found guilty is not part of your deliberation. You need to base your verdict on words from the defendant. You were instructed on defendant liability because the defendant says Raven pulled the trigger. The defendant is equally responsible for the actions of Raven."

"On October twenty-third, 1971, Captain J.T. Smith died from injuries inflicted based on the confession of the defendant. The only just verdict is guilty on all counts."

The trial ended at one fifteen pm on Friday. I stuck around the courtroom that afternoon in case a quick verdict was reached. The jury sent a question to the judge asking if the police could lie in order to obtain a confession. The answer was yes. The jury was sent home at five pm, told to reconvene the following Tuesday since Monday was Martin Luther King Day and the court was closed.

CHAPTER FIFTY

Saturday with the Schmidts

One of my favorite parts of the eleven days I spent in Rockville was getting to meet and know Roger and Diane Schmidt. The Schmidts testified on the first day of the trial, and then came back and spent every day of the trial in the courtroom. We would get together and talk during recess. I found them to be very engaging, intelligent, and inquisitive. After fifty-two years they still had a deep desire to learn what had actually happened the fateful night of October twenty-third, 1971, just one month after they had moved into their house in Manor Club. Since that time many things had changed: they now had two grown children and several grandchildren. They had both retired from successful careers. But the one constant was they still lived in the same house they did fifty-two years before. Neighbors had come and gone, houses had been remodeled and updated, but the Schmidts loved their life in Manor Club and remained there.

They invited me to spend Saturday morning with them, to show me their house and the golf course and country club. I took an Uber from my hotel over to their house early Saturday morning and my attention was first directed to the ultra-long curving driveway leading up to their house. It was easy to see how a lot of police cars could have lined up in the driveway the night of the murder. The driveway was flanked on both sides by tall, leafless trees, making it easy to spot neighboring houses in the distance. The driveway led up to the garage where a free standing basketball hoop was framed by two cast-iron chairs and fronted by a concrete planter. The Schmidts met me outside and pointed out the

Anderson's house across the street where Diane had gone to get a ladder to get into the second floor window of their house.

The Schmidt's house was red brick with white window panes and a white overhang. There were windows all around the two-story house with beautiful large windows looking out onto the golf course. We walked to the back patio and they showed me where the burglars had used a "jimmy" to break into their house. The defect in the door jamb looked the same as fifty-two years before, since the Schmidts had never repaired it.

We went on a tour of the house and it was a beautiful home that I could tell had been lived in and loved by its occupants. There was a wood paneled long bar in the family room with various beer and liquor signs behind it as well as an electrified Schmidts sign sitting on one end. The gorgeous curving wood staircase leading to the second floor was the most outstanding architectural feature of the house in my opinion.

Roger did show me one portable radio in a black leather case from the nineteen sixties which he had come upon recently. Larry Smith had talked about taking radios in the burglary and this was the only radio Roger had. Roger was uncertain if it had been part of the pile of goods taken from their house. They also showed me the aluminum step stool that had been stolen which showed signs of over fifty years of use. I also saw the ceramic jack-o-lantern that had been recovered from the burglars' pile. Upstairs we walked into their then baby daughter's room to visualize the open window that Diane had crawled through that night. It was a very small space that Diane had pushed herself through; she was and still is extremely athletic.

From the second floor windows I could look out on the golf course, its green grass and most of its trees bereft of leaves. With no leaves to block my view I could see the large clubhouse in the distance, painted white with a dark roof. The clubhouse certainly didn't seem far from the

Schmidt's house and was only separated from the house by the golf course. On a dark, rainy night without any light it was easy to imagine the burglars moving items from the house to the parking lot of the clubhouse undetected.

We walked out of the house and onto the golf course. Diane showed me the large pond to the left of the house which had been drained looking for the murder weapon. As I looked out over the golf course I realized that it was also lined with pine, spruce, and cedar trees, the "evergreen trees" which retain their leaves or needles throughout the year. These would make it much more difficult to see someone running across the golf course.

We got to the parking lot area and the Schmidts showed me the grassy area just off the parking lot where their property had been piled. The incredulous look of having to identify your own personal property in a public location away from your home was reflected in their eyes. We looked up the circular driveway at the clubhouse and then walked around the parking lot. It had started to rain fifteen minutes before, and I could see shallow puddles starting to form.

We got into the Schmidt's car and began to drive around their neighborhood. They related their story of October twenty-third to me, but now I could picture everything more precisely. They showed me the streets that Smith said he ran on as he escaped the Manor Club and made his way to Maggie's. I saw the hills near the country club where the neighborhood kids would sled in the winter. They showed me a house on the corner a few blocks from their house which they told me was the Becker's house.

I asked Roger to stop the car so that I could get a long look at the Becker's house. It was set back quite a distance from the road and had beautiful big trees around it. It was a red brick house with a composite roof and chimney. There were Christmas lights strung up over the entire front porch of the house and a huge wreath hanging in the middle of the white paneling which formed a triangle over the front door. Four white cane chairs were positioned on the front porch with two on either side of the door.

We kept driving and got to Maggie's and the pet cemetery area. I first saw the pet cemetery which was fenced shut and had tiny headstones close to one another. There were areas where there was just grass where someone could sleep.

Maggie's turned out to be the Church of Saint Mary Magdalene in Wheaton, Maryland. It was a small, picturesque church across the street from a large shopping center. The church had brick walls and a large composite triangular roof. The Schmidts and I went inside and walked around. Of the places we could get to inside, there was nothing that looked like a separate youth center or Maggie's. There was a cornerstone with 1959 engraved in it so I felt that the church I was seeing now was at least similar to the Maggie's hangout in 1971.

The Schmidts showed me around the area including Aspen Hills where the Beltway Snipers murdered six of their seventeen victims in October of 2002. They then took me to one of their favorite restaurants and treated me to brunch which was delicious. After we ate they dropped me back at my hotel. I thanked them for their incredible hospitality and said I would see them in the courthouse on Tuesday.

CHAPTER FIFTY-ONE

The Verdict

The judge let the jury deliberate until seven pm Friday night and then sent them home for the long weekend. It snowed Monday and Tuesday, so the courthouse opening on Tuesday was delayed until ten am. I stood outside in the cold wind and waited in a long line for half an hour to get into the courthouse. I threw my coat and briefcase onto the conveyor belt to be x-rayed and then walked under the metal detector. I took the elevators to the sixth floor where I spent most of the day in the lobby outside the courtroom waiting for any word. I met a newspaper reporter who was covering the case and talked to him for a few minutes. I went for lunch to a nearby sandwich shop with the Philos and then returned to the lobby outside of Courtroom Six B. Occasionally I would walk into the courtroom to make sure I hadn't missed anything, but no verdict had been reached. I was scheduled to fly back to Dallas the next day, Wednesday, because I had procedures scheduled on my patients on Thursday. I was very disappointed when the jury, judge, and attorneys came into the courtroom at five pm and said that no verdict had been reached and the jury was going home for the evening.

On Wednesday morning I had an early breakfast with the Philos at our hotel and exchanged goodbyes. I took an Uber to Dulles Airport and flew back to Dallas. When I got home from the airport I called the Philos.

Me- "Anything happen?"

Bob- "We had lunch and then went over to the courthouse. At two thirty pm they said there's something going on and you might as well go into the courtroom. We went in and waited until they finally brought the defendant up and the attorneys were there. They conferenced at the bench for at least a half-hour with the white noise blaring. I could tell the judge was a bit agitated. I learned later that the judge knew that the jury was deadlocked on two of the three charges and that on the third charge-first degree or premeditated murder they had voted unanimously not guilty. They were deadlocked on the felony murder and on second degree murder."

"The defense attorneys wanted the judge to rule that there was a partial verdict as to the first degree murder and a mistrial as to the other two charges. She said no, she couldn't do that. It was either a mistrial on everything or she'd have to send them back. They were hopelessly deadlocked. Ultimately they brought the jury in and the judge asked the jury if they were hopelessly deadlocked and they indicated that they were. She thanked them for their service and said that she was going to declare a mistrial. They could gather their stuff and leave. She said there is no bond for the defendant. He is back in jail."

"We were kind of surprised at that and were asked to go down to the State Attorney's office and the State Attorney had come in with a bunch of other people. Newspaper and media people all gathered to hear what was going on. Donna had announced at the conference at the judge's bench that they were definitely going to retry the case and so the judge had asked to see two attorneys from each side in her chambers. She picked a new trial date with the attorneys. The judge said she wanted to get this done before she retired. They said they were going to pick a jury June seventeenth and eighteenth, June nineteenth is a holiday, so they would start the retrial on June twentieth."

"We then went down to the press conference where John McCarthy, the State's Attorney, said we are one hundred percent positive we're going to retry this case. After the press conference we headed back to our hotel, and I got online and changed our departure date to tomorrow."

Me- "Any idea of the jury vote?"

Bob- "We believe it was either eleven to one or ten to two guilty based on discussions that Carolyn had with one of the male jurors who wouldn't give his name."

Me- "What are your thoughts about retrying the case?"

Carolyn- "I've been going through this in my mind and I'm going, I just want this to be over. The man is guilty and I don't understand why we have to keep doing this. Evidently we've got to do it again. I just want it to be over. The juror I talked to said "There was a person in the jury who disagreed with the majority." Before he kept saying person or persons because he didn't want to commit himself."

CHAPTER FIFTY-TWO

Interview with a Juror

Carolyn Philo convinced one of the female jurors to speak with me, telling her I was writing a book on the case. I contacted her by phone one week after the trial ended.

Me- "Tell me whatever you want to tell me and I will listen to whatever you have to say."

Juror-"Okay. I was disappointed in the verdict. I'm not going to tell you about the deliberations except to say that we were very serious (Note: the juror mentioned the jury being serious and working hard three times in our interview. I've seen these words used to describe juries in almost every case I have read about that ended in a hung jury or mistrial. It's not that we non-jurors think the twelve jurors divided up to play three tables of bridge. It's more, I think, defensiveness on the part of the jury that their inability to reach a verdict was not the result of their incompetence or lack of caring). We worked very, very hard and there was frustration because there were differing opinions. It was very, very clear that we were not going to come to a unanimous verdict. It was clear the day before (Tuesday) and we continued to work until it was clear we weren't going to come to a unanimous verdict. That's what happened."

Me- "What was the vote? I've been told the capital murder charge you voted to acquit him of. What about on the felony murder charge and second degree murder? What was the vote?"

Juror- "How did you find that out?"

Me-"A source from the State Attorney's office."

Juror-"I'm really not going to talk about numbers, counts, except to say we took it very seriously and I'm quite impressed with the contrast of people who were on the jury. Unfortunately, we couldn't come to an agreement."

Me- "Did it stay the same from the very start of the deliberations until the end?"

Juror- "No, no, people changed their minds. I was one of those who changed. There were a lot of people who changed in different ways."

Me- "Was there anything particular in the case that influenced you in your deliberations?"

Juror-"There was a lot. My fellow jurors, listening to their perspectives. I think he's guilty of some of the charges and the evidence that was presented brought me to that conclusion."

Me- "What did you think about the interrogation where he confessed?"

Juror-"Well, I was uncomfortable with the techniques that were used. Yet, they were lawful. So, I couldn't use my own discomfort as a basis for making my decision, but if I think the law is wrong then my job is to work to have the law changed. I couldn't use that in my own judgement."

Me- "One of the questions the jury asked the judge was can the police lie in order to obtain a confession. Of course, the answer to that is yes. That must have been a concerning point for several people."

Juror- "You know, I don't even remember that. Something that the jury asked..."

Me- "Yes, you asked the judge."

Juror- "I don't even recall that."

Me- "Any thoughts about any particular people's testimony in the trial?"

Juror- "There were a lot of people. I thought the differing opinions between the expert witnesses was strong for the prosecution. It really was his three confessions."

Me- "Confession in 1973 when he was in jail, the confession he made...

Juror-"No, no. The confession in the four hour interview and when he confessed to his daughter and son."

Me-"Any thoughts about the relationship with the daughter and the son and what they said on the witness stand."

Juror- "I didn't believe them. I can't speak to their relationships."

Me- "Were there any witnesses that you felt were hostile or not really cooperating?"

Juror-"Everybody eventually answered all of the questions. I think the possibility that Raven wasn't telling the truth. But that's not up to me if that's the case. Someone in law enforcement or the justice system would go after that."

Me- "Did his changing his name bother you or the other jurors at all? And moving away, did that bother you?"

Juror- "I can't speak to the other jurors or what went on in the jury room, but no, that had very little impact on me."

Me- "The sticking points that the jury couldn't resolve, that kept them from coming back with a verdict, what were they?"

Juror- "Again, I'm not going to talk about the jury deliberations. Except to say they were very serious people working very hard. We spent a lot of time in that room and ninety-seven percent was doing the work."

Me- "Did the foreman of the jury do a good job?"

Juror- "I'm not going to speak to anything that happened in the room. My sympathies are with the family and this was obviously a dreadful loss."

Me- "Carolyn is eighty years old and her brother Melvin is eighty-four years old. They wanted resolution while they were alive."

Juror- "I hope that will happen for them. This case was not easy for anybody. It was not easy for me and I don't believe it was easy for anybody. We really, really worked hard and we couldn't come to a resolution."

Me- "It sounds like you tried to look at things and come to a verdict which was impossible. I can understand because there is no physical evidence and you don't have any..."

Juror- "We were very clear that we were to weigh circumstantial evidence as strongly as direct evidence. That was very clear, and we kept reminding ourselves of that. Everything was circumstantial. I will tell you that I believe this was a societal failure in addition to Larry's personal failings. This was a teenager who was out on the street, scrounging for food, and sleeping out on the street. It's a societal failure."

Me- "You're asked to say innocent or guilty. The background you can't take into consideration although I felt sorry for the guy. Society failed him in a big way."

CHAPTER FIFTY-THREE
Discussion with Rebekah, the Alternate Juror

I gave my business card with my cell phone number on it to the two alternate jurors, and within a couple of hours of the trial ending I heard from Rebekah, the thirty-nine year-old with training in social work who also did counseling. She was still in the courthouse in the jurors' lounge and was very agreeable to talk with me. The trial had consumed her mentally and emotionally, and I could tell how much she wanted to be in the ongoing jury deliberations. We found a quiet spot in the jurors' lounge and began to talk.

Rebekah- "I really enjoy my work with my clients, particularly thinking about how their childhood has formed a way to view the world and has formed them to be who they are today. I couldn't turn that off."

Me- "How does it relate to this case?"

Rebekah- "I think it's everything. Because really the turning point in this case is whether or not his confession is valid and to be honest, I'm not sure. Aside from the techniques that the officers were using, I saw a seven year old him. Locked in at that age. The same way he talked in that 2022 interview is the same way he talked in 1973. Compulsive lying. Different than pathological lying. Both are learned behaviors. Pathological lying is when you have a thought-out story you want to tell in your head and you're very good at manipulating and you can. You're very good at lying and people have a hard time catching you when you're lying. You begin to actually believe the lies. Compulsive lying is a learned behavior when you're young when telling the truth results in such trauma that you feel that your only option is learn to always lie."

"What we learned about his childhood: alcoholic mom, dad not around. He's seven and has two younger siblings and an older sibling and they're in foster care even before age seven. When he turned seven and they were adopted by the Becker family, he talked many times about being the black sheep, not being accepted. Through all of that I'm assuming this compulsive lying was developing this whole time. So compulsive lying is a lying behavior when you're young, but it's talking circles. You'll say something and then thirty seconds later you'll say something else that doesn't make sense. You have a really hard time repeating the same story. You say what you think the other person wants to hear. You can hear that in 1973-'When I have said enough that they'll stop asking me questions I can get my leniency and move on'. He pauses and thinks at times you shouldn't have to pause. Right or left; he has to pause and think about something that should be automatic. But something that he should pause at he won't pause but launch into a narrative and go on and on and on and on. Giving details that are so specific but they're contradictory. Same exact thing. I didn't believe any of the diagnoses of the psychologist that the defense called."

Me- "Why not?"

Rebekah- "A big reason is because I thought he was speaking the same way in 2022 as in 1973. But, also, I agreed with the psychiatrist about him not having dementia and not being depressed. So, I do not appreciate at all what the psychologist had to add except the testing. The IQ was very interesting and confirmed what I thought to be true."

Me- "I agree with you. In order to diagnose dementia, you have to rule out so many other things that can cause that. The depression part, I've been around a lot of depressed people, and I'm sure you have too in your field, and he didn't seem depressed."

Rebekah-"That was a stretch for sure. The fact that he included those diagnoses made me value nothing of what he said."

Me- "Did you know anything about this case before you came into jury selection?"

Rebekah- "Not at all."

Me- "The media, the news conference."

Rebekah- "No. Monday morning the trial started. Even before that first morning break, it was so heavy because I knew nothing about the case. The first five minutes of the opening statements I was like "Woah."

Me-"Any thoughts about the attorneys?"

Rebekah- "I actually wrote today the first time the older defense attorney (Kevin Collins) spoke, I wrote down I don't like him. I don't like his tone; very off-putting. I felt like yelling at him a little bit. The three young defense lawyers did a good job. I thought Judge McCallyity wasn't very patient with them, they were learning. I thought the two state's attorneys did a stellar job. They seemed to leave no stone unturned. What I think they did better than the defense was the defense would repeat the same thing that was already said. I was shocked at how competent the young defense attorneys were."

Me- "What about Donna, the lead state's attorney and what did you think about her rebuttal at the end and her cross examination of the psychologist?"

Rebekah- "I actually joked with her afterwards that I was shaking. I was like, oh man, and my hands were shaking a little bit. I think it's appropriate. It felt like a movie. This could be scripted. You could have cut the air with a knife, so thick, so intense. But it was spot-on. His diagnosis was not good."

"The witness was not proving his case and I was surprised he couldn't handle himself better. I think it was spot-on and proved the point she was trying to make."

Me- "What about her rebuttal at the end?"

Rebekah- "Her voice was elevated. Whenever somebody raises their voice at me I'm recognizing that you really need to make yourself big right now because you don't think you're powerful enough. I always shut down a little bit when somebody raises their voice. That's why it bothers me that the defense attorney did it, too. I have to look away, it's all very emotional. Trying to pull the emotion out of us. I hate that; let me form my own emotions. I need the information, not the emotions."

Me-"Carolyn Philo, the first witness called who was the daughter of the murdered sheriff. Did she elicit sympathy from you?"

Rebekah- "I know my tendency is to have emotions. I've been prepping myself not to do that. I try to separate myself as much as possible because generally I even....that's my job. Hearing their story. This whole week I just want to hear how the family is doing. That's just who I am. I already have an ear to that. In the opening statement I was really turned off by how Donna started, "In 1971 Officer Hall kissed his family for the last time...in 1971 Officer Hall put on his raincoat for the last time." Very much pulling on our emotions. That bothers me. Feeling like you have to connect with my emotions because you don't have enough facts. Even Carolyn's testimony felt a little bit that way to me because she was the first witness called and all that. I wrote down this is the first time this case has gone to trial, no wonder she's so emotional. No wonder that there's still grief for her. She will never forget that day, Monday testifying. That's what was in my mind. We know how he died. That's why she was there, to solidify the fact that he died."

Me- "What about the theory of trauma causing a stoppage in one's maturity. Do you think Larry got to age seven and then never went further?"

Rebekah- "When you're at whatever childhood age you're not capable of forming relationships. You're too self-absorbed. You can't have stable relationships. That's what I think about the defendant. He was seven when he was adopted but when did the trauma start is the question. I don't know if he ever had a stable environment. When a person is drinking so much that their brain is pickled, a true alcoholic, then they will function better when they're drinking alcohol than when they stop because it's all the brain knows. Same way, he only knows trauma, he only knows lies. His life has been on the run and unstable. He doesn't know how to be in a safe environment. When a loving adoptive family brought him in, he didn't know what to do with that. Scary to him, something to run from. He did not have the skills to be able to accept their safety."

Me- "What do you think about the idea that one family adopted four children at the same time? They took all four of those kids from another family. Also, shouldn't they have tried counseling for Larry rather than throwing him out of the house?"

Rebekah- "He talked about a time at age twelve when his parents sent him to a facility and there was a psychiatrist involved. I have no idea what adoptions were like in that era. So much has changed since then."

Me- "What do you think about his two children testifying and did you notice they weren't there for the rest of the week? Did that make an impression on you?"

Rebekah- "We heard their testimony early on. Their testimony was so different from the recording. It would have felt better had they said yes, that's my voice, that's what I said. But this is why I said it. But just something believable. Not just, "That's my voice but that's not what I said." What, is there some sort of AI switching the recording around? No. From that moment the daughter and son lost all credibility for me. I did not give any weight to their testimony. I think they have learned compulsive lying just like their father. If I just lie about it, it will go away. Let me tell a different story."

Me- "I thought the daughter was a little belligerent. Did you pick up on that or did you think her affect was appropriate?"

Rebekah- "I thought it was completely inappropriate. The day she was interviewed in 2022 she's going about her normal life, cheery, happy, almost in a joking way about her dad. So inconsistent. She was so sullen as a witness. She was, "Surely this recording is wrong." Initially she seemed to think that her dad shooting and killing someone was within the realm of possible. She wasn't totally crippled by it the next day: "I can't come into work; I was crying all night." Realistic for her to believe this happened versus she was just crippled. The state's attorney told me after the fact that the children didn't want to come. I'm not surprised."

Me- "I felt bad that there was no one there for him in the courtroom. No family. You live this life and all that matters is your family and the people you love, and there was nobody there. What did you think about his appearance? Anything you took from the way he looked and acted?"

Rebekah- "I remember when they were calling the jury. I took note of who he was and I thought I can't tell anything about him. His head is shaved. I couldn't even tell what ethnicity he was when they were asking a few questions about whether you be biased. He was very distant, flat. One of the Coke machine boys was talking and for the very first time he was playing with his beard and took his glasses off. He normally would just sit there and stare. I thought he should become agitated hearing about the crime scene for the first time. He was so flat the whole time. Only one time in the whole trial did I see him take off his glasses."

Me- "O.W. Sweat told me that of all the murder cases in his long career this was the only one that he never solved. He honed in on Shoemaker who was the son of a policeman. According to Sweat, the father would not let the son be interviewed by the police. It was interesting to see how some of these teenagers turned out. Some went into the military giving them that discipline that was missing in their lives. What were your thoughts about the testimony of the two guys from the Coke machines?"

Rebekah- "They seemed solid. All five of them were consistent throughout and none of them fled."

Me- "Katie Leggett was one of the interrogators who was also involved in the interrogation of the Lyon sisters' murderer. What did you think about the interrogation? The circumstances: the room, the proximity of the detectives. At one point Lisa Killen had her chair so close she could have touched him."

Rebekah- "It was three hours and forty-five minutes. The actual physical proximity I don't have a problem with. He was free to leave at any time. I was squeamish at times as to how much he was being manipulated. She talked about using minimization and alternative theories. I know that police can do anything. But it just felt so different. Especially for someone with such a low IQ who doesn't know any better. That's the piece that was hard. It felt like he was being taken advantage of. I have a seven year old at home. I was thinking during the interrogation that it could be my seven year old in the chair and the questions would be framed the same. Saying, "It's okay if you did this", and "that's who he is." It just felt bad. My seven year old would not know any better to defend himself or to say, "I don't want to answer your questions anymore," or "I want a lawyer." That's what made me squeamish. She knows exactly where this is going to go. Not necessarily because he did it, but because he's very good at lying and telling a story until it makes the other person happy with the story."

Me- "I felt at the end of the interrogation he felt good, "I'm done with this, it's off my chest."

Rebekah- "They are happy. They stopped asking me questions. That means I gave them the answers they wanted. I'm glad I could help you, okay."

Me- "Any other issues?"

Rebekah-"What about his brother, Leslie? What about him? Had he been recorded in the seventies he could have said the same number of incriminating things. Or anybody else could have. And said a couple of things that were rumored to be true but weren't released to the media. Maybe Leslie had a similar IQ, similar coping mechanism. Maybe if he was still alive he would have all of this happen to him and we'd have been sitting in this exact same spot. This is the piece that makes me not be positive that he's guilty. I know we've explored a lot of people, but what about Leslie? He's not here to tell us."

Me- "We don't really know his life's arc. We don't know that much about him other than he was Larry's brother and he made those phone calls."

Rebekah-"Maybe he did a lot of robberies after that and was never caught. Maybe he was in on a lot of things. I so much want closure for the family. It's my profession to help people find closure. Even me, I went to my car and I had to come back. I don't feel closure. Back to Leslie. I couldn't see myself giving closure unless I was positive and I was hoping that the jury deliberations would help me to understand things the way they were understanding them. I was undecided. I was hoping the others would pull me towards believing he was guilty beyond a reasonable doubt. I still have reasonable doubt. I don't think he's guilty beyond all doubt, But I don't know about reasonable doubt. Leslie, for example, why couldn't it have been him when he was initially interviewed and said it was his brother. That's all we know from the police report. I know a lot of stones were left unturned, but what about the name that wasn't dropped or the other person?"

Me- "The officers who questioned Larry in 1973 in person apparently didn't communicate with the lead investigator, O.W. Sweat. He knew nothing about this."

Rebekah- "It had only been two years."

Me- "Lack of communication. They should have brought Leslie in and questioned him. O.W. Sweat knew how important the two shots fired was. That was held back. The officers who interviewed Larry in 1973 had no idea about that."

Rebekah- "I think Larry was probably there. I don't believe any of Larry's testimony including what he said about experience with guns. I believe he'd handled guns before. In the same way that I disregarded Larry's daughter and anything she said, I felt the same way about Larry. He was so twisted in 1973. He may say many things and a lot of them are totally false and we know they are false. Daughter says he told her he was with two friends and his brother. Those other guys are cleared. How do we accept part of it to be true and not all of it? His story just didn't fully make sense to me."

Me- "Does it serve any purpose to put him in jail now, fifty-two years later? He rehabilitated himself as a family man and with gainful employment."

Rebekah- "It costs the government more to take care of him in prison. He was living in a quiet, secluded place. Our judicial system breaks down if we say okay, well if someone is fine now we don't have to prosecute them for what they did in the past. Regardless of what quiet life he's living, he should be charged for a crime hei might have committed."

Me- "I think he was there that night. I don't know if he shot him."

Rebekah- "They were doing a lot of burglaries. "Did you run from the scene that night?" He answered, "Normally I would run back to Maggie's Place." Maybe that's why he couldn't keep it straight because he was involved in so many burglaries. In the interview I couldn't tell if he was talking about this specific night or he was just filling in the gaps."

Me- "Burglaries were his vocation."

Rebekah- "He's in survival mode. Trying to fill in gaps to make people happy. I really don't know what reasonable doubt is."

Carolyn and Bob Philo with J.T. Hall memorial plaque at the Montgomery County Police Department (Photo courtesy of Carolyn and Bob Philo)

Montgomery County Police Chief addresses reporters Sept. 7, 2022, announcing an arrest in a 51-year-old cold case. (WTOP/Kate Ryan)

Deputy Sheriff Hall's daughter, Carolyn Philo, on left.

Manor Country Club
(©Manor Country Club)

Suspect Larry David Becker AKA Larry David Smith in 1973 and 2022.
(Montgomery County Police)

K9 Officer Robert Philo   Deputy Sheriff, J.T. Hall
(courtesy of Carolyn and Bob Philo)

Michael Weisberg

BOOK TWO

CHAPTER ONE
Four Bypasses and Two Funerals

My life changed dramatically between January when the first trial ended and June eighteenth when the second trial began. The changes kept me from attending the second trial, but instead, I relied on my nightly conversations with the Philos to know what was happening. Because that was the only way I received information at that point, the verdict turned out to be shocking and disturbing. But before I go to the trial, let me recount the events in my life that kept me from being an on-site observer of the trial.

In January the health of my mother-in-law, Barbara, started deteriorating. She was hospitalized with pneumonia and then moved to skilled nursing units at various facilities. She never made any progress. Early on she said she'd had enough and didn't want to go on living the very limited lifestyle her condition had imposed upon her the previous six months. She was a very social, loving woman of ninety whose greatest joy was interacting with her family and friends. Most of her friends had died by this time, and the few who were left were battling their own traumas. My wife, Sheryl, and her sister, Saundra, still visited Barbara regularly as did my daughter, Carly, who lives in Dallas. Nothing seemed to lift Barbara's spirits for long. As a doctor I recognized she was in the slow downward spiral to death.

Barbara decided to go on hospice and was moved to the T. Boone Pickens Hospice Center in Dallas on March fifteenth. My brother, Perry, was in town to visit our ailing mother, Joan, and I took him to the hospice center to see Barbara. When we entered her room, I looked at

Barbara and realized she was having agonal respirations. She was totally unresponsive to each of us telling her our last words of love and blessing. We left her at eight pm that night and received a phone call at ten pm that she had passed away.

Barbara's passing left a void in our lives. It had become more difficult lately to get her places, but we still tried to have her over to our house regularly and Sheryl and Saundra took her out to lunch weekly. We comforted ourselves by reassuring each other that the life of someone as fun, happy, giving, and loving as Barbara was no longer achievable in the condition she had deteriorated into. I never thought I'd agree with such a bold assessment given my own father's daily proclamation that life was beautiful and man needed to press forward until God took the gift of life away from man's clenched fist. However, knowing Barbara and what made her happy, I was willing to hope and pray she was in a better place.

Barbara's funeral was beautiful. All three of her daughters spoke as did Carly who also read speeches from my sons who lived elsewhere. All three of my children had seen their grandmother the week before when she was still alive, and we didn't feel the boys needed to fly back to Dallas for the funeral. As I listened to the speeches I thought of Barbara and felt she was there watching. Interestingly enough, during my daughter's poignant remembrance, she said she felt the presence of her grandmother standing next to her. At the end of her talk, she felt a hand on her shoulder to comfort her, even though there was nobody there.

* * * * * * * *

In 2019 driving back from Houston to Dallas on I-45 I was involved in a horrific accident. The driver of an eighteen wheeler driving the opposite direction from Dallas to Houston fell asleep at the wheel, crossed the grassy divide, and began crashing into cars on our side. My wife was driving and I was in the front passenger seat with two of our children sleeping in the back seat. The truck hit four cars head on and two of them went flying by our car. My wife tried to turn our car to get over the divide and out of danger, but there were stiff wires that refused to yield and let us escape. Instead, the wires rotated our car perfectly so that I was in direct line to be hit by the truck. There were a few moments of breathless silence as I looked straight ahead and refused to acknowledge that the source of my death was about to crush me. All at once the impact came, and the truck smashed into and through our car exactly one foot in front of me. The airbags deployed as our car spun around like a top, with glass shattering and metal crunching. I watched the truck go halfway through our car close enough for me to touch, and the next thing I knew, people were all around the car screaming at me to get out.

I looked around and saw my daughter, Carly, outside the car standing in shock. She had been sitting behind my wife on the driver's side and had been cut by the car's broken shards of glass. Her legs were a bloody, Jackson Pollock painting. Brent, my son, who had been sitting behind me, and my wife soon joined Carly and yelled at me to get out of the car. I could hear people yelling that the car might blow up or catch fire at any second. I stupidly tried the door on my side which was pushed in and unable to be moved. I had severe pain in my chest and right side as somehow I used my arms and legs to push myself over the console to the driver's seat, and then I was pulled out of the car by my son, wife and daughter. I couldn't stand up straight.

We were taken by ambulance to the nearest hospital in Huntsville, Texas, and on CT Scan I was diagnosed with multiple rib fractures, fracture of my sternum, and blood around my heart. Incidentally found was a large amount of calcium and plaque in my coronary arteries which supply blood to the heart. The emergency room gave me a shot of Fentanyl and said I could go home to Dallas, but I needed to follow up with my own doctor.

Michael Weisberg

My broken bones slowly and painfully healed over the next six months, but my radiologist colleague, Mark Spivey, reviewed the CAT Scan and told me I needed to get my coronary arteries investigated further. I had absolutely no symptoms but went and saw a Cardiologist who did an echo stress test that he read as completely normal. He said to come back yearly.

That was in 2019. I had normal stress tests in 2020 and 2021, but like most doctors who neglect their own health, didn't go back until 2024. By then my first cardiologist had retired, and I had the stress echo done with another cardiologist in the community. I felt great during the stress test, but there appeared to be a tiny abnormality in the apex of the heart that the cardiologist thought could be due to a blip in the machine. He asked a partner who specialized in reading echoes for his opinion and he agreed that something wasn't right, but it was possibly just the machine. They finally decided that I needed a CT angiogram of my coronary arteries and referred me to the Heart Hospital to have it done. The Heart Hospital gave me an appointment three weeks later.

How my mind works... Variables:

1. Cardiologists uncertain of results of echo; may just be blip in machine

2. Scheduled for further testing to evaluate, but three weeks later

My Conclusion: Definitely a blip in the echo machine and needs no further evaluation.

Reasoning: No cardiologist would wait three weeks to have further testing done on their patient if they felt their heart at risk.

I talked to my wife and told her my decision not to pursue further evaluation since I felt great and could exercise at any level I wanted. That day I rode my recumbent bike and got my pulse up to one hundred and forty.

A Second Shot

The next day Waenard Miller came to see me in the office. Waenard was a retired cardiologist who had started a large cardiology group in Plano. I told him my story and my decision. He shook his head no and spent the next ten minutes telling me why I needed to have further testing, something no one else had done. He even told me the story of a young doctor who we both knew who had died of a heart attack while cycling after having been treated for heart disease. I had so much respect for Waenard and his ability and his genuine concern that I scheduled the CT angiogram of my heart.

I went to the Heart Hospital for my CT angiogram after following all of their instructions regarding eating and taking a Beta blocker the night before and the morning of the test to slow down my heart so they could see things more clearly. I walked into the radiology suite and the secretary took my information and put an identification bracelet on my left wrist. The last thing she said was, "Your insurance pays eight thousand dollars for this test, so your portion will be thirty-three hundred dollars." I looked at her like she was crazy and I might have said, "You're fucking kidding me!", but without the "F" word. I have excellent private insurance so I next said, "I owe what?" She calmly replied, "You owe thirty-three hundred dollars. You can pay the full amount now or we can set up a payment plan for you."

I said, "I'm not paying that much more. I'm not having that test." I ripped the identification bracelet off my arm and stormed out the door. I'd already decided to switch cardiologists and have the CT scan done at my own hospital.

I went and saw a different cardiologist who practiced at my hospital. He reviewed all of my records including my high coronary calcium score and scheduled me for the CT angiogram that week at the hospital I had practiced at for thirty-four years. I checked in and was asked to pay my part of the CT angiogram, which was three hundred dollars.

That afternoon I went back to look at the results with my radiology guru, Mark Spivey, who I also consider a friend. Technically the radiologist does an overread of the CT looking at all of the structures except the heart. However, Mark looked at my heart and told me point-blank that I had some significant blockages. He ended his comments by looking at me and saying, "But didn't your father just live to almost ninety-eight years-old?" I interpreted this as meaning that my heart was going to stand in the way of my living a long life, so something needed to be done immediately. I knew a lot of men my age who had stents, and I was comfortable with the notion of that fixing my problem.

My new (third for those counting) cardiologist called me that night and went over the results with me. He said I needed a cardiac catheterization which he didn't do but gave me the name and number of the cardiologist in his group who did them. I contacted this interventional cardiologist, and he said he was extremely busy and booked out, but he would try to get me on his schedule in three weeks.

I went looking for my fourth cardiologist. If I had blockages in my heart and needed stents, I didn't want to wait three weeks to get fixed. I called a surgeon I've known and respected for years on a Thursday night for advice, and within ten minutes the cardiologist he recommended called me back and said I was on his schedule for cardiac catheterization the following Tuesday.

I woke up from the catheterization with the cardiologist in my room telling me that my blockages weren't amenable to stents. I would need bypass surgery. I had a sixty percent blockage of the left main artery, two ninety-eight per cent blockages of the left anterior descending artery ("widow maker"), and an eighty percent blockage of the circumflex artery. I'd gone to medical school at Baylor College of Medicine in Houston and had done a one month rotation with Michael DeBakey's Heart Surgery Team at Methodist Hospital, so I'd seen or participated in over one-hundred open heart surgeries. I was nervous but not frightened. I wanted the problem fixed so I could resume my normal life.

On April eleventh I underwent open heart surgery. The surgeon used my internal mammary artery to bypass the blockages in the left main artery and the two blockages in the left anterior descending artery and took a portion of the saphenous vein from my left leg to bypass my circumflex artery. He also drained the blood around my heart left over from the car/truck accident. I was in the hospital for four days and sent home. I didn't do well. I could hardly move and my breathing was painful and ineffective. My wife, Sheryl, needed to get up with me every hour when I woke up at night to check my oxygen saturation which hovered around eighty-nine to ninety per cent. Sheryl would arrange the various cushions and pillows she had bought to try to place my body in the most advantageous position, but it was to no avail. One night I slept in a recliner in the living room, which moved backwards to let you lie down and forwards to help you get out of the chair. I had to pee in the middle of the night, so I pushed the button to move the recliner forward. Apparently I ended up catapulting myself to the floor; I don't remember, but my wife heard me fall and helped me get up. The next day the bruises on my arms and legs and my body's increased soreness reminded me that I had indeed fallen.

At two weeks we visited the cardiologist and I could barely walk from my wife's car to his office. He came into my exam room, listened to my heart and lungs, and told me I was doing well and left.

At three weeks I went back for my first post-operative visit with the surgeon. I was miserable. The surgeon ordered a chest x-ray prior to the visit and I pushed myself to stand up to do it. The surgeon showed me the chest x-ray, and my left lung had a good-sized pleural effusion (fluid around the lung). Two days later, using ultrasound guidance, a pulmonologist drained twelve hundred and fifty cc of blood from my left lung which weighed two and a half pounds (I weighed myself before and after the procedure). I had the weird sensation of my left lung re-expanding after the blood was removed which was somewhat painful.

Almost immediately I felt better and was more active. I slept through the night and I was able to climb stairs. I started Cardiac Rehabilitation at my hospital and worked my way up to forty-five minutes of exercise. I did have one episode of atrial fibrillation at the start of my first visit to rehab, but I used my medical training and made myself cough and my heart went back into normal sinus rhythm.

* * * * * * * *

My ninety-three year-old mother had become more and more demented over the last year since my father died. I had her living at a memory care home two minutes' drive from my house. After my three weeks of hell, I tried to visit her if not daily, then at least every other day. She was going downhill and could barely communicate. She couldn't pronounce many words and was increasingly frustrated with her inability to ask and answer questions. She was completely bed- bound having lost the ability to use her legs. She had lost almost all of her orange hair (yes, it was orange, not red) which she had been known for wherever she lived. She was completely bald except for a few strands of gray hair which the caretakers at the home pulled back and unsuccessfully tried to anchor behind her ears.

The one thing she could still repeat was "I love you." I said this to her multiple times during our visits, and she would repeat it back to me. When I would leave she would always try to say, "Do you have to go, can't you stay five more minutes?" The words were garbled, but I understood enough to stay five more minutes.

I went back to work full-time on Monday, June third. I was now back to my regular routine of visiting my mother every Saturday and bringing her lunch and sweets. She loved everything sweet from cookies to candy to pies to cake. I was planning to see her on Saturday, June fifteenth, when my phone rang at six am that morning. It was the hospice nurse telling me my mother was dead. The door to all of the occupants' rooms were locked during the night, and when the attendant went to wake her he found her dead.

I got dressed and called my brother Perry in Florida to tell him the news and went over to the memory home. I walked into my mother's room and she was lying on the bed in her usual position as if she was expecting me. I gave her a kiss on her cold forehead and sat down in a chair right next to her. Her right pupil was blown and her right eye was wide open even though the left eye was closed. A blown pupil meant some kind of event had happened to her brain during the night, either a stroke or a brain bleed that had increased intracranial pressure. I only hoped she hadn't suffered. I tried to close the eyelid, but it wouldn't stay closed. The black enormous pupil which had replaced her brown eye kept staring at me and staring at me. My sister and her husband soon came into the room and said their good-byes. About fifteen minutes later the attendants from the funeral home arrived and took my mother's body back to the funeral home.

My mother died on Saturday, and we had the funeral on Sunday. My brother came in from Florida, and two cousins, Martha and Seth, flew in from Houston and Denver respectively. It was a typical Dallas summer day, about ninety-five degrees with no air movement. We had a graveside funeral with the rabbi from our synagogue presiding. About twenty of our relatives and friends watched the funeral on Zoom.

After some initial prayers by the rabbi, my sister spoke first and told one story about how my mother had changed my sister's birth certificate to show she had been born a month earlier so she wouldn't have to start school a year later. My sister then read a poem and sat down. My brother first talked about how the first time he remembered my mother saying she loved him was five years before after he told her he loved her. He told a few stories about my mother and his relationship with her. He had become closer and more attached to her as she became more demented and she was dependent on him for his nightly phone calls to entertain her and to reassure her that her children still cared about her.

My brother sat down and I spoke. I had jotted down some general statements about my mother on the notes section of my I-Phone, and I used each of these as a starting point to talk about her life. I talked about her growing up in Brooklyn, New York and having been raised by her grandparents due to having a mother with mental illness and a father who was a travelling salesman. I told about her being a brilliant student skipping grades, and how she was one of the first female graduates of Yale Law School at age twenty-three. I talked about her bravery for flying over to see Israel between law school and starting a job as a lawyer doing labor relations for the state of New York.

I went on to tell the story of my mother and father meeting in Miami Beach while on vacation and becoming engaged three hours after they met. They were married for sixty-seven years until my father died. I reminisced about living in Huntington, West Virginia where my mother gave up her career to raise her three children in a kosher home. I talked about how she loved to play the card game bridge and taught my brother and I to play when we were seven and five years-old so she would always have a foursome available. I talked about her moving our entire family to West Palm Beach, Florida because she no longer wanted to live in what she felt was an unaccepting community to her in Huntington. We lived in a tiny apartment in West Palm Beach for five and a half years while my brother and I went to high school and my sister attended elementary school. She and my father had no good plan for living, for us going to school, or for my father working when we moved, and I think the many problems we encountered and the hardships we experienced impacted all of our lives. Finally, I talked about all of the volunteer work she had done and how she and my father had moved to Dallas to be near their children and grandchildren. My last words were, "Mom, we will always love you and think of you and be grateful for your presence in our lives. Rest in peace."

In the span of three months, I had lost my mother and mother-in-law, two people who had impacted my life and who I loved and will always love. I had survived two-ninety-eight percent blockages of my "widow maker" as well as two other significant blockages and had returned to working full-time since my first day back, June third. I felt that the horrific traffic accident five years before had given me a second shot at life, and I wanted to make the most of it. I wanted to finish the book about the murder of Deputy Sheriff J.T. Hall, but I couldn't make it back to Rockville, Maryland for the second trial due to ongoing recovery from my surgery and patient backlog due to the seven weeks I had missed work. I agreed with Bob and Carolyn who were going back for the re-trial that starting June eighteenth they would act as my eyes and ears and we would talk nightly by phone. During my seven week recovery from surgery, I had typed over three hundred and thirty pages of the book based on research, interviews, and the first trial. I wasn't going to stop now, even though people would soon appear who didn't want the book written.

CHAPTER TWO
Re-Trial Day One
Tuesday, June 18, 2024

After jury selection, the second trial of Larry Smith began with opening statements by the prosecution and defense on Tuesday, June eighteenth. Bob and Carolyn weren't in attendance, so I had no eyewitnesses for the statements. Bob and Carolyn chose to spend time with Carolyn's brother Melvin and his wife Judy at their home in Virginia. One of the best things about the trial was how the Philos and the Halls got to spend time together in their eighties, and re-kindle their love and friendship.

Carolyn told me she had spoken to Donna Fenton and that the opening statements would be given that afternoon and the court would be closed Wednesday for Juneteenth Holiday. Carolyn would meet with Donna Wednesday morning to go over her testimony since she would be the first witness. The prosecutions' plan was to put on Carolyn, then the Schmidts, and then Corporal Lisa Killen uninterrupted. Carolyn said Donna felt there were too many interruptions in Lisa's testimony in the first trial, so in this trial, it was planned to be non-stop Lisa testifying making it easier for the jury to follow. The charges against Larry David Smith at this trial were:

Count One: Felony Murder
Count Two: Murder- First Degree
Count Three: Burglary-First Degree
Count Four: Conspiracy-Murder-First Degree
Count Five: Conspiracy -Burglary-First Degree

CHAPTER THREE
Juneteenth Holiday
Wednesday, June 19, 2024

I talked to Bob Philo by phone, and he was excited by the prosecution's plan to present witnesses. By putting on Lisa Killen Thursday and Friday he felt the jury would go home for the weekend with a real outline of the entire investigation. On Monday the prosecution was going to bring in other witnesses to back up Lisa's testimony. "I think much better positioning and much less confusion," Bob told me. I asked about Donna's thoughts on jury selection this time and Carolyn answered that Donna was very pleased with it. We discussed that the same defense team would be representing Larry Smith and Bob said, "I have to say I admire them because they're doing the best they can, which is what he is owed. They're doing it for free."

Since they were staying at the same hotel we stayed at for the first trial, I asked the Philos if any of the staff there asked for me, the "Big Tipper". They both laughed. They went on to tell me that Donna was alone in the courthouse on the holiday and had to let them in. Donna had spent a couple of hours talking to the state's psychiatrist. Bob told me that Donna's opening statement the day before was one and a half hours and one of the jurors fell asleep. She approached the bench and the judge said for everyone to be quiet to see if the juror would wake up with nothing going on and he did.

At the end of our discussion that night Carolyn spoke:

Carolyn- "I sat down with Melvin and I held his hand. I said I need to tell you something. You've been a good son to mom and dad. You've been a great brother to me. You're a wonderful husband and I don't think you could have been a better father. You need to know that. People love you. He started crying and said, "Thank you so much, Carolyn. Thank you."

Me-"Wonderful you said that. You've got to tell people that while they're still alive. Don't wait until they're dead. Don't show up to the funeral after not doing anything for years."

Carolyn- "That's how I felt. It was a good visit."

CHAPTER FOUR
Retrial Day Two
Thursday, June Twentieth, 2024

I talked to Carolyn and Bob after getting home from work. The big news from the trial was that the juror who kept falling asleep was dismissed from the jury so there were now eleven seated jurors and three alternates. The dismissed juror was a forty year-old man whose excuse for falling asleep was that he worked a night job.

Carolyn testified today and said she was more emotional and tearful than in the first trial. She messed up J.T.'s year of birth saying he was born in nineteen thirty-eight instead of nineteen eighteen. The Schmidts both testified, and then Jerry Boone, the officer in charge of the crime scene, testified by Zoom. After Jerry Boone finished, Corporal Lisa Killen was called to testify. She told how she zeroed in on Smith as a suspect from comments he made in his nineteen seventy-three interview with police that he shouldn't have known unless he was there. She went chronologically through her testimony, bringing up the important points. Both Bob and Carolyn agreed that the prosecution's case had a better vibe this time.

CHAPTER FIVE
Retrial Day Three
Friday, June 21, 2024

When I called Bob and Carolyn on Friday they were eager to talk. The judge had come in that morning and said they would be quitting at four forty-five that afternoon. The prosecution showed the interrogation tape leading to the confession which ended at exactly four forty-five. Bob and Carolyn felt it was very helpful that the jurors would have the whole weekend to remember that Larry confessed. They both felt the trial was going much smoother.

Bob went through the presentation of Smith's escape or escapes from custody, but the details were still confusing and contradictory to me. Exactly which escape or sentence Smith was trying to have reduced when he interviewed with the police in nineteen seventy-three will probably always be a mystery to me and others. When Bob brought up the subject of a second escape by Larry from custody I responded that I had no idea he had escaped a second time. Bob ended this part of our discussion by telling me about the huge, four by eight foot board the prosecution had constructed which included a blow up of the hand-written ledger from the records at the Maryland Department of Corrections. It contained the judges who sentenced Smith, the correctional officers' names, and where and when his escapes from custody occurred. Lisa Killen had to stand up to point to the things they were asking her to point to.

Another thing that occurred that day was that the jury seemed extremely interested in following the interrogation. One of the jurors raised his hand and asked the judge if there was any way to make the screen size bigger so they could see Smith's reactions and his expressions related to the questions. Clearly they were paying close attention to what Smith did and what he said. Smith was given headphones to wear while the tape was playing in order to hear the tape better. He had put on quite a bit of weight in prison and his hair was much longer touching his shoulders.

Bob felt this trial was going better than the first. He felt the prosecution had filled in some gaps that needed to be filled in. We ended up again talking about the confusion regarding where, when, who, and how Larry had escaped from prison and what he had done while free.

CHAPTER SIX
Retrial Day Four
Monday, June 24, 2024

I realize that when you are writing about a trial from the viewpoint of only two people who are there the story is going to be slanted in the direction they want. Therefore, as I went back over the conversations with the Philo's, I tried to categorize what they said into either fact or opinion. Both are important. The facts are what the case will be decided on. Their opinions are what got me involved in writing this book and have sustained my interest for the two years I have been working on it.

On Monday Lisa Killen finished her testimony and then Detective Katie Leggett took the stand. After Katie was the detective who transported Smith from jail to the airplane in a car, was with him on the plane, and then was with him in a car from the airplane to Montgomery County Jail. Bob made an interesting observation about the defense's tactics. Although they weren't attacking the witnesses' testimonies, "they still seemed to be raising the point he was dumb, stupid, and didn't know what he was doing." Carolyn mentioned there were a total of thirteen witnesses and they had gotten through ten without much rebuttal. The four officers from New York came in to testify as did Larry's son and daughter.

Other possible suspects were brought in. Greg Swarr, Rizzo, Shoemaker. The only one of the "Coke Machines Gang' left to testify on Tuesday would be Robert Canaveri, and then the State would bring the medical examiner and then rest its case. They would see who the defense called as witnesses before deciding who to call for rebuttal. Certainly, the defense would again call their psychologist to testify as to Smith's intelligence and psychiatric condition, so the state would bring back their psychiatrist for rebuttal.

Carolyn remarked that the state was not calling Bobby Ray Edwards, "Raven," to testify at this trial due to an ongoing investigation. This sounded unusual to me, but I wasn't sure what to make of it. Carolyn also told me about the controversy of the caliber of the gun and bullet that killed JT. Smith said it was a forty-five caliber gun and the bullets recovered were thirty two caliber. How could that be?

Towards the end of our conversation Bob said, "To me the defense seems to hammer two things:

1. Smith never said he did this or that until they planted that idea in his mind. They say all he did was repeat what they (Lisa and Katie) told him. 2. What was Smith's capacity?"

Not to be outdone, the defense brought in a huge chart blowing up the drawing Lisa had done during the interview with Smith. It was a kindergarten style drawing showing the locations of the burglarized house, the country club, the golf course, where the sheriff's body was found, etc. The poster, which was as big as a queen-size bed, took two of the younger defense attorneys to hold. When they got it admitted into evidence and set it down in front of the bailiff and clerk, the bailiff and clerk were completely blocked from the view of the rest of the courtroom.

CHAPTER SEVEN
Retrial Day Five
Tuesday, June 25, 2024

Day number five of the trial was explosive and completely outside the boundaries of anything that had preceded it in either of the trials. In order to present the evidence and motions in an understandable fashion, I will first use my conversation with Attorney Robert Philo that night as he reported from the trial and I tried to understand what was going on. Then, I will present the defense's motion to the judge and her subsequent ruling.

Bob- "The medical examiner testified and Robert Canaveri was next. He was the last witness for the state so they turned it over to the defense and the defense summoned Bobby Ray Edwards 'The Raven'. He was named as an unindicted co-defendant in the latest charging document and they did that because they charged conspiracy to commit burglary and conspiracy to commit murder. You can't have conspiracy with just one person. They said in the indictment that Smith conspired with Edwards to commit burglary and murder. Because it's unindicted that doesn't really charge him, but it puts him on notice that he's a suspect and might be charged. Since he was subpoenaed by the defense, he sought counsel. The counsel told him to show up to comply with the subpoena, but then you can claim the Fifth Amendment. You don't have to testify against yourself if you don't want to. Under these circumstances there was a hearing where the judge went through with him to make sure he understood his rights even though he was represented by counsel. Ultimately he said he understood his rights and he was going to claim the Fifth Amendment which the defense couldn't really object to. The defense got mad and told the judge that the state was conspiring to keep them from having a witness testify by naming him an unindicted co-conspirator. There was a big argument about that. The judge overruled them and said you knew about this before, they told you they were going to do that. The defense is saying now we can't call him and we need him. I don't know and I don't think anyone knows what he would have said to help the defense. They were arguing that there was a ruling in California and the judge said, "We're not in California, we're in Maryland." They cited a similar situation in a case in California and the federal judge ruled in that case the state had to grant immunity so the unindicted co-conspirator could testify without jeopardy. The judge said, "I'm not going to rule that this court has the right to tell the state what to do with regards to immunity." That took a long time."

Me- "Wait a second, Bob. Raven was one of the people Smith said was there that night. He's taking the Fifth because he's guilty?"

Carolyn- "That's what we think."

Me- "He's taking the Fifth. He could actually say, if he was granted immunity, I was there and I saw him shoot the sheriff, etc. and that would be it. So why doesn't the state grant him immunity?"

Bob- "I think they are still hoping that they can get more evidence, one way or another, and they can actually try him. Try Raven also. It's a close thing. Smith said Raven was there and Smith said Raven shot J.T. at one time. Apparently there's no evidence other than Smith's statement that Raven was there. If there was, and he's committing the burglary, then he's as guilty as Smith. Doesn't have to shoot him. They just need some evidence other than Smith's statement that Raven was there."

Me-"What happened first? When did the state decide he was an unindicted co-conspirator? That had to be before the trial started, right?"

Bob- "Yes. When they went back and re-indicted Smith with first degree premeditated murder. We're going to charge him with second degree murder and then, as a part of that, felony murder. Then they decided to charge Smith with burglary. Then they decided to charge him and an unindicted co-conspirator, Raven, with conspiracy to commit burglary and conspiracy to commit murder. Why they did that I don't know except to say Smith conspired with somebody or else you don't have conspiracy."

Me-"When they did that, the defense said we're going to call him as a witness because maybe he's the murderer? Why did the defense want to call him?"

Bob- "We don't know, and they never had to say on the record why they called him."

Me- "Did Raven come up in front of the courtroom and answer questions with every answer being, "I'm taking the Fifth Amendment?" Did the defense attorneys get to ask Raven questions?"

Bob- "No, they weren't allowed to."

Me- "So if you take the Fifth, you don't have to face the defense, you're excused."

Bob- "Just so you'll know, at the same time after the defense said we're going to rest, the judge said that means you're not going to call Smith and they said that's right. The judge did the same thing with Smith to make sure on the record that he knew he had a right to testify and he had a right not to testify. Smith spoke up clearly."

Me-"What happened between the first and second trials to make the state charge Raven?"

Bob- "They didn't actually charge him. They named him in the indictment as being at least one of the people Smith had conspired with, hence the conspiracy. Has to be at least two people getting together to agree to do something."

Me- "After the trial is over I need to talk to Donna Fenton to see what was going on in her mind. By saying he's an unindicted co-conspirator it makes it more obvious that Smith is one of the people who was there. Raven is his best buddy. Could this be the guy he was protecting until his confession? By saying Raven is an unindicted co-conspirator it brings Smith further into the crime."

Bob-"In some ways I think it does. Smith has essentially admitted that he was there. Certainly, he admitted that he pulled the trigger, but it was an accident."

Me- "Did they finish with witnesses today?"

Bob- 'Yes. Each side will have one and a half hours for closing statements tomorrow and then twenty minutes of rebuttal for each side. The defense put up their psychologist and a firearms expert as witnesses. The firearms expert was clearly qualified and gave good testimony. His whole point was based on his looking at bullets and the fact they had rifling on them which meant the thirty-two caliber bullet had not been fired through a thirty-eight or a forty-five caliber gun. He explained why. But the whole point of the thirty-eight and forty-five is nobody really knows what the gun was and Smith said he thought it was a thirty-eight. It was handed to him twenty minutes before he pulled the trigger in the dark, so how could he know if it was a thirty-two or a thirty-eight?"

Me- "I thought the bullets had disappeared and there were no bullets in evidence."

Bob- "He testified from the FBI's report. While I think it was interesting, I don't think it proved anything. If they had recovered the gun and it really was a thirty-eight, then his testimony would have been important because the bullets they recovered didn't come from that gun. Since the gun wasn't recovered and nobody specifically said it was a thirty-eight, I don't think it hurt anything."

Me- "Whole thing with Raven is interesting to me.

Bob- "I learned something today that kind of pisses me off. Becker-Smith in the 1973 interview with three detectives was interviewed the next day and O.W. Sweat was there for that interview. That came out in testimony today!"

Me- "Oh my gosh!"

Bob- "I was sitting there thinking, if he was there and he knew there were two shots and he knew there was a flashlight what the hell happened? I got very angry. They were talking about whether or not the recording of the interview covered the second day. That's when it came out. The second day when he was interviewed there is no recording of that interview. Kind of strange, when you think about it, you record one day and not the next."

Me- "That's weird."

Bob- "I can forgive someone for being biased and a failure of communication. But if you were there the second day and he sat there and said he heard two shots and there was a flashlight and you, O.W. Sweat, knew that was correct and information that hadn't been released, why didn't Smith get arrested?"

Me- "That doesn't make sense to me."

Bob- "He was so focused on Shoemaker.""

Me- "Who said he (O.W. Sweat) was there the second day?"

Bob- "It came from defense counsel. The whole thing was you played the tape from the first day, where's the tape from the second day? The state said the tape covers both days. The defense pointed out at the end of the tape, where there is no more speaking afterward, one of the detectives says this concludes the tape on such and such a day which is the first day. They had carefully listened to that tape."

Me- "I thought the second day they took him out to the scene of the murder and he showed them locations, but they didn't interview him. Maybe that's why they didn't tape it. There wasn't an interrogation and it was just a visit to the site."

Bob- "Once the case is over maybe the defense will give more information about that. I'm assuming they know he was there because Smith told them he was there."

Me- "That's a real curve ball. You would think he (O.W. Sweat) would have at least listened to the first day's tape. Even if all they did the second day was take him out and have him show them where everyone was. O.W. seems confused now and mixes up some of the forty-plus murder cases he was involved in. Did you know when you went back to Maryland for this trial that they were going to name Raven as a co-conspirator?"

Carolyn- "No, we didn't know any of that. That was shocking."

Bob- "We knew they weren't going to bring the first degree premeditated murder charge We knew there was going to be a burglary charge. We didn't know about O.W. Sweat being there the second day. The defense did play Raven's testimony in the first trial, but he really didn't say anything there."

Me- "So many inconsistencies. Maybe due to fifty years. After you listen to the first trial you realize after Rizzo makes those two controlled calls who does Smith want to know about and try to get ahold of? Raven."

CHAPTER EIGHT
Retrial Final Day
Wednesday, June 26, 2024

Bob and Carolyn were eager to talk to me about the last day of the trial and eager to share their opinions about what the outcome would be.

Bob- "We had closing arguments, instructions to the jury on the law. Closing arguments went very well for the state. John told the story again. Then the lead attorney for the defense got up and said the whole thing was wrong, their client wasn't even at Manor Country Club that night and everything was focused on him by mistake and they told him what to say. He kept saying the State had cherry-picked its evidence and he must have said that at least thirty times. To prove it he pulled little excerpts out from different testimony which curiously was cherry-picking that part of it. That's really the only defense they had. He pooh-poohed the testimony of the psychiatrist and said she only spent an hour with Smith. Smith was a poor eighty-three IQ and easily persuaded. They did bring in O.W. Sweat was lead detective in all this and he was there for the 1973 interview; why didn't he do something about this?"

Carolyn- "Collins put up five different things on the screen and Donna objected. It had to be taken down and the judge told the jurors to disregard it."

Bob- "Same thing happened in the first trial. Slide on screen and Donna objected so they made him take that down. When he got done Donna did the twenty minute rebuttal. She laid into him. Went to lunch and then gave them instructions. They had a dinner break and went home and will come back tomorrow."

Me- "Who filled the seat of the juror that was removed and what was the racial/gender makeup of the jury?"

Carolyn- "They didn't pick a young woman who was cracking her knuckles and playing with her hair and looking around. She got released."

Bob- "The jury had young people, middle-aged. More women than men. One female African American. Couple of either Hispanic or mixed-race. I think it's going to be another hung jury. The sympathy factor there. He was duped. They put words in his mouth. I just have the feeling that at least one person there is going to believe that. On the other hand, if they really analyze it, there's no question there was a burglary and there's no question that he was involved in it even if he was duped about the shooting. He certainly wasn't duped about being there. He said he was there. I could conceivably see guilty only on the burglary charge. If someone points out that someone was killed while they were committing that burglary it's felony murder and they don't have to prove he was the one who did the shooting. I don't know."

Me- "Such an unusual case. No physical evidence. I think Raven taking the fifth amendment would be very damaging for him. If Raven wasn't there he should say this is my alibi."

Carolyn- "A couple of days ago something was said about Raven and they said they couldn't comment on that because that's an ongoing investigation."

Bob- "They think Raven might have done it. Defense says you have hamstrung us because you didn't charge him but we can't get him to testify because he's going to take the fifth and you did this as a trick.

Why didn't you charge him? The answer is it's an ongoing investigation. I have to say the defense closing was as good as it could be."

Carolyn- "Donna went over to Smith in her rebuttal and pointed at him and said this is the man that killed Sheriff Hall. She was super! She was really wound up."

Me- "You're staying up there until the verdict?"

Carolyn- "We're staying here until we hear the verdict. I asked Donna today; can I hug you yet? She said no, not yet. No, no. Don't talk to me yet."

Me- "The first time was such a disappointment for her and for Lisa. They both took it so personally."

Carolyn- "One thing that I found contradictory was that Collins brought up that Lisa and Katie said that Smith's apartment was clean and the bed was made. But the trooper who went to pick him up to arrest him said, "Well, it was really messy." That was a contradiction. Collins brought that out. Katie and Lisa said it was very nice yet Trooper Solls who just came back within a couple of hours said no, that's not the way it was."

Bob-"Of course Collins said the trooper had nothing to gain and was not invested in the case whereas Katie and Lisa were. He hit pretty hard on that."

Carolyn- "Nothing more was said. Donna didn't bring that up again."

Bob- "She did bring up that his daughter had said she went to his apartment every day and she had to make the bed, that kind of stuff. But she didn't go to his apartment September first, and when they got there his bed was made. So it wasn't as if she was having to go over there and make the bed every day."

Carolyn- "Donna brought up twice that when the troopers were taking him back to his apartment he asked to be let off a block away so his neighbors wouldn't see he was dropped off by a police officer."

Bob- "That goes to how smart he is."

Me- "Have you been talking to Melvin every night?"

Carolyn- "Yes. Brian is coming up tomorrow. He said he started with this and he wants to see it through. I told him I hate for him to have to drive up. He said he's coming."

CHAPTER NINE

False Confessions

In the second trial the defense tried a new tactic. They wanted to introduce the concept of False Confessions and bring two expert witnesses in to testify on Larrry Smith's behalf. They wanted to educate the jury on the science of what leads to a false confession and why it was possible in this particular case. The state wanted to exclude any witnesses to lend credence to this theory, even questioning whether it truly qualified as a science. The briefings went back and forth until the judge's verdict was rendered. It all started with a brief from the Innocence Project as Amicus Curiae (friend of the court) in support of defendant Larry David Smith's opposition to the state's motions to exclude expert testimony at trial. I use quotation marks when they are used in the brief.

The brief was written by Lauren Gottesman of the Innocence Project and Elizabeth Pearce Zoulias, Acting District Public Defender who was the Local Counsel for Amicus Curiae. I have taken verbatim what I consider the most vital and interesting arguments from their brief:

...research demonstrates the threat that unreliable evidence poses to the truth-seeking function of criminal trials. Nearly twenty-four percent of the individuals exonerated by post-conviction DNA testing were convicted based, at least in part, on their confession-even though they were innocent.

The Innocence Project has a compelling interest in advocating for the admission of expert testimony regarding the phenomenon of and risk factors contributing to false confessions. Such expert testimony never includes an opinion on the voluntariness or truthfulness of the statement at issue, as this would infringe on the jury's role as arbiter of the facts. Rather, expert testimony in this area provides jurors with objective, scientific information about the counterintuitive, psychological research regarding risk factors relevant to the case in question. With such testimony, the jury becomes-if anything-more capable of reaching its own conclusions as to the reliability of the confession evidence... Thus, the admission of expert testimony regarding the scientifically established risk factors for false confession at issue in a case is critical, and particularly so when, as here, the confession is the only direct evidence against the accused.

...jurors have a difficult time relating to the idea that an innocent person would "admit" to having committed a crime...a robust canon of scientific research has developed, resulting in extensive, well-accepted literature on the risk factors for false confession.

...the science underlying the phenomenon of false confession is quintessential material for expert testimony...founded upon reliable, evidence-based methodologies that have produced decades of scientific, peer-reviewed literature...the Innocence Project urges this Court to admit the expert testimony of Dr. Melissa Russano and David Thompson.... for the purpose of educating the jury about the well-established science underlying the phenomenon of false confessions. To hold otherwise would improperly deny the jury a critical tool for reliably assessing the only direct evidence against Mr. Smith-a confession elicited in response to deceptive, coercive interrogation tactics that have been proven by scientists to have the power to induce the innocent to confess.

...because such expert testimony is reliable, admissible, and relevant to the only evidence against Mr. Smith, to preclude it would be to violate Mr. Smith's constitutional right to present a defense.

..."when someone voluntarily admits to wrongdoing, in light of the adverse consequences that will follow, people trust that confession"... Without expert testimony as a guide, jurors are also much less likely to understand how, for example, police deception and promises of leniency increase the risk of false confession..."only 56% of (lay) participants believed that (police deception about evidence) puts innocent people at risk to confess-in contrast to 94% of experts" and that "only 65% believed that explicit promises can have that same effect-in contrast to 99% of experts"...confession experts' in disputed confession cases are significantly more aware of the interrogation tactics and personal vulnerabilities as risk factors in disputed confessions than laypeople.

Consequently, "confessions have more impact on verdicts than do other potent forms of evidence" to such an extent that "people do not adequately discount confessions-even when they are retracted and judged to be the result of coercion." In fact, 22% of exonerees whose convictions rested on confession evidence now understood to be false were convicted despite the availability of exculpatory DNA evidence at the time of trial-such is the power of a confession over jurors.

Additionally, the psychological impact of certain interrogation tactics, such as the "bluff technique"-a tactic at issue here-are particularly counterintuitive and thus unlikely to be identified as coercive without expert guidance. The "bluff" tactic refers to a technique in which interrogators pretend to or imply that they have "evidence without asserting that this evidence necessarily implicates the suspect." For example, if officers tell a suspect that blood or other forensic evidence was collected from the scene and will be tested-thus raising the specter that such evidence may incriminate the suspect-when such evidence either does not exist or will not or cannot be subjected to forensic testing, officers are engaging in the "bluff" technique...experts have determined that such "bluff" tactics can increase the rates of false confessions by as much as 60%-a rate comparable with that of false confessions provided in response to more explicitly deceptive tactics.

...many courts throughout the nation admit relevant expert testimony on the literature underlying coercive interrogation tactics... "a false confession expert can play an important role in explaining to a jury that a 'phenomenon that causes innocent people to confess to a criminal offense exists', and 'the parameters within which one can evaluate a confession to determine its veracity.'"

The science regarding the phenomenon of false confessions and interrogation coercion is grounded in over a century of psychological research examining human behavior and social influence...social scientists have developed various reliable mechanisms with which to study false confessions..."it is the combination of real-life case studies of false confession, experimental research emerging in the 1990's, and community studies that have advanced the scientific basis of the psychology of false confessions."...This "convergence of results-meaning that various studies using different scientific methodologies have produced similar results-adds to the reliability of the research findings. Consequently, today, "the scientific study of false confessions has become a mature subdiscipline of psychology."

Conclusion

...amicus respectfully urges this Court to deny the prosecution's motions to preclude the expert testimony of Dr. Melissa Russano and David Thompson and to admit their respective testimony to educate the jury about the relevant, counterintuitive science underlying the phenomenon of false confessions. Without such testimony, the jury will not have a critical tool with which to reliably assess whether and how the interrogating officers' coercive, deceptive tactics impacted the confession evidence.

Judge McCally read the arguments submitted by the defense asking that expert testimony regarding false confessions be admitted in the trial and then reviewed the prosecution's rebuttal. She ruled "The Court finds the topic of false confessions is not appropriate to present at trial.

CHAPTER TEN
The Retrial Verdict
Friday, June 28, 2024

The trial went to the jury on Wednesday afternoon on June twenty-sixth. They deliberated on Wednesday and then all day Thursday. Late Friday afternoon the jury was about to be sent home for the weekend when they asked the Court for a little more time because they were close to a verdict.

At 6:06 pm, EST, while making phone calls at work the following text message appeared on my phone from Carolyn Philo:

"Not guilty on all counts"

Carolyn and Bob left the courthouse after hearing the verdict and went back to the hotel to pack up and leave town. They didn't want to talk to anyone. I was shocked by the outcome, but I went back to making phone calls to patients.

CHAPTER ELEVEN

Discussion with Dillon Grimm, Defense Attorney Who Spoke to Jurors After the Verdict

Dillon Grimm is a sixth-year associate attorney with Covington whose practice focuses on defending complex class action suits in state and federal court. He also represents clients in a range of commercial litigation matters. He graduated from the University of Virginia with highest distinction in 2013 and was elected to Phi Beta Kappa. He graduated cum laude from Harvard Law School in 2018 and was editor of Harvard Civil Rights-Civil Liberties Law Review. He agreed to discuss his meeting with the jurors after the verdict was read with me.

Me- "What did the jurors say swayed them as far as the verdict?"

Dillon-"I did talk to three or four jurors after the trial. I can give you some of my recollections of what they told us to the extent that that would be helpful. A few things came to mind when I went back and thought about what they told us after the trial. They were very focused on the evidence. Multiple jurors told us that they were very focused on the details. There was a lot of evidence that came in during the trial and we could tell during the trial that they were sort of taking everything in and focused on it. After the trial they confirmed to us that they were looking at it very closely and reviewing it very closely. They also were very focused on the burden of proof. That's something that we talked about in our opening statement and multiple jurors told us that was the lens through which they were viewing the case. Did the State meet its burden? Was there proof beyond a reasonable doubt that the defendant was guilty? They were coming at it from that angle and reviewing all the evidence with that in their minds: has the State met its burden?"

"A couple of other things that I recalled them saying to us were that in our presentation and particularly in our closing statement we tried to be very detailed with the evidence and we showed a number of clips from the interrogation video and multiple jurors told us they appreciated that in our presentation. We embraced all of the evidence; we told them in the closing statement to review it all and they told us it was helpful we played the clips and we gave them "time-stance". Through the clips we were able to show that virtually everything our client said during the interrogation was fed to him by the detectives. They said they appreciated the specificity in our presentation. I'm just looking back at a couple of notes I jotted down. They said that they reviewed the evidence again meticulously while they were back in the jury room and they deliberated for basically three full days. They were back there for a very long time. They told us that they went through all of the evidence with a fine-toothed comb. They told us they watched the interrogation video again and they watched it in a way...they would watch a little bit, pause it, talk about it, and start it again.. When they went through it they told me that what they were doing was seeing who brought up details first. That was an important theme that we talked about in our closing. If you watch the interrogation video, our client doesn't bring up details first. They are fed to him by the detectives, so we provided some examples of that in our closing and encouraged the jury to go look at the tape again for themselves. They said that they did that and when they did they saw that we were right. The details of the crime were fed to our client. The last thing that they told us was that consistent with their focus on the burden, they didn't feel that the State met their burden and that's what it came down to."

Me- "Why do you think the second trial's outcome was so different from the first trial? The first trial, I was told, was ten to two and eleven to one to convict. Why do you think there was such a change?"

Dillon- "I think that part of it could just be you get twelve people from the community as the jury and some of it might just be chance or you get twelve different people on any given day. That might be part of it. I also think in the second trial we focused more on the theme of our client being convinced that he committed this crime and we focused more on showing how all of the details of the crime were fed to him. I think that we certainly argued that in the first trial, but between the first and the second trial we crystallized that theory. You probably know how we tried to offer false confession experts at the second trial and they were ultimately excluded, but that was also helpful for us in preparing for this second trial. Even though the expert testimony wasn't admitted, working with these experts helped us refine our theory of the case. We were able to put on a more persuasive case the second time to show in really granular detail that this wasn't from his memory, this was something that was fed to him."

Me-"This was your first murder case. Did you enjoy working on it? Did you enjoy working with the team that was assembled for the Defense?"

Dillon-"It was an A-Plus team. I can't say enough good things about Jonah and Danny and Kevin and Nick Xenakis who was involved more earlier in the proceedings. Also, we had a couple of really great paralegals who I would be remiss not mentioning, Larissa England and Sarah Applebaum. The team ran like clockwork. Jonah, Danny, and I were the three associates on the team and we worked well together. Kevin was instrumental in guiding us throughout the process. The team was great. It was great to represent our client and vindicate his interest in court. It was also great professionally to get us in court and do some direct examination, some cross examination. It was an incredible experience overall for me."

Me-"How was the work divided among the four lawyers?"

Dillon- "Kevin supervised the team and provided our strategic direction. Jonah. Danny, and I mostly divided up the work among us. For example, I worked with our psychologist, Dr. O'Connell, and I did his direct examination at trial. I worked with Dr. O'Connell to prepare him and to put him on the first trial. Similarly, Jonah and Danny took on witnesses and we divided up the opening."

Me- "How did you feel about your chances of winning after the second trial ended and before the verdict came back?"

Dillon-"We felt positive after our closing statement. We felt like it was an effective trial. We felt like we left it all on the field. We made all of the points we wanted to make. We had the great series of clips from the interrogation and we felt positive that we put on the best case that we could. I think we felt consistently, cautiously optimistic during the trial, recognizing that it's tough to tell. The jury was pretty inscrutable during the trial. We could tell they were paying attention. Sometimes you can read folks' faces and see if they might be trending in your direction or not. We couldn't tell at all. Even though we felt positive about the trial, during the trial a lot is up in the air."

Me- "Did you try to get a different type of juror this time? Was there a different focus? Did you have a consultant working with you to tell you what type of person to pick for the jury?"

Dillon-"We did not have an outside consultant or a jury expert or anything like that. Our paralegal. Larissa England, has a lot of experience working with Kevin and has helped him pick juries. so she provided a lot of help in that respect. I don't think we came with a different mindset about a jury for the second trial. I think in a trial like this you're just looking for someone who has an open mind and is willing to look at the facts and think critically about them and whether the State has met their burden."

Me-"Tell me your impression of Larry Smith."

Dillon- "Larry was great. He was understanding. We worked very closely with him in terms of what we were thinking and he trusted us and that what we were doing was the right way to proceed. He also was steadfast in wanting to fight this and I think that was great that he believed in us, he believed in the case, and ultimately we prevailed. He was great to work with. Just getting to know him a little bit personally I found he's a nice guy who had been living a quiet life for a long time and then got caught up in this. He had put a lot of stuff behind him a long, long time ago."

CHAPTER TWELVE

The Prosecution's Response to My Questions

After the verdict was announced. I reached out by email to Donna Fenton, the lead attorney on the case, for questions I had regarding her thoughts on the case and the outcome. The following are the exchanges by email starting with Carolyn Philo:

Carolyn Philo-July 8, 2024 Good afternoon. I talked to Donna, she said to please email her and yes, she will talk to you. Not sure why she wanted you to email her first.

Michael Weisberg-July 9, 2024 (Donna) Thank you for agreeing to talk to me regarding the Becker-Smith case. I work full time as a physician, so nights or weekends are best for me. However, I can adjust my schedule as necessary...I am looking forward to hearing from you. Michael Weisberg

Michael Weisberg-July 12, 2024 (Donna) if you have any available time this weekend to speak with me that would be great. My phone number is 214-------. Michael Weisberg

Carolyn Philo-July 15, 2024 Good evening. Donna. I mentioned that Michael Weisberg would like to talk to you about the book he is writing about my Dad. I hope you don't mind I have given him your phone number. Thank you again for all your hard work on my Dad's case. Hugs, Carolyn

Donna Fenton-July 16, 2024 (Michael) Good morning. So sorry for the delay in getting back to you. I'm out of town in Nashville. Can we talk next week? Need to confirm time with John and Lauren as I want them on the call as well. For now, everything would have to be off the record. Thanks! Donna

Michael Weisberg-July 16, 2024 (Donna) Thank you very much for getting back to me. l am writing.a book about the Smith case and would need statements I could use in the book for our discussion to be of benefit to me. When do you think you could talk "on the record"? I appreciate you getting back to me. Michael Weisberg

Donna Fenton-July 16, 2024 Would really depend. Now that the verdict is a NG we have liability concerns that we have to be careful about. Lauren-thoughts?

Michael Weisberg-July 23, 2024 Donna, I have a list of questions that I would like you to answer. If there are some you don't feel comfortable answering. I certainly understand. I would greatly appreciate your responses as I am close to finishing the first draft of the book and would love to hear your perspective. Thank you in advance. Michael F. Weisberg. M.D.

1. Tell me about your background. Growing up, high school, college, law school and how you decided to become a lawyer and a state's prosecutor. Your hobbies, family life and anything else you would be able to share.

2. How were you chosen to take this case?

3. Have you gone up against Kevin Collins before and what are your thoughts about prior encounters?

4. How did your strategy in the second trial differ from the first trial?

5. Were you surprised by the verdict? Why?

6. Did you or John talk to any jurors about the trial? What did they tell you about deliberations?

7. Can you give me contact information for any of the jurors?

8. Have you ever prosecuted a case like this before with no physical evidence or witnesses?

9. Ever any plans for other witnesses? Who?

10. Why did you name Raven an unindicted co-conspirator for the second trial?

11. What were you looking for when you picked the jury for the second trial?

12. What are you working on now?

I would appreciate it if you would answer these questions and email your responses back to me. All the best to you and your team. Sincerely, Michael F. Weisberg

Lauren DeMarco Director, Public Affairs Montgomery County State's Attorney's Office: July 24, 2024

Hi Michael

Here is an on the record comment from me:

The Hall family has suffered tremendously and we are extremely disappointed as the State firmly believes justice was not served in this matter. We thank our prosecutors and Montgomery County Police for their tireless work on this case.

We have no comment on the other questions—and I do not have contact info for any jurors.

Lauren DeMarco
Director, Public Affairs
Montgomery County State's Attorney's Office

CHAPTER THIRTEEN

Interview with Kevin Collins, Lead Defense Attorney, After the Verdict

Me-"Tell me about your background, where you grew up, your family, education and anything else you want to include."

Kevin- "I'm first generation college educated. My dad was a plumber and my mother was a nurse. They believed deeply in education. I have a brother who is a tax lawyer, a twin sister who's a cardiologist and my older sister has been the comptroller at a number of big companies. They believed in education. At times my brother and I believed in having too much fun. We went to an all- boys Jesuit high school in the District of Columbia called Gonzaga. It is better known now for having two number one draft picks in this past NFL draft including Caleb Williams. I went to an engineering school in Worcester, Massachusetts. I was an engineer for a couple of years and then started law school at night at the University of Baltimore. It's one of two state law schools in Maryland. I did very well there. I ended up clerking at the State Supreme Court when I graduated in 1992. I had an affinity and a liking for criminal procedure. I was a research assistant for a professor who's now deceased. He was sort of a dean of criminal procedure and wrote a prominent treatise and I was his research assistant. I clerked in the Attorney General's office in the criminal appeals division during law school. Clerked in State Supreme court when I was done. Ended up at a big firm called Venable for about twelve years and then moved over to Covington and Burling in April, 2005. That's kind of my background. I've always enjoyed doing trial work. I've been on the Board of the Public

Defender for about twelve years or more. I was appointed and re-appointed by a couple of different governors. Through that, I guess, it gave me some insight into the public defender's office and I realized these lawyers were overworked, underpaid, and understaffed. What big firms do is they provide an outlet for the public defender, particularly busy district offices that are just overwhelmed with work. So, I started doing these cases, public defender referred cases probably in 2006 or 2007. I've been doing serious criminal cases for about seventeen years. I was a partner at two different law firms, Venable and Covington. I've tried a lot of different cases. I'm nominally a patent litigator so I try patent cases, but I'll try any kind of case, frankly, including homicide and criminal cases. That's my background. I'm married to a physician who is a cardiologist at Johns Hopkins and who I met through my twin sister. My sister and my wife were doing fellowship together at Duke. We have two kids and we both work a lot!"

Me- "How old are your kids? Are they in college? Are they going to be lawyers or doctors?"

Kevin- "I have twins. I have a special needs kid and I have a junior at Northwestern. She's probably going to go to law school although for a while she was trying to figure out if she wanted to follow in her mother's path or her father's path. She's a really fine writer so she's in Northwestern's Medill School which is typically regarded as one of the top journalism schools in the country.

Me-"The twin who has special needs is at home?"

Kevin- "Yes, he's at home. He'll be with us as long as we're above ground I think."

Me- "You told me this past weekend you played golf. Is that your hobby? Do you have other hobbies?"

Kevin- "Not really. I just try and unplug at times. My wife is from Minnesota so her family hunts and fishes. I typically do a Canadian fishing trip most June's other than when we were interrupted by Covid for five years. Hunt and fish a little bit, golf. I used to play a lot more golf but kids and the practice of law sort of got in the way of that. I enjoy politics, reading, and mostly what we do now. We're kind of plugged in twenty-four/seven, so to relax I try to unplug."

Me-"I read where you were on the Law Review at your law school."

Kevin- "I was the associate editor. I graded on. I did very well in law school; applied myself and worked very hard. The University of Baltimore is not super highly regarded outside of this area, but there are a lot of really good lawyers who have gone to that law school, a lot of judges, a lot of prosecutors, Very practice-oriented law school and I'm grateful that I went there."

Me- "If you could, take me from the time where Larry Smith confessed and waived extradition from New York to Maryland to your first appearance in court for him."

Kevin-"I got a call, I don't remember when it was, but the public defender called me and said I've got a case and it's going to require some resources. Interesting case. Could you guys take a look at it? We do what we do in all of these cases, we run a conflicts check to make sure we don't have any issues and to make sure we have sufficient staffing to support it. Obviously this was going to take some resources because you're going back to understanding a factual situation that occurred fifty some years ago. So typically, when these cases come in, a public defender has got a lot of cases or they just need to refer it out. He gave me a call and said would you look at doing this case. That was....how does a gastroenterologist end up getting involved in writing stories?"

Me-"I was an English literature major in college and I won awards as a writer. I always wanted to be a writer. But I also spent time in Boston

Children's Hospital when I was five years-old and wanted to be a doctor from that point on. I was a very sick child. I had these two career goals and I've tried to do both things in my life. I enjoy both, I love both of them."

Kevin- "Well, that's great. My computer seems stuck."

Me- "What I want to know is if it was his decision to withdraw his confession or did you tell him to do that?"

Kevin- "What occurred was on September first, 2022, the officers interrogated him and elicited his statement where he implicated himself in the crime. We think it was a false confession. As we went through the videotape, the more you watch it the facts... at the end of the day he basically admitted to accidentally shooting the sheriff which made no sense. The sheriff was shot in the back of the head. In any event, the detectives elicited this statement and once he got to Maryland, the public defender was representing him for a little bit and he entered a plea of not guilty and we took it over from there."

Me- "Did he change his mind? Did Larry change his mind?"

Kevin- "No, I don't think so. I think the officers convinced him that he was involved in a shooting that he had no recollection of."

Me-"He just thought about it more."

Kevin- "I think you have to understand Larry has an IQ of eighty-three. He has terrible memory issues and he also is pretty compliant. I think it's a stretch to say he changed his mind. I think the officers elicited incriminating statements and once he got counsel he entered a plea of not guilty and that's where we ended up. I think a rational person would say he changed his mind, but I don't know that Larry ever...my sense is the officers with their questioning techniques and feeding him details that he then adopted. They convinced him that he was involved in a shooting."

"The second trial was very different from the first trial. We learned a lot. In between the trials we retained two false confession experts. False confessions are a real thing and there's a real science to support it. Unfortunately, Judge McCally didn't allow either of those experts to testify. She thought that was invading the province of the jury. I respectfully disagree with that but those two expert opinions I think would be very interesting and helped shape the second trial. I think the jury concluded that there was not evidence beyond reasonable doubt for any number of reasons, but Larry has an IQ of 83, he doesn't remember anything, and even in the alleged confession he gets all the basic facts wrong. He got them wrong in 1973; the location of the incident. I mean, certainly he was aware it was at Manor Club. He grew up there. Other than that, the weapon was wrong, the caliber was wrong, where the altercation occurred was wrong. I mean he got everything wrong. The only things he got right were totally unrelated to the shooting. In the second trial it was a very different trial in the way the evidence was presented. I think it would have been a slam dunk, a very easy decision for the jury had the false confession experts actually testified. The judge didn't see that that was appropriate and again, it doesn't matter now. Their expert reports are a matter of public record. We filed them in the event we lost because we thought it's an acceptable area of science, but the judge did not think the jury should hear it."

Me- "Tell me more about how your strategy changed for the second trial."

Kevin- "The first trial was more about Larry was coerced into making these statements. The second trial was Larry was convinced that he was involved but I think it's a subtle distinction. We tried it differently. The State kept harping on there were three confessions: the statement in the precinct up in New York to the detectives and then his statements to his children later that day and the day after. They tried to make the same sort of case, but it all melted into one. Larry was convinced by the detectives that he was involved in the shooting which he didn't remember anything about because he got all of the basic details wrong. That's how we tried the second case."

Me- "More looking at what Larry said. All of the details from 1973 and from his confession were wrong. And it wasn't that he was smart enough to make some things right and some things wrong. He didn't know what he was talking about."

Kevin- "Right. The two pieces of evidence established that. In 1973 he gave a series of interviews when he was trying to get himself out of a jam. He was charged with burglary. He was trying to tell the police he knew something about the shooting. All the basic details he got wrong like the gun, the location of the shooting, how it occurred, the uniform, the clothes that Deputy Sheriff Hall was wearing. He said that he was wearing a standard brown uniform and it was a clear night. Of course, it was raining and Sheriff Hall was wearing his bright yellow raincoat. In 1973 the detectives who knew everything about this crime concluded two things: 1. Larry was lying in an effort to gain leniency; 2. Larry didn't witness the crime. He didn't know what he was talking about. He lacked first-hand knowledge. Then when Corporal Killen re-opens the investigation on the fiftieth anniversary she decides just the opposite. She decides that based on the 1973 statement that he's a self-admitted eyewitness when in fact the detectives in 1973 concluded just the opposite. Corporal Killen and Lieutenant Leggett then set out-they had those sting calls and they tried to get Larry to implicate himself but he really doesn't until they show up and knock on his door on September first. There are so many pieces of evidence that show that Larry didn't know what he was talking about. Larry keeps calling this guy Russo when his name was Rizzo. He didn't even know this guy. This guy is making sting calls and he keeps calling him Russo. Russo keeps telling him we're involved in the shooting and he just denies it. He continues to get everything wrong.but the detectives, again, we didn't fault the detectives, they're trying to solve this cold case and the murder of a law enforcement officer. Yeah, I just think they got it wrong. Sometimes well-intentioned people make mistakes and I think that's what happened here."

Me- "In 1973 there were two days of interviews. The first day was taped and the second day wasn't. Is that correct?"

Kevin- "He was interviewed, if I'm not mistaken. April fifth and April sixth. Let me send you my slides."

Me- "I've done an hour and a half interview with O.W. Sweat who was the initial officer and I understand that at the second trial you were able to bring out that he was there the second day. Is that true?"

Kevin- "He was there."

Me- "That wasn't brought out in the first trial. Why not?"

Kevin- "I don't know. I think there were a lot of objections that were sustained. We tried to get into that, but sometimes the judge makes a call and you're not able to do it."

Me- "At that time, in 1973, O.W. Sweat had been in charge of that case for two years. He knew more about the case than anybody. So, if he said the guy, Larry, didn't know what he was talking about that is key. Is that correct?"

Kevin- "That is absolutely correct."

Me- "That's a slam dunk right there to me."

Kevin- "Absolutely."

Me- "I talked to O.W. now, and he's got some memory issues. I talked to him for an hour and a half and really didn't get anything out of it. But when I look back at the responsibility for the case, if I had known that he was there the second day and he cleared Larry I would have said goodbye."

Kevin- "That's exactly what happened except Corporal Killen drew the exact opposite inference. She said Larry was a self-admitted eyewitness. Even though Sweat concluded in his words. "He didn't put eyeballs on the offense."

Me- "Wow!"

Kevin-"They basically clear him, then these detectives go and convince this elderly guy with cognitive issues and memory issues that he's involved in a shooting. It seems crazy when you listen to the statement. They convince him that he accidentally shot the sheriff. How do you accidentally shoot the sheriff in the front when the fatal wound is in the back of the head. It's just logistically the facts don't make any sense. Yet the State ran with this case. They called it a confession. Confession, confession. confession. It just didn't line up with the evidence."

Me- "He did the 1973 interview because he wanted leniency on his burglary charge. It wasn't an escape charge, is that correct?"

Kevin-"You know, Michael, it's unclear because the records are so crappy. It's probably for both. It might have been for burglary. The burglary occurred in August of 1972 and it's unclear when the escape was. It's unclear if the escape was from a work-release program or from the detention center, but either way he was trying to curry favor with the detectives and get out of the jam he was in. I'll walk you through this. I think it's a pretty decent summary."

Me- "While you're looking for that, can I ask you if you've ever had a case like this before where there's no evidence. No fingerprints, no DNA, no eyewitnesses. Have you ever been on the defense for a case like this before?"

Kevin- "Yeah, I've done a lot of murder cases. I've done, probably north of fifty criminal jury trials. There are a lot of cases that are circumstantial. The answer is yes, but I haven't always gotten the same results. Sometimes there's....just sent you my closing slides minus my notes."

Me. "Thank you. Quick questions now. What was your impression of Larry Smith?"

Kevin- "He has a low IQ. He has memory and cognitive issues."

Me- "Good guy? Nice guy? Hard to say?"

Kevin-"My impressions were in line with what he tested at with Dr. O'Connell. I didn't spend a lot of time with him. I think he had a hard life. He's been on disability for the better part of two decades. Lived by himself. My view of him is consistent with Dr. O'Connell which is low IQ, significant cognitive and memory issues."

Me- "Have you gone up against his team of lawyers before, Donna and John?"

Kevin- "Donna many times. John, my first trial with John. But Donna and I know each other very well."

Me- "Any thoughts you want to tell me about going up against Donna? Typical case compared to what it's been in the past?"

Kevin- "I've tried a lot of serious cases against Donna. She's a formidable prosecutor."

Me-"How did you feel your three young associates did in the trial?"

Kevin- "I thought they were off the charts great."

Me- "How much experience have they had?"

Kevin- "For them it was their first trial."

Me-"Were you surprised by the first trial's verdict?"

Kevin- "No, because I thought the jury was hung early. The first note indicated that they were hung. There's a jury note received in that case indicating they were unanimous on count one but stuck on the rest of the counts. To me what that indicated was, count one was first degree premeditated murder. So, the only rational inference is they found him not guilty of count one. Otherwise, they would not have been dealing with the other counts. They basically told us in the jury note they were stuck and they were out a good bit of time."

Me-"Was there something you looked for in the second jury that wasn't there in the first jury that you think helped you when you were picking jurors?"

Kevin- "No. I would have liked to have seen a lawyer on the jury. I don't think we had one. We're not allowed to keep a lot of details on our jury, like all of our jury sheets go back. I don't know if we had a lawyer on the second jury. I'm trying to remember if we had one that went to law school. On the first jury we had a couple of lawyers and, you know, it's hard for lay people to understand burdens of proof and the need for the government to prove its case beyond a reasonable doubt. That's the feedback we got from the first jury. There were a couple of lawyers who kind of held the line and for that we're grateful. We ultimately got to the right result in the second trial. I mean, obviously the State doesn't agree. Have you watched the interrogation at all?"

Me- "I have watched it."

Kevin-"The more you watch it, the more it doesn't make any sense. What we found out from these false confession experts is particularly for people with memory issues. When the detectives feed particularly false facts they're kind of adopted by the defendants in these situations for whatever reasons. Ultimately in this confession, the defendant makes some incriminating statements in a pretty difficult environment. The more we watched it the more we said this doesn't make any sense."

Me- "The State told me that on the other charges besides first degree premeditated murder the jury was eleven to one or twelve to two guilty. Is that not true?"

Kevin- "I don't know. Michael. There were more in favor of finding guilt than acquitting. The first trial was very helpful in terms of us thinking of how to retry the case. Ultimately we embraced this interrogation because basically that was the only evidence and it didn't make any sense. The incriminating statements he made, when you look at powerpoint slide fourteen, Larry got all the basic facts wrong: the location of the bullet, the location of the body, who was there, the weather, Sheriff Hall's clothing, and the murder weapon. In his statements in 1973 and 2022 he identified three different types of weapons none of which matched the bullets."

Me- "Do you think that having a firearms expert at the second trial helped you?"

Kevin- "We believe he helped because Corporal Killen, as I said in my closing argument, I think they engaged in tunnel vision. All of this evidence pointed in different directions and pointed to Larry not being involved. But there were also statements by Corporal Killen and some of the state's witnesses that overstated the evidence. The bullets I think were lost as the result of the FBI doing their own analysis. Like Corporal Killen opined and testified that it was possible for a thirty-two caliber bullet to be fired from either a thirty-eight or forty-five caliber gun. I think. if I'm not mistaken, the caliber of the bullet that killed Deputy Sheriff Hall was a thirty-two."

Me- "That's correct."

Kevin- "Our ballistics experts said there's not a chance in hell that a thirty-two caliber bullet could be fired out of a thirty-eight caliber revolver or even a forty-five. It might get down the chamber, but it would not have the marks and grooves that are normally imparted to a bullet that's spinning down the chamber. If you're familiar with geometry, they have all kinds of different marks. This is where I think Corporal Killen was more of an advocate and to me oversold what the evidence was. I don't blame her. She's trying to solve the case, but she overstated what the evidence was."

Me- "Did you talk to the jurors after the second trial to get an idea of their thoughts?"

Kevin- "I did not because the next morning I was flying out to Minnesota and I didn't wait around to talk to the jurors. Some of my colleagues did and we have a great picture of Larry with the associates."

Me- "What did Larry say to you after the verdict?"

Kevin- "He understood enough to know when the acquittals were read and he grabbed my hand. He's not an emotional guy, but he understood enough to know he got his life back. He grabbed my hand and I grabbed his hand. When the jury came back with that verdict, all of the questions were answered in the right way for him, otherwise he would spend the rest of his life in jail. He was very happy, very appreciative."

Me-"How did you find out that O.W. Sweat was present that second day in 1973? How did you get that information? Was that something the State was trying to keep from you?"

Kevin- "No, the more we looked at the evidence there were detective notes, they were like reports. They talked to Larry on the fifth and sixth. I don't know what days of the week, but they talked to him on two consecutive days. Here's what happened. On the fifth they recorded that statement that ultimately was on the reel to reel tape that then was reformatted into a digital version so that it could be played. That's what Corporal Killen relied on to say that Larry was on the scene. That was the first of three sort of interviews with Larry. Later on the fifth they took him to the crime scene and had him identify where certain things allegedly were. He got it all wrong. Well, O.W. Sweat interviewed him the next day and he confronted him with details, saying basically you got all this wrong. Are you sure it's this or are you sure it's that? He stuck to it. That's why O.W. Sweat concluded Larry did not have eyes on the offense, he concluded Larry did not witness. Corporal Killen hears the first part of these three interviews and concludes just the opposite."

Me- "Let me give you some names and give me your thoughts. Leslie Becker, Larry's brother. Do you have any thoughts about him or his role in this? In 1972 he told police to contact my brother, he knows about the killing of the officer."

Kevin- "I think Leslie is dead, right?"

Me- "He's dead."

Kevin-"I don't think any of these kids had anything to do with it. I don't know anything about Leslie. I think Leslie and Larry were involved in that daytime burglary in the Aspen Hill/Glenmont area and were locked up. We're going back fifty years. When law enforcement officers were shot, obviously it's a big deal now. But back then it was the talk of the community and I just think these guys heard a lot of different things. Particularly for Larry, he's living in basically a teen center at the time. I don't know that Leslie was involved. My sense is it was somebody else who hasn't been identified."

Me-"How did you feel about how the prosecution handled Raven in the second case making him an unindicted co-conspirator?"

Kevin-"I think that was a stunt and I think it was a really... We filed a paper on that. That, I thought, was not appropriate. I think that was an effort to preclude Raven from testifying. Raven testified at the first trial. He was a state's witness. He was Larry's best friend growing up. He testified that he wasn't involved and he had no knowledge that Larry was involved. Raven knew Larry before the shooting and had a relationship with him afterwards. To me that's a very helpful fact. The problem is when you call that guy a co-conspirator of a murder he can't take the stand and take the fifth amendment in front of a judge. One could argue it was an effort to prevent us from putting on favorable evidence. The judge disagreed, but I sent that motion before I filed it to any number of distinguished lawyers and even other judges and they were appalled at the conduct of the state's attorney in this case."

Me-"I couldn't understand it."

Kevin-"I called it a stunt. I called it a stunt in open court."

Me- "Is Mark Jensen, the driver, dead?"

Kevin- "Yes, I think the testimony was that he was dead. Don't quote me."

Me- "Because he would have been someone that probably would have been there, too. You keep hearing his name brought up but he never came to testify"

Kevin- "I think he died."

Me- "There was a difference in the look of Larry Smith between trials. At the first trial he had a shaved head and was thin. At the second trial he had long hair and gained weight. Any reason for that or just from being in jail it happened? Did you want to have him look differently?"

Kevin- "No, we don't have any say in that. He was living by himself and he was eating very small meals. I think in jail he was probably fed a lot of carbs and he can't exercise because he has a serious cardiac issue. There were arrangements made for the second trial. There was an issue with the elevator where the jury had to be kept on a different floor because apparently from the back of the holding cells Larry couldn't walk down a flight of steps due to cardiac reasons. He's got a serious heart issue. My sense was he was living a pretty spartan life in upstate New York. Not a lot of food, on disability, maybe Medicare and Medicaid. When he got to the jail he was fed a lot of baloney sandwiches with a lot of bread. That's the way it was."

Me-"Any additional thoughts about the second trial that made such a difference in the outcome?"

Kevin- "We were basically saying in our closing argument that this was a false confession and we told the jury to go back and look at the recorded statements as many times as you want. You're going to find that the facts that Larry says that implicate him were all fed to him by the detectives. I think the jury ended up watching it over and over again and I think they concluded the same thing we did. It didn't make any sense. In rebuttal Donna gets up and starts saying there's no such thing as a false confession. That's just wrong. I don't think the jury bought what she was saying and I think the jury ultimately bought what we were saying. I think the main thing we embraced was we weren't as concerned about what he was saying. just the process by which it was elicited. I think that was the focus of what we were trying to get out."

Me- "Tell me about your firm's attitude towards this type of pro bono case."

Kevin- "We use this as development opportunities for young lawyers. We do a really good job. Our firm supports it. We don't charge for our time. It would shock you if I told you the equivalent of what it would have been in terms of fees had we been charging, but again we do it as a matter of public service and pro bono."

Me- "Do you have any thoughts about what you think happened to Sheriff Hall that night or anything else to say about that?"

Kevin- "I think Larry Smith is innocent. I think he was talked into making statements by hard- charging detectives that wanted to solve a case. I'm not alleging bad faith; I'm just saying they were trying to close an unsolved mystery of the murder of a law officer, Larry wasn't involved because everything he said about it was totally wrong. I mean he knows Manor Country Club and he grew up in a house near there. He lived around the area and that was all he knows."

Me- "Do you think there is any way Larry would talk to me?"

Kevin- "We asked and he said he wasn't interested."

CHAPTER FOURTEEN
Déjà Vu All Over Again

It was amazing to me how similar the two most famous cold cases in Montgomery County were. I read *The Last Stone* by Mark Bowden a second time just to make sure that so many of the details of the Lyon sisters' abduction, rape, and murder by Lloyd Welch were identical to the murder of Deputy Sheriff J.T. Hall. Obviously both cases occurred in the 1970s in Montgomery County, Maryland, and both cases went unsolved for years. However, there were many other striking details that connected these two seemingly unrelated crimes.

The Accused Men Were Very Similar

Both Lloyd Welch, who was convicted of first degree murder in the Lyon sisters' case and Larry Smith were in their late teens when the crimes occurred that they were associated with. At the time the crimes occurred, both men had dropped out of school for a period of years and were living on the streets and in the woods of Montgomery County. Not a lot of details of their homeless existence were available, but both had a history of malfeasance. Lloyd had a history of burglary, assault and battery, while Larry was involved in day time burglaries.

Both men had screwed up parents. Lloyd admitted he "had a screwed up father" and "never knew my real mother." From Mark Bowden's book *The Last Stone*, Lloyd says, "My father killed my mother when I was two." His father, Lee Welch, driving drunk, had crashed their car, killing Lloyd's mother, Margaret Ann, who at the time was pregnant with twins. Lee was convicted of manslaughter and went to prison." From Bowden's book we also learn that Lloyd's father abused him. Larry's mother was an alcoholic who was so inept at taking care of her children that it was safer for them to live in a series of foster homes. Larry's father was a truck driver who was never around except to impregnate his mother.

A major turning point in both men's lives occurred at the age of seven. Lloyd was living in a foster home at age seven when Lee, his father, reappeared with his new wife at the foster home and took Lloyd back to live with them. Although this sounded like a positive development in Lloyd's life, the physical, mental, and sexual abuse he suffered at the hands of his father made his life a living hell. At the age of seven Larry Smith and his three siblings were adopted by the Becker family which ended their constant movement from one foster home to another. Again, this seemed like a positive turn in Larry's life. Instead, just like Lloyd, Larry's seeming good fortune turned bad as he could never fit in with his new family and was eventually thrown out of the house to live on the streets.

Finally, when the cold case team confronted each man, neither could remember having an interview with the police thirty-eight and fifty years before, respectively. From *The Last Stone*, Lloyd Welch, "I just don't remember going to a police station and giving a statement and taking a polygraph test. I mean, I honestly don't believe that. I mean, well, not believe. I just don't remember it. It was at a mall? What mall?" Larry throughout his conversations with Rizzo and the detectives denied ever having an interview with the police in 1973.

Two Detectives in Cases Overlap

Chris Homrock was the detective who got the Lyon Sister Case moving after thirty-eight years. He joined other detectives on the cold case team in 2011 and by 2013 he was the only one left on the squad. He went back through the entire case file and found the six-page transcript of Lloyd Welch's statement given one week after the Lyon sisters' abduction, Chris had a suspect in mind, Ray Mileski, who had a history of similar offences and had died in prison. Mileski had a limp and in Lloyd's statement he said the man who took the girls had a limp. Chris assembled the team of detectives to investigate what other information Lloyd Welch could provide as a witness, and he oversaw the investigation.

For the J.T. Hall murder Chris Homrock was now a detective sergeant in the Cold Case Division who was given the responsibility of opening up and investigating the murder. He again put together the team of detectives to work on the case, choosing Lisa Killen, Sarah White, and Katie Leggett.

Katie Leggett was the other detective who was part of both cold case teams. She entered the Lloyd Wech case as a polygraph expert and did such outstanding work on Lloyd's lie detector test that she became a permanent part of the team. By the time the Hall murder case was reopened. Katie was a full-time cold case detective who knew the ins and outs of dealing with a case that had been scrutinized and abandoned by many capable detectives.

Both of the Accused Made Statements Early On

Larry Smith was in prison in 1973 for burglary when he went to the prison officials and told them he had information on the Deputy Sheriff's murder. This was eighteen months after the murder had occurred, and the case was still fresh and on the minds of the Montgomery County Police Department.

Lloyd Welch went back to Wheaton Plaza Mall one week after the Lyon sisters disappeared. He initially told his story to a mall cop who called the police. Two detectives came to the mall immediately and drove Lloyd to police headquarters to give his statement. Neither Larry Smith or Lloyd Welch would have been linked to their respective cases if they hadn't gone to the police voluntarily early on.

Both of the Accused Were Dismissed by the Initial Detectives Who Interviewed Them

Lloyd Welch gave a detailed story about what happened to the Lyon sisters at the Wheaton Plaza Mall. In The Last Stone's first chapter he told of seeing "two little girls who fit the Lyon sisters' description... talking in the mall to an older man with a tape recorder." Lloyd offered a detailed description "of the man." Lloyd related that "he'd overheard the man explaining to the girls that he recorded people's voices and then put them on the radio. This same story had been in all the news reports." "Lloyd said he later saw both girls leaving the mall with the man and had seen them again outside as they drove off." Lloyd went on to describe seeing the man outside the mall with the two girls, and the three of them getting into a "red Camaro" which he said had "white seats"..."a dent in the right rear end, and the taillight busted out." Lloyd then "went on to offer a startling spate of additional details about the car". "In a final flourish, Lloyd added that the man he had seen leaving with the girls "walked with a little limp".

"Lloyd was then given a lie detector test which he flunked. Flustered, he admitted that he'd made up everything about the car and about seeing the tape recorder man with the girls outside the mall...The detectives dismissed him, no doubt annoyed". "The six-paged typed transcript of the interview went into a ring binder with all the other stray bits. A one-page report was written up. At the top, (Detective) Hargrove wrote, "LIED."

Larry Becker-Smith's conversation with the police was recorded on a reel-to-reel tape. He said he was a witness to the shooting of Deputy Sheriff Hall and named the shooter as well as all of the boys who were present at the country club that night. However, he got so many of the details wrong that the detectives interviewing him did nothing. They thought Becker was trying to reduce his sentence for burglary and escape and knew nothing about the shooting. He went back to jail to finish his entire sentence and the reel-to-reel was mislabeled and put into the J.T. Hall cold case file.

Something Found by Cold Case Detectives in Case File Led to Lloyd Welch and Larry Smith Becoming Persons of Interest

When Detective Chris Homrock looked at the Lyon Sister cold case file, sitting on top was the six-page interview with Lloyd Welch. He immediately deduced that this could be a valuable piece of evidence and set out to find Lloyd. Also in the file was a police artist's sketch of a suspicious young man who had been harassing young girls at the Wheaton Plaza Mall on the day the Lyon sisters were abducted. The sketch had been done using the description of this man given by a teenage girl who the man had been following along with her friends. When the cold case detectives looked at the sketch, it looked eerily similar to the photograph they had of Lloyd Welch at that age.

Detective Lisa Killen went through the cold case file of Deputy Sheriff Hall slowly and carefully. Almost all of the file had been looked over by many detectives and there was nothing new to be learned. However, the reel-to-reel tape labeled "Interview with Richard Hobart' needed to be listened to and accounted for since Hobart's name and the license plate number of his parent's car appeared in J.T. Hall's notepad. Once the tape was transformed to a format she could listen to, Lisa and then Katie both agreed that Larry Becker was a person of interest who they needed to find.

Katie Leggett's Interrogation Technique Uses the Same Strategy in Both Cases

In both cases, Katie Leggett's interrogation method stood out as a determining factor in getting a guilty verdict for Lloyd Welch on first degree murder charges and getting Larry Smith to confess to killing Deputy Sheriff Hall. When I read through her interrogation of both suspects, I found significant overlap in the words and methods used.

Interrogation of Lloyd Welch by Katie Leggett as recounted in *The Last Stone* by Mark Bowden:

"She (Katie) said she had made mistakes in her life and that he (Lloyd) was really no different from her in a fundamental way. We've all done things that could have really wound us up in bad situations."

Katie-"I've actually had people write letters from prison thanking me for treating them the way I do... As I've grown up I've realized that I'm not perfect, so who am I to judge other people?"

Katie-"...I think you're a decent guy."

Katie-"In my heart of hearts. I believe there's some part of you that knows something more than you are giving us. I don't think you're a bad guy. I think you've made mistakes in your life."

Katie- "Is it possible you have seen them again since then?" "I can't say yes or no on that," said Lloyd... "You can interpret it any way you want." Katie-" No! What you just said is, you can't say yes or no." "Yeah, but I can't!" Lloyd complained loudly. Katie-"Again, that's like being kind of pregnant!"..."It's not an answer.. You're probably smarter than me, to be honest with you, because you've lived a lot of life, okay? The bottom line is it can't be both ways."

"Katie noticed the change. She said Lloyd's body language showed he was being deceptive and suggested that he was scared."

"She (Katie) buttered Lloyd up at length, going on about how much better a person he was than the rest of his family...They (the detectives) were on his side!"

"We're sitting here trying to give you the benefit of the doubt," she (Katie) said. "The last thing we want to do is pin this on somebody who didn't do it."

"Katie sometimes tried to simply overwhelm Lloyd. She would start talking, throwing out ideas, her words flowing in great improvisational gusts, easing from one concept to the next, alternately flattering, reasoning. bargaining, confronting, empathizing. Mark (another cold case detective) called it her superpower: he joked that sometimes suspects would confess just to shut her up."

"Katie played stubbornly on his conscience, stressing how certain she was that he had one, what a truly decent fellow he was at heart, how in her eyes he was always trying to do the right thing, tenaciously egging him on to display this inherent decency."

Kate to Lloyd-"You're a smart guy. You're one of the smartest people I've met."

Interrogation of Larry Smith by Katie Leggett

Katie-"My brain is crazy and I forget everything."

Katie-"You have a very good memory, better than mine. Don't remember burglary?"

Katie- "I don't want you to get jammed up with murder."

Katie-"I do believe you became a very good man...You have to know by television shows you watch that the police already know the truth before asking questions. Don't insult my intelligence by lying to me."

Katie-"This is shit going sideways....You're a completely different person now than you were then. Larry has lived a good life..."

Katie-"I think you're in a good place."

Katie-"That's like being kind of pregnant...You're struggling with something."

Katie-"I want to make sure I'm not upsetting you."

Katie-"Do you feel like you're ready to tell me who shot him? I don't want you to stop here. I know you ran but you saw him get shot first. Either you or somebody next to you shot him. I'm feeling what is cost or benefit of you telling me the truth. We already know a lot of the truth. We know you saw it because you said it yourself... took the time to get to know you. I think you're a good guy who has cleaned up his life. I'm not here to mess with that. Imagine how your daughter would feel if you got shot. There's a story here. The security guard wasn't even supposed to be there. I want to know if it was an accident or someone went boom-boom!"

Katie- "I want you to trust me."

Katie-"Do you feel we treated you fairly?"

Katie- "The family just wants closure."

Katie (after Larry's confession of shooting Deputy Sheriff Hall) "I very much appreciate you. I had a vibe you were a good guy...It's important to me that people feel they were treated with respect."

Katie- "Do you feel you were forced?"

Katie-"Do you feel you were respected?"

Each Case Had a Police "Hold-Back"

It is not uncommon in criminal cases for police to hold back evidence from the public. The police can then see whether or not the suspect is able to discuss this evidence in their interrogation which would signal their guilt.

In the Lyon sister abduction and murder, the clothing the Lyon sisters were wearing had never been made public. Lloyd Welch correctly described the clothes the girls were wearing.

In the Deputy Sheriff Hall murder it was never made public (at least from available newspaper stories) that there were two shots fired at the deputy sheriff that night and that he held a flashlight. Larry Smith mentioned the two shots multiple times and relayed the fact that J.J. Hall held a flashlight in his interview in 1973.

In Both Cases Evidence Held by The Police/FBI Went Missing and Was Never Recovered

In the Lyon sister case a tooth was found belonging to a twelve year-old girl (age of the older Lyon sister, Sheila) buried on the mountain in Virginia where the girls' bodies were thought to be burned and buried. It was supposed to be sent back to Maryland for analysis, but it disappeared and was never found.

In the Deputy Sheriff Hall case the deputy's flashlight and the two bullet fragments (one from inside Deputy Hall's head) disappeared while being held by the FBI and were not available as physical evidence for Larry Smith's trial.

CHAPTER FIFTEEN
CONCLUDING THOUGHTS

"Life is a dream, Michaela," my father always said. He had a way of adding -la or -ala to his children's names to make them sound more Yiddish. I became Michaela and my brother, Perry. was Perryla. I have thought a lot about my father's summation of life since his death, looking to find the meaning since he never explained to me why he felt this way.

What did he mean by life is a dream? Most likely he meant that life shared all of the good that a dream has to offer. Unlike a nightmare, a dream is a pleasant experience which allows you to explore and participate in things you'd never be able to do awake. Life, like a dream, has endless possibilities, but also like a disappearing dream when we awaken our lives are finite so each moment must be treasured and enjoyed.

But what else could "life is a dream" mean? Could it mean that in both life and in dreams we are really asleep and we stumble from one occurrence to the next without fully comprehending or appreciating what took place? If life is a dream, why are we able to quickly terminate the bad or uncomfortable dreams by simply waking up, but we are unable to do this in life. In life we have to deal with the bad, the evil, our failures as well as possible and we don't have that magic turn-off button of waking up that a dream has.

I prefer to look at life as a journey; we start off as knowing nothing and relying completely on others and then our journey takes each of us through our own unique stages of life. Life's big journey is made up of a succession of smaller journeys, and I like to look back at my writing of A Second Shot as a two year journey in my life that I will always treasure.

What makes a journey fulfilling and a great experience? First, there are the people you meet along the way. Carolyn and Bob Philo became my friends, my confidants, and substitute parents during the two years. We spent a lot of time together and got to know each other well. They consoled me after the deaths of my father, mother-in-law, and mother, and always put my health and well-being before anything I might write. They still check in with me by phone or text to make sure my heart and health are doing well. Their daughter, Carrie, was always a delight to be around. She is super- intelligent and had great insight into this case as well as into people in general. She gave me a lot of background information I used in this book and was always receptive to questions.

The members of the Philo/Hall family are outstanding people. The dinner at the country club I spent sitting between cousins Frank and John Michael stands out. They were smart, street-wise men with great senses of humor. They had seen it all in their law enforcement days and were able to bring their careers into focus for me. I always enjoyed seeing them, talking to them, and learning from them.

Katie Leggett is a remarkable detective. She has a lot of amazing skills, but I think her ability to empathize with people and to "read" them stands out. I was in awe listening to her for the two hours we talked on the phone. She doesn't hold anything back; she tells it like it is. If there is a Cold Case Detective Hall of Fame, she should be one of the first inductees.

Kevin Collins is a brilliant trial lawyer who opened my eyes to the possibility of Larry Smith being innocent. He also taught me that what we observe in the courtroom during a trial is just the tip of the iceberg related to what is really going on. There are motions filed, expert witnesses proposed and prepared, strategies and presentations being sharpened like a pencil all outside of the courtroom that we know nothing about. Kevin impressed me with his knowledge, his integrity. and his devotion to his craft.

So this journey was a ship filled with people on board who made it fascinating and who brought out all kinds of emotions in me.

Every journey I've taken in life has furthered my education. I want to grow in knowledge as long as I'm alive. The amount of things I learned on this journey was staggering. I had considered law as a career briefly when younger, but never pursued it and never immersed myself in it until this case. I have an appreciation for the role of the judge now in orchestrating a case from beginning to end and I see what lawyers go through on a regular basis. I learned a lot about overcoming tragedy and loss from the Philos. Their son, Eddie, who J.T. Hall made sure to always look out for, dealt with debilitating schizophrenia. Carolyn and Bob stood by him and helped him until he died too young. Carrie and her husband also did everything in their power to enhance and prolong Eddie's life.

I learned that in any trial you have to be open-minded going in. Prior to Larry Smith's first trial I'd had a year of thinking he was definitely guilty and the trial was just a formality to register his guilt in the courtroom. I learned about false confessions and the science behind them which I knew nothing about before. When Carolyn Philo told me the murderer had confessed and was being extradited from New York to Maryland I thought game over, let's just hear how brilliantly the cold case detectives solved this case after fifty years. I learned that a confession, like any other piece of evidence, has to be carefully examined and critically considered.

The homeless crisis is raging throughout our country now, but it was present in a certain segment of the population in the 1970s. Both Larry and Lloyd (from the Lyon Sister case) had to deal with living on the streets from their teen-age years. Both men were survivors, but it certainly stunted their educational and psychological growth. It led me to wonder what we are doing in 2024 to the thousands of homeless people in our country and how will they and their children develop. I concluded that one of our top priorities as a society should be to get these people off the streets and into houses.

My Thoughts About the Verdict

I think that both the prosecution and the defense did outstanding jobs in presenting their cases to the jury in the Hall Murder Trial. There were very strong points that argued in favor of each side.

From the prosecution's case, I was swayed by the three confession idea. If Larry didn't participate in the murder of J.T. Hall, why would he tell the two closest people in his life, his daughter and son, that he did after confessing to the detectives. I was also swayed by the prosecution showing that in the interview in 1973 Larry kept saying two shots and that the security guard carried a flashlight. Both of these were accurate pieces of evidence that I could not find publicized at that time.

Katie Leggett made a statement to me that I took to heart: "I've never seen an innocent person confess to murder." Katie is an extremely erudite person who may seem to ramble on in an interrogation but knows exactly where she is going. Her statement weighed heavily on my mind when I considered the outcome of this case.

What factors would lead me to believe Larry Smith was innocent? First, a jury of his peers found him innocent of all charges. They had no bias or preconceived notions and they deliberated in a manner that I think was superior to the jury in the first trial who I could only conclude "worked hard." The second trial's jury broke Larry's confession down into workable pieces and tried to decide if each piece was from Larry's memory or from the detectives' mouths. By doing this they concluded, as Kevin Collins said, that Larry had been "fed the facts."

The second thing that would argue for innocence is the whole notion of false confessions. I was amazed when I read about the incidence of false confessions in our judicial system. Larry would seem to be the poster child for a lot of the characteristics found in someone who would make a false confession: his low IQ, his poor memory, his medical issues, his desire to please, and his compulsive lying would all be red flags that his confession needed to be examined with the most delicate, finely tuned instruments available.

FINAL WORD

History is written by the victors.
Sir Winston Churchill

In the end, I feel Larry David Smith was innocent of the murder of Deputy Sheriff J.T. Hall. Both sides made compelling cases and the arguments given by each side seem to cancel out the opposing arguments. What is the deciding factor for me in analyzing this case? It all goes back to one of the first people I interviewed for this book, Detective O.W. Sweat. O.W. Sweat was in charge of the case and knew far more about it than anyone. He had a spotless record: he solved every murder case he investigated until the one case came up that he wanted to solve the most, the Deputy Sheriff J.T. Hall murder. Sweat was an impeccable detective who was so good at solving murders that the department's lieutenant tried to get all the murders assigned to him. In 1973, eighteen months after Sheriff Hall's murder, the man with the most knowledge about this case and the man with the greatest reputation of closing murder cases was present when Larry Becker-Smith was interviewed by the police. Sweat got to go with Becker-Smith to the murder scene and see Becker-Smith point out just what he witnessed on October twenty-third, 1971. Sweat's conclusion: "He (Becker-Smith) didn't put eyeballs on the offense." In other words, Larry Smith was not there.

The verdict was, of course, a tremendous disappointment to the Philo and Hall families who have waited over fifty years for justice. I have gotten together with Carolyn and Bob a few times since the trial ended and they have resumed their normal lives. They don't talk about the case or the verdict. They appreciate all the work the detectives and prosecutors did on their behalf and speak of Lisa Killen and Donna Fenton like they were family. Their daughter, Carrie, has moved with her family to Houston which is where Carrie's son and daughter live with their families. I keep asking Carolyn when she and Bob are going to move to Houston and she replies, "But all of my doctors are here." I understand. I've gone from being a writer chronicling the most important event in Carolyn's life to being her doctor again. And that's the way it should be.

POSTSCRIPT

by Carolyn and Bob Philo

So, what did we, Carolyn and Bob Philo, learn from all this? First, as a family member of a victim of an unsolved crime, never assume it can't be solved and never give up reminding the police that it needs to be solved. Although it has been ages since I, Bob, left the Montgomery County Police Department in 1973 to practice law, we both continued to stay in touch with the department and the officers that we knew and the ones who we came to know by active participation. We make annual trips to attend the Law Enforcement Memorial Ceremonies in Montgomery County and the annual conventions of the Montgomery County Police Alumni Association, even though we moved to Texas in 1980 and the trips back were long. But face to face serves as a better reminder of things undone.

Carolyn was faithful to call the Montgomery County Police Department from time to time to see what was going on with the cold case. Sometimes the answer was "nothing" or "we have no new leads"; occasionally it was "we have a new detective assigned to the case and he is going over the file." We knew that there was very little physical evidence to point to the identity of the shooter. It was raining that night. There were no fingerprints at the scene or in the nearby home that had been burglarized. It was known that more than one person must have been involved in the burglary based on the amount and size of the items stolen in the burglary and carried across the golf course to the parking lot where J.T. was shot. There was no such thing as DNA evidence in

1971. And no one had doorbell cameras then - no CCTV either. But the lack of those things was not a reason to give up hope.

Second, we were reminded through our conversations with other police officers who were working there in the 1970s that the lead detective had focused on and was "sure" that one of the five boys who had tried to break into the coke machine that night, Norman Shoemaker, Jr., was the shooter. Why? Because he was known to be "bad" (even though his father was a Maryland County Police Sergeant) and his father refused to let the lead detective interview his son about the shooting.

For decades some MCP officers believed Norman Shoemaker, Jr. was the shooter as rumors circulated. Ultimately, after 50 years, a new look at the files and thorough review of all the evidence (including the reel-to-reel tape which had not been reviewed before) and following an interview with Norman, he was cleared. But no one knew that until Smith was arrested. Carolyn and I personally apologized to Norman for all the years he was a known suspect.

Cousin Frank Hall explains the constant problem of tunnel vision by an investigator. Every law enforcement officer needs to understand that they can suffer from it and how it affects the ultimate outcome. In this case, it certainly delayed the resolution; it could (and should) have been solved in 1973 when Becker/Smith was captured after his first escape and then interviewed.

Third, another thing law enforcement officers need to know concerns facts about a crime which are not released to the public. In this case the fact that there were two shots fired at J.T. and that he had a flashlight needed to be documented somehow so that if the case went cold those working on it later would know what information was withheld. If the three detectives who interviewed Becker/Smith in 1973 had known about the two shots and the flashlight the first day of the interviews when O. W. Sweat was not present, they might (and should) have realized that Becker/Smith knew two things that had been withheld, and he must have been present when J.T. was shot. But the purpose of their interview was not to find the shooter, they were trying to determine if Becker/Smith had any credible information to justify some leniency in punishment for escaping.

But there is a problem with putting the withheld-from-the-public information in a crime report. Those reports are generally available to the public through formal freedom of information requests under state laws. It may be necessary to put that information in a special kind of report rather than in the initial or follow-up crime report. It may be necessary to obtain the State Attorney General's official opinion on how to do that so that such reports are exempt from discovery by the public.

The fourth thing we learned from the two trials is that police officers need to be more careful how they word opinions in their reports that someone did not do something, or say something, or see something. In this case, the three detectives who interviewed Becker/Smith in 1973 apparently knew little if anything from the police reports of the murder. Yet they concluded and wrote in their report that he wasn't there at all. And the next day, when O. W. was present with Becker/Smith at the crime scene reenactment, he concluded that Becker/Smith "never had eyes on" the murder. When that came out at the second trial, it probably significantly affected the jury's verdict. When police are writing their opinions in reports, using terms like "based on today's interview, it appears that..." are much better than "he wasn't there" or "he never had eyes on."

Fifth, another "police issue" learned at the trials. It is very important to keep written logs of any evidence that is transported or sent somewhere else to be examined and what happened to that evidence - was it returned, and if not, why not. In this case one (or both) of the bullets shot at J.T. along with his flashlight which was hit by the first shot, were sent to the FBI for examination there. But they are not in the evidence file and there is no record of what happened to them. The "missing evidence" was highlighted by the defense during cross examination and in their closing argument. It was very likely another factor in the second jury's not guilty verdict. Good documentation of what happened to the bullet and flashlight - even that they were both damaged by acid from the bullet's penetration of the flashlight - would prevent doubt about what occurred.

Sixth, today's juries, exposed to so much CSI television shows and news about how DNA identified someone responsible for a ten-year-old cold case murder, expect to see real, hard evidence to convict. But does the lack of that evidence justify a finding of not guilty when there has been a confession, or in this case multiple confessions? Had the State been able to produce the flashlight and bullet(s), would the jury have reached a different result? Had the murder weapon (gun) been found and the caliber matched the bullet, would the "red herring" testimony of the defense expert witness about what caliber gun could have fired the bullet been needed? Did that testimony also sway the jury? Did the jury really understand that a shot-from 100 or more feet away with a handgun hitting a flashlight pointed at a suspect on a dark rainy night is evidence that the shooter was a good shot and that the second "kill" shot was not an accidental shooting? How do you prove that?

Seventh, I don't know how the State could have explained the simple concept of felony murder in more understandable language to the jury. Becker/Smith was still in the act of committing a burglary (felony) when he (or an accomplice standing with him at the edge of the parking lot) shot and killed J. T. But, in my mind, the State did prove at a minimum those facts beyond any reasonable doubt.

Finally, on a personal note, believing that Becker/Smith is guilty of murder and knowing that my faith and my Savior require that I forgive him, I struggle to do so. Maybe it would be easier to forgive if he would now admit what he did that night. He did admit it two years ago to the detectives and to his children. And his daughter said he would never admit to something he didn't do. Do I need to forgive someone for something they maintain they did not do?

What do you think? Guilty or not? Forgive? Ultimately, he will face God and so will we all.

ACKNOWLEDGEMENTS

This book would never have been written if it hadn't been for the persistence of Carolyn Philo in keeping her father's case open and her persistence in having me write the book. Thank you, Carolyn, for all of your help and more importantly, for your friendship. Robert Philo is one of the most knowledgeable people I have met concerning police matters and the law in general, and I appreciate all of his guidance and ideas. Carrie Crutcher, the Philo's daughter, was involved in this project from my first meeting at the Philo's house, and she deserves credit for giving me a unique perspective on many issues involving this case, and also for her wonderful sense of humor. Frank Hall, John Michael Kuster, Melvin, Judy, and Brian Hall were all family members who took the time to talk to me about James T. Hall and to reminisce about life in law enforcement.

I also want to thank Kevin Collins, lead defense attorney, for spending time talking to me and for answering my countless questions. I greatly appreciate Kevin's transparency in discussing the case and his introducing me to areas of the law I never knew existed. Kevin's junior associate, Dillon Grimm, provided me with input from the second trial's jury and also spent time enabling me to see the entire case from his perspective. I also want to thank the two jurors who talked to me directly, especially Rebekah, who gave me insight into several of the nuances surrounding the first trial. I want to thank Diane and Roger Schmidt for their kindness and hospitality. They not only opened their house to me and recreated the burglary that occurred there fifty-two years before, but they also walked the entire crime scene with me and drove me to other important locations in the case such as Maggie's and the pet cemetery.

Thank you to Detective Katie Leggett for discussing her thoughts on the case with me and for giving me a better understanding of cold case detective work.

Thank you to the greatest publisher/publicist, Judy Tashbook Safern, for all of her encouragement and ideas which helped the book come together. Getting to know and work with Judy and her team was one of the best parts of writing this book.

Finally, thank you to my wife Sheryl for your unwavering love and support. These last three years have been an incredible journey, and I am thankful that you were the person who accompanied me on this journey.

Michael Weisberg

ABOUT THE AUTHOR

Michael Weisberg was born in Huntington, West Virginia on March 10th, 1959 to Fred Weisberg. whose valor enabled the Allies to win World War II, and Joan Weisberg, who placed second to Elizabeth Taylor in the 1950 Miss Brooklyn Beauty Pageant. As a child, Michael actually believed both of these stories and many others told to him by his late father who was the world's greatest storyteller.

Michael graduated from Vanderbilt University in 1981 with a major in English literature and a minor in Linguistics and an appreciation for the music of Johnny Cash. His lifelong dream of becoming a physician was realized when he was accepted to Baylor College of Medicine from which he graduated in 1985. He completed a residency in Internal Medicine and then a fellowship in Gastroenterology. Many of the colorful characters and incredible events portrayed in Michael's novels, *The Hospitalist* and *In The End*, are based on his experiences and encounters during training.

His first novel, *The Hospitalist* (2014), was a prescient and humorous thriller about the practice of medicine in modern times. In 2016, Michael gave a Tedx Talk on How the Art of Medicine Became a Business in the 21st Century at the Bomb Factory in Dallas before 800 wildly cheering spectators. His second novel, *In The End* (2019,) goes on a search for the meaning to life and deals with critical topics in modern America such as poverty, discrimination, abortion, homosexuality, and the value of a good haircut.

Michael lives only with his wife Sheryl in Dallas, Texas since all three of his children have grown up and moved out. His hobbies include calling his children, learning how to use an iPhone, listening to rock and roll music, and walking his adorable and occasionally obedient dog, Piper.

Michael Weisberg